INFAMY

DR JERRY TONER is Fellow and Director of Studies in Classics, Churchill College, Cambridge University. He is the author of *How to Manage Your Slaves* and *Release your Inner Roman*, which were published under his pseudonym Marcus Sidonius Falx.

INFAMY

THE CRIMES OF ANCIENT ROME

JERRY TONER

P

PROFILE BOOKS

This paperback edition published in 2020

First published in Great Britain in 2019 by
PROFILE BOOKS LTD
29 Cloth Fair
London ECIA 7JQ

www.profilebooks.com

10 9 8 7 6 5 4 3 2 1

Typeset in Dante by MacGuru Ltd
Printed and bound in Great Britain by
CPI Group (UK) Ltd, Croydon CR0 4YY

A CIP catalogue record for this book is available from the British
Library.

ISBN 978 1 78125 386 1
eISBN 978 1 78283 124 2

CONTENTS

THE VERDICT

THE CHARGE

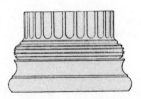

ROME ON TRIAL

The king knew a threat when he saw one. When a rival's daughter gave birth to twin boys, he saw at once that they could grow up to challenge him. So he did what any sensible king would do: he ordered that they be thrown into the Tiber. Unfortunately for him, the river had flooded and no one could get close to the banks, so his faithless men dumped the babies' cradle at the water's edge, assuming this would be enough to drown them. As it turned out, the flood waters quickly retreated, leaving the crib on dry land. The infants found themselves in a wild place, swampy and full of fig trees. A thirsty she-wolf came to drink from the river and discovered the crying boys. Instead of devouring them, she offered the hungry babies her teats to suck on, gently licking them with her tongue as they fed. Soon after, a shepherd called Faustulus found the boys and took them back to his wife, Acca Larentia, who brought them up as her own, naming them Romulus and Remus.

As the boys grew up, they became extraordinarily strong. They used to go on hunting trips in the woods, and would even attack robbers if they stumbled upon them. Natural leaders, they were soon followed by a crowd of young men, eager to join in their adventures. Eventually, the twins acquired such a following that they were able to confront the tyrant who had tried to drown them at birth. There was a scuffle, but the king had missed his opportunity for an easy win and at this juncture he leaves the record. Thus are the mighty fallen.

The brothers were now gripped by an urge to found their own city close to where they had been abandoned. The cities nearby were all overcrowded, and so many people were keen to join these inspiring young men that the project seemed destined for success. Alas, each boy wanted to found the city in a slightly different place. Romulus favoured the Palatine hill and Remus the Aventine. A seemingly trivial issue brought matters to a head: who should the new city be named after? The boys were twins: both equally senior. Unable to agree, they each went ahead and built their own settlements in their chosen spots before they decided to resolve the argument by consulting the gods.

Here was the method they hit upon. They would count birds, each on his own hill, and the gods would make clear which brother was right by sending the most birds his way. Each of them prepared a sacred space on their respective hills and began to watch the sky. None appeared to Romulus, so he tried to trick Remus by sending word to come straight away. Remus would naturally think that he was conceding defeat. The messengers, ashamed at this dishonesty and perhaps wondering if they had chosen the right brother, took their time. Remus counted six vultures on the journey. He thought he must have won – but at the very moment he arrived, twice as many birds appeared before Romulus. Both sides claimed victory. Remus said he had won because the birds appeared to him first. Romulus argued that he had seen more. With passions running high, blows were thrown and Remus was killed. Romulus was free to name the city after himself. Rome had been founded.

The historian Livy tells us the precise date this took place: 21 April 753 BC. But despite his accuracy, Livy was writing some 750 years after the event. He had no real idea. And there were many other versions of the story. Some claimed that Remus had ridiculed Romulus's wall and had jumped over it shouting insults about how ineffective it was before his brother grew so angry that he killed him. One even claimed that the guilty party was not Romulus but one of his supporters. The earliest known account by a Roman historian, Quintus Fabius Pictor, was written in about 200 BC, half a millennium after the supposed event. The three sources which are best known today are the roughly contemporaneous accounts of Livy and Dionysius of Halicarnassus, as well as Plutarch's life of Romulus from the early second century AD. None of the various versions agreed on when Rome had been founded: 814, 753, 752, 751, 748, and 729 BC were all given as possible dates. All these accounts were written after Rome had become the dominant power in the Mediterranean world and in reality tell us a lot more about how the later Romans saw themselves than they do about what actually happened when the city was first established. It may be that there is a kernel of truth to some of the tales. Perhaps Rome was established by a man whose name was Romulus. Perhaps a pair of twin brothers did quarrel over where to found the settlement and even came to blows over what to call it. But what is really telling about these myths is what they reveal about how the later Romans understood themselves. The foundation myth was thought to explain why the Roman character was as it was; and it answered the questions of why the Romans had been so successful and what had made them so great.

The myth provided answers to these questions, but not all of them were particularly palatable. Why did the story need the horrible crime of fratricide at its core? After all, killing a close family member was deemed to be particularly shocking by later Roman society. These heinous criminals were not killed simply by beheading or burning but were sewn into a sack together with a dog, a cockerel, a snake and an ape, and then thrown into the sea or the river Tiber. It was an exaggerated form of execution that reflected the fundamental importance of the extended family within Roman society. That such a dreadful crime played so important a part in the tale suggests that the Romans recognised a profoundly disturbing side to their personality. The later Romans saw within themselves a ruthlessness that explained how they had conquered the Mediterranean world. The murder of Remus represented a Roman's ability to put the state above everything else, even his own brother. Power was all that mattered and if getting political control meant killing family, then so be it. The story underlined the Roman capacity for violence and showed that they understood the brutality that ruling often involved. It also revealed that the Romans knew their own ancestry to be a curious mix. If the city founders were born of a princess, abandoned as infants, then brought up by shepherds, was it any surprise that the Romans could be so tough? They expected none of the usual luxuries of royal life. In many ways, Rome's slightly dodgy upbringing served as a metaphor for the whole Roman people. Some – the senators – were noble, but most – the plebs – were no-nonsense down-to-earth folk, and, taken as a whole, the Romans displayed the characteristics that were needed to govern the known world.

The Romans also knew that they were not entirely trustworthy. There was something of the overly ambitious pleb about them. Hadn't Romulus even tried to con his own brother in the counting of the birds? Didn't he do this even though the gods were involved? The Romans liked to believe they had the gods on their side – a cosy arrangement known as the *pax deorum* 'the peace of the gods' – but here was their mythical founder openly trying to cheat in a religious matter. Later Romans recognised that they were perfectly capable of carrying out such disgraceful acts. One version of the myth even claimed that the very idea of a wolf was a fiction. The Romans used the Latin word 'lupae' to describe not only female wolves but also prostitutes, and in this version of the story Faustulus's wife was in fact a prostitute. It was as if the Romans believed there was some kind of shameful secret in their ancestral closet: a secret which helped to explain who they were.

Of course, the foundation myth also explained their

good points. The abandoned children had been so strong it was clear they were special. They grew up into handsome, noble young men who were courageous and daring. They courted danger and were scared of nobody. The brothers were equally friendly with their peers and their inferiors but they sneered at the king's agents. If anyone was threatened by violence they would intervene on their behalf. Like the extraordinary she-wolf, who had chosen to suckle rather than devour them, they looked after those under their care. Of the two, it was said that Romulus seemed to exercise better judgement, and to have political sagacity, while in his dealings with neighbours he gave the firm impression that he was born to command rather than to obey. Both men were passionate in everything they did, whether it was exercise, hunting or driving off robbers and thieves. It was no surprise that they were famed throughout the land and that their descendants had conquered the Mediterranean world.

But the Romans also knew that their success came at a cost. In the poet Ovid's account of the myth (*Fasti* Book 4), the ghost of Remus appears to his adoptive parents and talks of his anger at his death, but also of how there should be no doubt about his love for his brother. When Romulus hears of this, he struggles to hold back his tears, but manages to do so, keeping his grief locked up inside. He is determined not to weep in public and to set an example of fortitude. The Romans understood that success meant repressing individual concerns and sacrificing all for the good of the state; and they were prepared to put up with all kinds of violent crime when they had to. Above all, they understood that there was something else of the wolf about them: a vicious streak, threatening and wild, that itself seemed to have been imbibed along with the milk. The Romans knew they were sons of a bitch.

This book puts Rome on trial. Plenty of people have seen Rome as a place of infamy, riven with savagery, sin and corruption. One modern writer described the gladiatorial combats of the Colosseum as 'bloodthirsty human holocausts' and 'by far the nastiest blood-sport ever invented', even claiming that 'the two most quantitatively destructive institutions in History are Nazism and the Roman Gladiators.' Rome's wars of conquest involved what Edward Gibbon described as 'a perpetual violation of humanity and justice' and today would have landed them in the international War Crimes Tribunal at the Hague in Holland. Corruption, as one eminent academic has argued, was so endemic in the Roman empire, with governmental aims being thwarted for private gain by high-ranking bureaucrats and military leaders, that it contributed to the empire's fall. And in more modern popular entertainment, whether Robert Graves's *I Claudius* or the HBO television series *Rome*, the Roman empire has become synonymous with sexual depravity of all kinds. But others have held up Rome as an example of an ordered and successful society. They have seen the *pax romana* of the empire as having delivered centuries of peace and freed millions from their worst fears: invasion, defeat, death or enslavement. The authority of the Roman state inspired much of the architecture of governmental and judicial buildings in the Western world today, from the Old Bailey in London to the Capitol in Washington DC.

What kind of place was it in reality? Was it a well-ordered society where the emperors, on the whole, did a good job and the people were largely content to support the empire? Or was it a brutal gangster enterprise, where crime was ubiquitous, the law primarily existed to serve the interests of the mighty, and opposition was crushed? Was it a society where crime sat at its heart in the same way as it did in the myth of the city's foundation?

The emperors themselves reflect Rome's split personality. We have infamous 'bad' emperors, like Nero and Caligula, who epitomise the arbitrary tyrant. Immune from prosecution and above the law, these rulers broke all the rules of social behaviour. Are they the exceptions? Other emperors seem to have tried hard to deliver justice. The Roman historian Suetonius says that the emperor Claudius, for example, did not always follow the letter of the law, but modified it according to his own notions of fairness, even if sometimes this meant having serious criminals thrown to the wild beasts when the law said they should not suffer such a severe punishment. Once, when he convicted a man of forgery and someone cried out that the criminal should have his hands cut off, Claudius immediately agreed and summoned the executioner with a knife and a block. Was this good governance or just an emperor showboating to a bloodthirsty public? Suetonius also says that Claudius displayed a strange inconsistency in judging cases. Sometimes he was careful and shrewd, other times rash and inconsiderate, and occasionally just plain silly. In a dispute about whether a man was a citizen or not, a pointless argument arose between the lawyers about whether the man should appear in a toga or a tunic, since only citizens could wear the toga. Wishing to appear impartial, Claudius made the man change clothes depending on whether the defence or the prosecution were talking. Suetonius says that such acts meant that Claudius was discredited and held in general and open contempt.

Or consider how Tiberius acted when the official Plautius Silvanus, for reasons not known, threw his wife Apronia out of their bedroom window. Brought before the emperor, Silvanus claimed to have been fast asleep and so thought that his wife must have committed suicide. Without any hesitation, Tiberius went straight to the house and examined the bedroom where he found visible signs of a struggle. Rather than act arbitrarily, he referred the case to the senate and a judicial committee was formed. So far so good. But Silvanus's grandmother Urgulania, a friend of the imperial family, sent her grandson a dagger. This was interpreted as being a less than subtle hint from the emperor, and the accused duly arranged to have his arteries opened (Tacitus *Annals* 4.22). Once again, we have a colourful picture, an anecdote that provides us with what seems like an atypical event but which also provides evidence of the mix of justice and arbitrariness that often characterised imperial rule.

Even so, how relevant were the emperors to Roman society as a whole? Cut off and distant, would the emperors have had much impact on the average Roman's life? It certainly seems to be true that some ancient writers express gratitude towards their emperors, directly crediting them with Rome's peace and prosperity: 'Caesar seems to provide us with profound peace, there are no more wars any longer, nor battles, no brigandage on a large scale, nor piracy, and at any hour we may travel by land or sail.' (Epictetus *Discourses* 3.13.9). Some academics have argued that this kind of sentiment reflects a fundamental law-abidingness within the empire. Sure, they say, the law was harsh but it was seen as being applied to all for the good of all. The Roman historian Velleius Paterculus describes how the emperor Augustus made justice a key quality of his new kind of imperial government after the chaos of the final years of the republic:

Justice, equity, and hard work, long buried in oblivion, have been restored to the state. The magistrates have regained their authority, the senate its majesty, the courts their dignity. Rioting in the theatre has been suppressed and every citizen has either been filled with the desire to do right, or has been forced to do so by necessity. (*History of Rome* 2.126)

He goes on to claim, 'When was the price of grain more reasonable, or when were the blessings of peace greater?' It is, he says, the *pax Augusta*, the Augustan peace, which has brought security to every corner of the empire. It is the emperor himself who leads by example, by teaching his citizens what is right by doing it.

High praise indeed. Is it warranted? Suppose we take these descriptions at face value. Then we see a world that, even with a legal system less developed than our own, succeeded in generating peaceful coexistence among the millions of inhabitants of the Roman empire. The Roman empire lasted so long, in this view, because there existed

a generally accepted consensus that Roman rule was justified. The inhabitants of the Roman world internalised the
ideology of the ruling class and thereby became willing
participants in empire rather than its subjects. The
problem with this is that it ignores the massive power
imbalance between the two sides. How else can you
address an emperor but with flattery? In the same way,
crowds of Iraqis danced for joy whenever Saddam Hussein
put in an appearance while still in power but acted very
differently once he had been toppled. So too, we might
imagine, did Romans tell their emperors what they
wanted to hear. They might well have thought something
different in private.

What about the Roman people? Were they basically
law-abiding? Were they too interested in 'bread and circuses', in the words of the satirist Juvenal, to care about
abstract concepts such as justice? We shall examine
whether the people managed to exert any influence on
the emperors and whether the emperors ever responded
to popular demands for law and order. We shall look at
what kind of conversations they had in the taverns of
Rome and what they said about those in authority. Talking
freely was a dangerous business under an autocratic
emperor and we shall see how people often couched their
criticisms in safely anonymous terms.

We will be the detectives in this case, and in reaching a
verdict on the Roman empire we will have to gather evidence from right across its world, looking not just at the
emperors and senators at the top of society but also at the
peasants, workers and slaves at the bottom. We will pore
over a huge range of sources in the search for Roman

illegality. The great law books that were put together in the later empire provide many examples of cases that reached the courts and are packed with detail. Papyrus evidence from Egypt gives fascinating information of cases at a local level. There are also examples of fictional crime, both in the rhetorical exercises used in teaching and in ancient novels. Roman writers and historians often discuss the crimes of the elite, while surviving oracles and magic spells tell us a great deal about ordinary people's fears. Christian texts contain gruesome accounts of the deaths of martyrs at the hands of the Roman state, and later, when the Roman state had itself become Christian, show how it reckoned with previous practice. We shall find that all of this testimony has problems. We will have to weigh up the evidence as best we can.

We will have to reach a judgement on Rome and decide if the Romans were really any worse than us. Was it a society guilty of letting the vast majority of its population live a life exposed to all kinds of crime? Did Rome inflict this criminal culture on all those it conquered? We will look at how all those involved in crime in Rome, whether accused, witness or accuser, were treated and at how their gender, status and age affected that treatment. It will involve investigating ancient crime from many angles, from what was thought to cause it, to how they tried to prevent and punish it, to how it was experienced and feared. We shall uncover how crime – whether religious, sexual, violent or treasonable in nature – cut across all levels of Roman society and how it was perceived differently by each of them. As the city of Rome developed into the massive hub of a global empire, we will see how different crimes, ranging from treason to adultery, came into focus and how new ways of dealing with them had to be found. We shall examine what role the emperors played in all this, adjudicating questions as diverse as what kinds of food it was legal to sell in cook shops, to the punishment of slaves. Finally, we shall see whether the later Christianisation of the Roman empire made any difference. Did Rome become a reformed character under the influence of Jesus's teachings or did the Romans stay the same brutes they had always been?

T
H
E

E
V
I
D
E
N
C
E

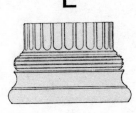

Chapter I

NERO'S MUGGINGS AND OTHER VIOLENT CRIME

At night the emperor Nero used to disguise himself as a slave and go wandering in the streets and the taverns of Rome. This was before the Great Fire of AD 64 – which he was accused of starting himself – when the streets of the old city were narrow, twisting and dark. The emperor lurked in the shadows until an unsuspecting victim passed by and then leapt out and violently assaulted him. If any resisted, Nero stabbed them and threw their bodies into the sewers. One victim who had the nerve to fight back managed to overpower the emperor and pummelled him to within an inch of his life. Nero later forced the man to commit suicide. Nero would even break into shops and steal from them. Once safely back at his palace, he would auction off his booty to the highest bidder, making the imperial residence a marketplace for stolen goods. When it became well known that the emperor himself was indulging in such a wanton crime spree, many others began to copy his example. It was said that there were so many marauding gangs that at night Rome became like a city captured by the enemy (Suetonius *Nero* 26).

Nero was still a young man at this time. He had become emperor when only sixteen and people may have been prepared to give him the benefit of the doubt at first. They would probably have dismissed his nocturnal activities, as well as his lust, extravagance and cruelty, as the mere follies of youth, were it not for the fact that they seemed to be an ingrained part of his character. The moment darkness fell, the young emperor seemed incapable of resisting these sinister pranks. They revealed an almost psychopathic love of violence and a complete disdain for all the normal rules of behaviour. The Romans could be fairly forgiving of their sons and do not seem to have been overly concerned if they sometimes drank too much, got into the occasional fight, or had sex with prostitutes. As Cicero once said, whoever would condemn such behaviour would be very harsh indeed. So long as the behaviour was relatively contained, it was seen as a way for young men to let off steam before settling down to the serious business of adult life (young women, needless to say, had a very different set of attitudes applied to them).

Nero was something else. He felt compelled to break not just some rules but every rule, whether it related to sexual behaviour, property rights or the use of violence. And he felt the need to break them constantly. Every evening he would, like a hoodied youth today, put on a wig or a cap to try to conceal his identity and head out to experience the thrill of the dangerous street life that filled Rome at night. It was obvious that he hated being confined to the palace, where his mother and senior advisers would lecture him by day about what he should be doing to be a good emperor. Later on, Nero was to rid himself of all these old people. But for the first few years he did what he was told by day, then did what he wanted by night. He seemed to be scared of being found out and he learned how to use the Thapsia plant to conceal the bruises he acquired during his escapades (Pliny *Natural History* 13.126). He was still trying to keep up the pretence that he could behave as an emperor was expected to. But once he was out on the town, he became completely reckless, and didn't care what risks he took. He almost had his eyes knocked out in one of the fights and could easily have been killed. It was as if he had some kind of youthful death wish. But he was also a coward. After he had nearly been killed by one of his victims, he took bodyguards with him when he went on his night-time adventures. They would follow at a distance, unseen, and step in to protect him if it looked like one of his opponents was getting the upper hand in a brawl. Psychopath and coward: it all underlined how unbalanced the young Nero was.

What is even more extraordinary about these stories is that we have Nero, the man who was head of the Roman legal system and the ultimate judge and source of Roman law, delighting in being a violent mugger. Of course, the stories of Nero's criminal behaviour also served to show how bad a ruler he was – and his defects were certainly more pronounced than most. But for all the rhetoric surrounding Nero, and however good other Roman rulers were, how was it possible for Nero to get away with it at

the same time as presiding over an increasingly sophisticated legal system? What does the mugging emperor tell
us about the reality of life in Rome? Did the violence done
by Romulus against his brother continue to permeate the
later Roman world?

Roman Violence

Today violence tends to be categorised into several sub-
groups representing a variety of aggressive behaviours:
physical, sexual, psychological, and emotional. The
Romans gave considerable thought as to what constituted
an injury (*iniuria*), and their understanding was very different from ours. As one jurist explains: 'Injury is
committed not only where anyone strikes another with
his fist, or with a stick or a whip, but where he reviles him
in a loud voice' (Gaius *Institutes* 220). Reputation had
enormous importance for Romans since it reflected their
social status. To be publicly defamed by another without
good reason was as hurtful as any physical blow. This also
applied to any written attacks, either in the form of prose
or poetry. Slander and libel are lesser offences for us, and
I think I would be rather flattered if someone took the
trouble to vilify me in verse (not an invitation). And while
contemporary libel laws do display something of this way
of thinking, in that the famous can sue to claim damages
for harm done to their reputation in written or broadcast
defamatory comments, we also know that libel is a rich
man's game. Most people are insufficiently well known
for a case to be worth the expense (which is why newspa-
pers can treat little people so badly). Most of us, if we

suffer insult in the street or verbal assault on the internet, just have to shrug it off. But we also believe that, while words might hurt a bit, they aren't as bad as sticks and stones. This is a big difference. Roman society saw the individual as being subservient to the wider community. What the community thought of a person – their reputation – meant much more than what the person thought about him- or herself. Anything that threatened an individual's standing in the eyes of society represented a grave challenge to that person's identity. It was a threat that demanded an aggressive response.

This close link between status and hurt meant that the Romans did not accept that a slave could suffer an injury, in the sense of their term *iniuria*. His master might suffer an injury if you chose to beat his slave as a way of embarrassing him (Gaius *Institutes* 222). This would also apply if you took the slave to a tavern and taught him how to play dice and so corrupted him. Flashing at women would have the same effect, as would throwing dung at them, because fundamentally what 'injuring' someone did was to challenge or reduce the social status or honour of the victim. Injury could also be committed against the general public, by, for example, tainting the water supply. This was considered a particularly serious crime because it disrespected the entire social order and so, as one law states, 'demands punishment of extraordinary severity' (*Digest* 47.11.1.1).

How Violent was Rome?

The satirist Juvenal provides an infamous picture of Rome as a den of violent crime. His third satire has a vivid account of the perils of the street (*Satires* 3.281–308). If you go to dinner without making a will, he claims, you are reckless. There are so many opportunities to die. If you are lucky you will just have a chamber pot emptied on your head. If not, you will find some angry drunk wanting to get into a fight – he will steer clear of the rich man who is protected by his retinue of slaves and pick on you. Or you will be attacked by some vagabonds with a knife. We get a similar picture from the historian Livy, writing during the reign of Augustus about an episode five centuries before, who tells the story of the down-to-earth Lucius and his brother Volscius, who were out for a night on the town when they ran into a group of drunk, partying young aristocrats, the kind of people who held such riff-raff in utter contempt. 'At first they laughed at us and abused us,' says Volscius, 'as young men when drunk and arrogant are wont to abuse the humble and the poor.' A fight ensued and the brothers were beaten senseless (*History of Rome* 3.13).

How accurate is this picture? Do we believe Juvenal's testimony? Very little is known about his life, but the very fact that he was composing elegant poetry suggests that he was highly educated and therefore from a wealthy background. If so, how likely was it that he was hanging around the dingy streets of Rome after hours? What's more he was a satirist, a writer who filled his creations with vitriol and exaggeration in order to make his point. He does not seem to be a particularly reliable witness and we cannot take what he says at face value.

Roman law books actually gave very little space to common assault or wounding. This might suggest that the streets were safe but it simply reflects that such minor matters were not worth going to court over. Law was written by the kind of rich men Juvenal complains of – men who were protected by their retinues. Everyday violence had no interest for them as a legal issue. When casual violence does appear in the legal record it often takes the form of a slightly bizarre, theoretical discussion. So in one example from the *Digest*, the huge compendium of Roman legal opinion collated under the emperor Justinian in the sixth century (9.2.52.1), we find the case of a shopkeeper who placed a lantern on a stone in the street in front of his shop at night. A passer-by took it and the shopkeeper followed him and demanded it back. The thief started to attack the shopkeeper with a whip and things really kicked off. The shopkeeper knocked out the thief's eye. Afterwards, the shopkeeper consulted a lawyer to find out whether he was guilty of inflicting unlawful harm, even though he had been hit first. The reply comes that, as the thief had been armed with a nasty piece of metal and had struck the first blow, he had to take responsibility for the loss of his eye. But if the shopkeeper had not been struck first then he would have been liable.

This is typical of the kind of street violence we find in the legal codes. On first sight we might decide that it shows just how casually violent the streets of Rome could be. Theft was rife and the only recourse the poor victim had was to fight for his belongings. But looking more closely we see that this is a theoretical case, dreamed up by an academic legal brain. It is part of a debate that echoes some of our own dilemmas about how far property owners should go in defending themselves against a

burglar. It is almost a caricature of how a member of the
elite might imagine the world of the street. But even if
that were not the case and the example was realistic, can
we extrapolate from this to create a picture of the preva-
lence of crime in Roman society as a whole? Can we
safely conclude that Rome was a world riven with brutal
crooks? I live in Cambridge, one of the safest cities in the
world, but casual, alcohol-related vandalism and violence
are still common in some parts of the town centre. If I
heard someone push over my bin late on a Saturday night
the last thing I would do is dash out and confront them.
If I wanted a fight I could go down to the big pub in town
where those looking out for such entertainment tend to
congregate. Nevertheless, this is far from the norm. The
fact that the Roman shopkeeper put the lantern outside
his shop could suggest that this was his normal practice
and that usually nothing happened – no theft, no
attempted burglaries, no fights.

Or consider the following case. Several youths were
playing with a ball in the street. One of them threw the
ball too hard and it hit the hand of a barber who was
shaving a slave at the time (it was common for barbers
simply to set up a stool on the side of the street and prac-
tise their trade there). The barber accidentally slit the
slave's throat. The question arises as to who is liable for
the damage. Is it the youth who threw the ball too hard;
the barber, because he was in the habit of shaving in a
public place where people would gather to play ball; or
does the slave have only himself to blame if he chose to
sit in a barber's chair in a dangerous place? Again, some
elements of the street scene provide interesting colour:

shaving customers in the street, the hustle and bustle, the slave going to a barber. But do we really think that death in this manner was common? It is a hypothetical situation invented for the legal issues it raises (9.2.11 pref.). (Which is not to say that the streets of Rome did not carry with them a variety of obscure risks. One law stipulates that snake charmers will be liable if any of their reptiles hurt anyone (47.11.11) – but were they really that commonplace and did their snakes often attack onlookers?)

Assessing how violent Rome was is especially difficult because the city was such an exception. At its height it had a huge population of around one million. The army was not normally allowed into the city, so order was kept by the *vigiles*, the Nightwatch, established under Augustus, whose primary purpose was to put out fires (always a major threat in a primarily wooden city), but who looked out for thieves as well. The wealthy who lived in large houses could protect themselves using slaves and by building high walls to keep out potential intruders. Outside Rome, soldiers were used more widely to maintain order, with many troops being posted in towns. This may have been sufficient to keep the peace most of the time. To be sure, the government was very keen to maintain public order in the sense of stamping out rebellions or stopping riots and tax revolts. But keeping soldiers in small towns suggests that the aim was to maintain order in a more everyday sense. The local centurion could be petitioned about relatively minor offences, and could keep an eye on troublemakers. This is not to suggest that a few military personnel would have kept the empire neatly in check, but it does counter the view that the government had no interest at all in small-scale, local crime. Even today, how often do you see police officers out on the street? But that does not automatically mean that the crime rate is high or that the authorities have no interest in crime prevention. The low number of police could reflect a generally law-abiding society or mean that the presence of a few officers is sufficient to act as a deterrent against most crime.

Forming a conclusion about the level of violence that existed in Roman society is also made difficult by our own modern preconceptions. Rome has often been associated with good order and government, something that has been reflected most obviously in the adoption of classical-style architecture for government buildings. This was particularly true in the nineteenth and early twentieth centuries when European imperial powers were keen to stress their links with the great Roman empire of the past. Newer powers were also keen to emphasise their mainte-nance of the Roman tradition. Consider the huge public monuments of Washington DC in America. The Capitol building, where Congress meets, was named precisely that to emphasise its comparison with the government buildings on the Capitoline hill in ancient Rome. The colossal Washington Monument is an Egyptian-style obelisk that harks back to the many such columns brought to Rome as symbols of its imperial power. This associa-tion of Rome with stable government, authority and good order has also filtered down to the popular level. As one of his followers remarks to Reg in Monty Python's *Life of Brian*, when he is forced to admit the many benefits that Roman rule has brought to Judaea, 'And it's safe to walk in the streets at night now, Reg.'

In reality, Roman power was not always so beneficial to those subject to it. Soldiers were not always a force for good order. The emperor Septimius Severus was blamed for making Rome unruly precisely because he stationed so many troops within the walls. Anyone who lives near an army barracks knows that soldiers out on the town can be a cause of small-scale disorder. Worse still, at least in the eyes of our snooty Roman source, Severus abandoned the practice of selecting the imperial guard exclusively from respectable areas of the empire such as Italy, Spain, Macedonia and Noricum (modern Austria), and accepted soldiers from any part of the empire based on talent alone. Fair enough, but it meant that the guard was now filled with recruits who came from very different cultures. The historian Dio complains that Rome was filled with a throng of motley soldiers who had 'the most savage appearance', the most terrifying way of speaking, and were completely uncouth and boorish (Roman History 75.2.4). Dio's snobbishness notwithstanding, it's true that soldiers were something of a law unto themselves and were notorious for preying on the local populations of the towns and cities where they were stationed.

A lot of the state's effort at preventing violence did not involve assigning officers or officials for that purpose. Instead, the government's response to violent crime was to make a terrifying example of those criminals it did manage to apprehend. As one law notes: 'It has been held by many authorities that notorious robbers should be hanged in the very same places they had pillaged, in order that others might be deterred by their example from perpetrating the same crimes.' The authorities also held that such highly visible retribution would be 'a consolation' to the relatives and friends of the victims, which was why it was important for it to be carried out in the same place as the crimes. The same reasoning applied to throwing violent criminals to the wild beasts in the arena (*Digest* 48.19.28.15). This is an approach which strikes us as disproportionate and shocking: all punishments should be proportionate as well as fit the crime. But we should remember that this is a modern way of thinking. Right up until the nineteenth century, it was a given that criminals should be made an example of in order to deter others. It was impossible to catch all criminals but, by punishing those that were caught in a dramatically brutal way, society was believed to have had some hope of affecting the behaviour of the criminal class as a whole.

Types of Violent Crime

Violent crime took a variety of forms. Murder seems to be universally condemned in human society and so it was in Rome. Roman law did recognise a distinction between premeditated murder and accidental killing. If someone struck another person with a sword there would be no doubt about his having done so with the intention of killing. But if, during a fight, a man hit another with a brass pot used in the bath it would not constitute murder, even though the weapon was made of metal. A lesser penalty would then be imposed (*Digest* 48.8.1.3). We will also see that burglars could be killed with impunity in certain circumstances. None of this seems different from cases of domestic violence or burglary that we often read about in the papers today.

What is striking is how many violent crimes in the Roman world occurred in the face-to-face context of local communities. One petition from Egypt in AD 47 describes an argument between a herdsman and one of his workers, who claimed that he was owed back pay. According to the worker, his boss first insulted him and his wife, then assaulted her with many blows, even though she was pregnant, with the result that her child was stillborn. The wife was left confined to bed and in danger of losing her life (*P. Mich.* 228). The text certainly gives us a clear sense of the competitive world most Romans inhabited. There is no cosy neighbourliness here. Instead, we find a society where everyone hung on doggedly to what little they had, while others strove hard to do anything to improve their lot. It is worth bearing in mind that this was not a world of substantial economic growth; the majority of inhabitants probably did not live much above subsistence level. Having few resources to fall back on, they were also vulnerable to any economic shock. It would not be surprising if this social context bred a highly competitive outlook, one which saw neighbours as competitors for the few resources on offer, not as friends with whom to share them. In another petition, we also get an idea that some kind of violent revenge attack has taken place against the property of an official called Aurelius Heracleides. Once, when away on business, one of his asses escaped, so some of his neighbours organised a search party but they found the animal tied up and dead, killed, presumably, by a local who held a grudge against the official (*SB* 6.9203). In

another example, a wife reported to the centurion that
her husband, Nemesion, a tax official, had left their home
in Philadelphia (in what is now the Egyptian Fayum) on
the afternoon of 2 March AD 207 and had not been seen
since, despite several searches (*P. Gen.* 17). His fate
remained a mystery but a violent end seems the most
likely cause.

A strand of such wantonly destructive violence runs
through the Egyptian material. One man reports that his
threshing floor near the village of New Ptolemis was set
on fire by persons unknown (*BGU* 2.561). Another, called
Petsiris, complains that he was beaten up by Patunion
after the latter found him driving a mule through his
newly planted vegetables (*P. Mich.* 5.229 dated AD 48).
Many disputes centred on land rights, the kind of neigh-
bourly conflict that can permanently sour relations. One
law refers to those who cut down fruit trees at night, the
kind of spiteful attack that a jealous or angry neighbour
might carry out against a bitter local enemy. People seem
to have been quick to turn to violence in the event of any
confrontation. In AD 218, Aphynchis complained that the
pastry chef, Achilleus, had attacked his slave and wounded
her on the lip. He went to confront the attacker and 'had
a discussion with him about his remarkable nastiness'. It
soon led to blows, with Aphynchis claiming, 'he then
attacked me too, and he assaulted me and swore at me.
Not only this, but he struck me on the head with a rock'
(*P. Oxy.* 33.2672.11–18). Another striking feature of these
petitions is just how many ways people found to attack
one another: with swords, clubs, implements and fists, as
well as words.

What also comes across clearly in many of the petitions is a powerful sense of injustice and outrage at the criminals' uncivilised and unacceptable behaviour. Often, the accusers dwell on the details of their wounds and make demands for offenders to be punished. Two words that feature a lot are the Greek terms for force or violence (bia) and arrogance or insolence (hubris). A commonly occurring phrase is that the accused acted 'like bandits'. The victims seem to feel that they have been treated in a manner well below that demanded by their status and that the offenders are ignoring the unwritten rules of civilised, communal life. The frequency of the complaints, however, suggests that acting in a violent and arrogant manner was also an inescapable part of living in an Egyptian village. Often the violence came at the end of a dispute between individuals known to each other. Other times it was more random. If a person was robbed they were often beaten up. Was this because they had tried to defend themselves, knowing that if they let their possessions go they would be unlikely to see them again? Does it reflect the need to fight hard to hold on to what you had? Or are these examples of petitioners trying to sex-up their claims in order to impress the judge with the gravity of the case? Probably all three. But it underlines the importance of status within the local community: what can seem small injuries to us were taken very seriously. This was a world where everyone was constantly jockeying for position.

The city of Rome also provides us with evidence for the violent side of street life, which seems qualitatively similar to that of Egypt. The philosopher Seneca warns that the lower classes were more likely 'to use force, to quarrel, to rush into a brawl, and to indulge their wrath' (*On Clemency* 1.7.4). Similarly, the historian Ammianus describes how the people in fourth-century Rome stood about in the public spaces arguing violently with each other (*Histories* 28.4.28–31). Some of this violence was linked to gambling, especially in taverns. Images, such as those in the bar of Salvius in Pompeii, show fighting gamblers being thrown out by the landlord. Cramped and poor-quality urban living conditions may well have exacerbated these violent tendencies. Some of the fighting occurred when individuals felt their honour was on the line, which is to say that they felt their local status and reputation was being attacked. Cicero argues that ordinary Romans had a less developed sense of honour than the elite but that they were still driven by it (*Divisions of Oratory* 91–2): 'nobody is so rustic that shame and insult do not motivate them.' In reality, individuals probably cared deeply about their reputation in the local communities in which they lived and they fought hard to protect their good name.

Indeed, rivalry between local communities could turn nasty. Tacitus gives two examples. One arose from what he calls 'a trifling incident at a gladiatorial show' (*Annals* 14.17) at Pompeii in AD 59. The locals and the townsfolk of nearby Nuceria started taunting each other, then the abuse turned into stone throwing, until finally swords were drawn and blood flowed. In the other, the rivalry between the cities of Oea and Leptis, on the coast of what is now Libya, first revealed itself with groups stealing crops and cattle from one another. The conflict escalated to the point where regular battles were taking place. Oea, being the smaller city, called in the Garamantes, a fierce tribe who lived on the borders of the empire. This allowed them to inflict heavy casualties on Leptis until they cowered within their city walls for protection (*Histories* 4.50). These were extreme examples, so much so that even a patrician historian like Tacitus, with no special interest in ordinary folk, thought they were worth recording. Nevertheless, they show how loyalty to neighbourhood could lead to terrible scenes.

One form of violent crime that seems to have been an endemic problem in parts of the countryside was banditry. The wealthy would travel with a retinue in order to ward off such attacks. Obviously, more humble people could not afford guards but they could try to attach themselves to such groups of wealthy travellers. So Epictetus advises safety-conscious travellers not to venture out alone along a road, if they have heard it is infested with bandits, but to wait until it is possible to travel in company with an ambassador, a governor's assistant, or the governor himself, so that they may travel safely (*Discourses* 4.1.91). Even then, prominent individuals did go missing. Pliny the Younger records how the equestrian Robustus vanished without trace and adds that the same thing happened to his fellow townsman, Metilius Crispus: 'whether he was killed by his slaves or along with them by bandits no one knows' (*Letters* 6.25). And Cicero complains in a letter to his friend Atticus that he failed to receive one of his letters because his friend, Lucius Quinctus, was robbed and wounded by the roadside (7.9.1).

Keep your Enemies Close

Inheritance could be the cause of acts of violent crime. In one case, a woman called Seia left five pounds of gold to her son, Titius, who then accused her of having arranged his father's death. Seia died before the accusation reached court and she was cleared posthumously. The legal discussion concerns whether Seia's other heirs are obliged to pay out the son given his false accusation (*Digest* 34.4.31.2). As usual, there is the problem of whether this example reflects a hypothetical situation, an exceptional case or an example of a broader social problem. It was certainly considered worth formulating another clause stating that any property an individual has acquired by criminal activity should not constitute part of their estate, for instance 'if he has caused a relative of his to be killed'.

Poison appears to have been a favoured medium (e.g. *Digest* 48.9.7). One of the questions contained in the *Oracles of Astrampsychus* asks, 'Have I been poisoned?' These oracles consist of a list of ninety-two questions that a worried petitioner could ask the gods in order to get their advice on what course of action he or she should take. The oracles were widely popular, with more than ten copies having been found in the rubbish dumps of Egypt alone, while a later Christianised version outlived the Roman empire. Each question has ten possible answers and, in the question concerning poison, four of the ten replies answer in the affirmative. While that percentage is not indicative of the actual likelihood of poisoning, it does show how people were prone to suspect foul play when they started feeling unwell.

Such suspicions could take on remarkable dimensions.

Dio tells of a shadowy group at the time of the emperor Domitian, who made a business of smearing needles with poison and then pricking people they had been paid to target. Many died with no idea of the cause. This happened not only in Rome but all over the empire. Dio claims that a similar outbreak of poisoning occurred during the reign of Commodus (67.11; 73.14). Curious. But rather than leap to conclusions about mass-murdering conspirators, we could note that both episodes occur at a time of otherwise heightened mortality during an outbreak of plague. In the example under Domitian, the fact that the phenomenon is described as happening everywhere in the world again suggests a more generalised cause, such as natural illness, rather than an empire-wide outbreak of malicious poisoning.

Perhaps this shows that when a spate of unexplained deaths occurred, people's natural reaction was to blame it on gangs, which featured prominently in Roman fear of crime in much the same way that they do today. Whether many of these gangs actually existed is hard to say because the evidence is so thin, but it certainly doesn't seem likely that they were responsible for these alleged poisonings.

Violence was an inbuilt feature of household life, whether directed at slaves, children or women. Augustine describes how many women bore the scars of beatings on their faces. Augustine's mother said they should think of their marriage vows 'as the instruments by which they had been turned into slaves' and tells the women 'not [to] be insolent towards their masters' (Confessions 9.9). It was accepted that husbands could act in this way. One old story had it that Egnatius beat his wife to death for drinking wine and was even praised for doing so (Valerius Maximus *Memorable Deeds and Sayings* 6.3.9). Some petitions give a flavour of the kind of intimidation men could use against women. In one from AD 381, a woman called Aurelia Eirene complains of being in a heated quarrel with a man 'who wished to end my life' and spoke 'at her face through his nose'. It sounds like he had his face right up to her (*P. Mich.* 18.793.2–5).

But women also acted as assailants. One account describes how a certain Didyme, the wife of Agathus Daimon, a cook, came to the petitioner's house one evening and 'finding me standing there with my family, did violence to us, in ways both speakable and unspeakable'. The petitioner gives her view of the assailant: 'she is a completely shameless woman, full of bravado.' The altercation grew even more bad-tempered and 'she reached such a peak of insanity that she attacked me, since she is naturally hot-tempered, and struck me, and swore at some of my granddaughters who were standing nearby' (*SB* 6.9421). It is worth bearing in mind that we only have one side of the story here and that the account may well be exaggerated. The victim suggests it was a motiveless attack but presumably there was a back-story. It is also interesting how it portrays the attacker as a stereotypical bad woman: mad, violent and foul-mouthed. Perhaps this was the way to get the male judge to take up the case? In any event, none of these examples seem hugely different from modern cases of violent assault. Often it is impossible to decide between two conflicting versions of what happened. But it was certainly a world where domestic abuse was commonplace and largely accepted.

Rape, on the other hand, was something of an obsession for our ancient authors. This focus did not stem from an exceptional level of concern for the safety of women. Rather it resulted from a daughter's status as being a part of the household under the direction of her father. Any assault on her represented an attack on the integrity and honour of the father, on her family as a whole, and, by extension, on the wider community. As one law tellingly states, a rapist should be punished even if the woman's father was ready to forgive the assailant for the injury done to *him* (*Digest* 48.6.5.2). Even if the father is so forgiving as to excuse an assault on his daughter, the crime was considered such an affront to the structuring of the social order that the attack on the father's own integrity could not go unpunished by society. One act of rape that was seen as perfectly legitimate and acceptable was a master's sexual abuse of his slaves. In Artemidorus's book on dream interpretation, to dream of having sex with a slave girl signified simply that the dreamer would derive pleasure from his assets.

It is tempting to use other comparative data on violent crime to shed light on what the Roman experience might have been. One problem is that crime rates vary enormously between societies. In the modern Third World, for instance, cities with many of the same characteristics as ancient Rome have lower levels of murder than do many American cities. Another is the uniqueness of Rome. Yes, it was a pre-industrial city, but it was much bigger than any other pre-industrial city outside China. The medieval period has some superficial similarities: there was widespread poverty, a high degree of inequality and a low level of policing. But the data for the Middle Ages is not much less problematic than the ancient evidence. One historical sociologist has argued that the annual murder rate in medieval London stood at about fifty per one hundred thousand of the population (it is now less than two). The problem is that it is very unclear how large the population of London was. Estimates for the fourteenth century range from not much more than thirty-five thousand to more than one hundred and fifty thousand, for the simple reason that we do not know how densely occupied most buildings were. Taking the highest estimates lowers the murder rate to something like ten per one hundred thousand: higher than London today but lower than many American cities. Perhaps the largest single difference is the modern availability of emergency healthcare. Wounds that would be easily treatable now would have killed in the ancient world. Comparing Rome with other societies is always a risky business and with crime the problems seem to be even greater than usual.

The ancient sources don't help much if we want a statistical picture of Roman crime. The best we can do is highlight some of its features. Violence against the person was probably at least as common as crime against property. This reflected the much lower level of property ownership and also a society where the use of force in personal relationships was more acceptable. Violence seems to have been as common in rural as in urban settings, although it took different forms: banditry as opposed to muggings. The wealthy are likely to have suffered less violence because they could pay for personal protection. The urban poor will have inhabited environments that were more crowded, offering plenty of opportunities for the criminal to strike. Rome's population was divided vertically not horizontally, meaning that areas of the city were less divided according to status and wealth than would now be the case. Modest residential buildings sat cheek by jowl with grand urban villas. There were no crime-ridden no-go areas. Women are likely to have suffered from assault from both within and outside the household.

Crime Fiction

One interesting type of evidence we possess are legal textbooks used by wealthy young men at law school. Known as declamations, these texts formed the backbone of higher education. They invited students to make speeches in fictional court cases on behalf of the defence or prosecution. The themes covered a titillating range of violent crime: murder, poisoning, tyrannicide, parricide, infanticide, the execution of children, torture, rape, and the mistreatment of wives and slaves. Here's an example from the declamations of Calpurnius Flaccus, an orator who practised in the first half of the second century AD. A young man was promised in marriage to a girl against her mother's wishes, who says she will die before she lets her daughter marry him. The girl then dies in circumstances suggesting poisoning. Her father conducts his own investigation by interrogating the household slaves under torture. A slave girl confesses that the mother was having an adulterous affair with the very young man who had been betrothed to her daughter. The father then accuses his wife of poisoning her daughter (*Declamation* 40).

These declamations often portray women negatively, with rape victims shown as exhibiting a cruel lust for revenge. It is striking how often women appear as victims of rape. One case concerns a girl who refuses to say anything about her ordeal: brought before the magistrate, she keeps quiet and weeps (16). During the trial, she is subjected to a cross-examination by the defence attorney. The lawyer describes the nobility of the defendant's appearance and how he is the kind of young man that any parent would pray to have as either a son or a son-in-law. It turns out that the accused had sought the girl's hand in marriage but had become impatient. He was, says the lawyer, just a typical lover, and, 'how shall I put this – did he rape her or did he marry her?' After all, she had lodged no formal complaint. Despite her refusal to give evidence, the magistrate has the rapist put to death. The girl is so distraught that she killed herself. This case is a work of fiction but it is clearly suggestive of the kind of casual attitude towards rape that many men seem to have had. As a lawyer says in another fictional rape case, 'What have you actually suffered, girl? So you lost your virginity, it's usual at your age, and in any case you were probably desperate to lose it!' (43).

These deliberations sound pretty outrageous to modern ears. In a sense, the Romans might have agreed. Tacitus complains that these declamations were ridiculously over the top, with subjects that are 'remote from all reality'. What was daily discussed in the classroom very rarely made it to the courts (*Dialogue on Oratory* 35). Why was it like this? It may be relevant that this material was aimed at teenage boys. Orators also had to attract pupils, so lurid content was a way of drumming up business. And doubtless the convoluted nature of the themes did genuinely challenge the legal skills of the aspiring lawyer.

What is perhaps more revealing is that these exaggerated speeches were used to train the empire's elite. In doing so they helped inculcate the social values of the ruling class, and are indicative of the imaginative concerns of the wealthy male, whose preoccupations differed greatly from those of a modern audience: there is no interest in the feelings of the victim, no attempt to look for proper evidence, just an endless concern about what was going on in the household behind their backs and a belief in their own ability to discern the truth by forming moral judgements concerning the character of others.

Attitudes to Violence

When Lucius Domitius was in charge of Sicily, Cicero reports that a huge wild boar was brought to him. Amazed at its size, he asked who had killed it. A certain slave shepherd, he was told. Domitius summoned the shepherd who came eagerly, expecting a reward. Domitius asked him how he had slain so huge a beast and the slave answered, 'With a hunting spear'. At once, Domitius had him crucified: slaves were not allowed to carry weapons. 'This may perhaps appear harsh,' admits Cicero, 'but Domitius preferred to appear cruel in punishing than to seeming negligent in overlooking offences' (*Against Verres* 2.5.7). What this story suggests, and many others confirm, is that the Romans didn't see violence the way we do (most of us, anyway). For us, it is abhorrent, barbaric. For them, it was the very key to civilised order.

And yet brutality had its limits, even when dealing with slaves. The story of Vedius Pollio (as told in Dio *Roman History* 54.23.1) shows both that very harsh punishments could be acceptable and that extremes of mistreatment were not. Pollio was prevented by the emperor Augustus from having a slave boy thrown to his man-eating eels. The slave's crime was dropping a vase. Progress! And it didn't stop there. Claudius built on Augustus's acts by declaring it illegal to kill slaves on a whim. Slaves were also given the legal right of appeal against abusive treatment. Did this mean that emperors wished to improve their conditions? I wouldn't bet on it. More plausibly, as emperors got more involved in all aspects of life, people simply looked to them to give guidance on where the limits should be set. A good rule of thumb, in Rome as in life, is this: never attribute to reformist zeal what can be explained by the simple consolidation of power.

One crime that the Romans thought deserved the most draconian punishment was the murder of a master by one of his slaves. The case of the death in AD 61 of the prefect of Rome, Pedanius Secundus, highlights the severity of the treatment. One of his slaves had killed him, either because Pedanius had reneged on a deal to free him or because the slave had fallen in love with one of his master's own favourites and didn't want to share. According to an ancient law, all of Pedanius's four hundred household slaves were condemned to death because they had failed to prevent the murder. At this point, things got interesting. When the four hundred were being marched to their deaths, the Roman people filled the streets and tried to block their way. They went so far as to besiege the senate house. The senate debated the matter, and even in this conservative institution many spoke against enforcing the traditional penalty. To no avail: the senate decided to kill them all. The verdict isn't so surprising, but it is noteworthy how this offended the ordinary Roman's sense of natural justice, so much so that they continued their protests. In the end, the crucifixions could take place only under armed guard (Tacitus *Annals* 14.42–5).

The penalty didn't just have tradition on its side. Arguably it was good behavioural economics, too. Condemning all the slaves in the household when a master was murdered ensured that they had an incentive to tell him about any plots that came to their attention. It also made sure that slaves were more likely to come to their master's aid in the event of an attack. That might be why reports of master-murder are so remarkably rare in the surviving sources: perhaps these brutal laws successfully terrorised the servile population. Or it might be that our sources only record a few high-profile cases in a sea of less distinguished dominicides. Whatever the cause, people weren't writing about it much.

Opposition to the execution of Pedanius's slaves notwithstanding, judicial violence seems in general to have been regarded as acceptable. The routine torture of slaves in legal proceedings is one of the most shocking abuses to the modern reader but was perfectly normal in Roman courts. Slaves were seen as too morally weak to be relied

upon to tell the truth. Torture was seen as a way of actually getting to it. The Romans did understand that
evidence obtained under torture needed to be treated
with caution, but examples of slaves lying to get the pain
to stop did not reduce what they saw as the benefits of the
practice. And so the atmosphere in Roman courts could
be tense. Transcripts of proceedings survive, recorded by
court shorthand writers, and give a flavour of the kind of
interrogations that took place. In one, dating from AD 136
(*P. Oslo* 2.17) the District Magistrate of the Prosopite district in Egypt questions two men accused of cutting down
some vines:

> District Magistrate: 'What did you say about these
> men?'
> Witness: 'The accused left the drinking party in the
> middle of the night, but came back to say they had
> cut down the vines of Imouthes.'
> Defendants: 'His charge is without foundation!'
> DM: 'Did you meet him at that time?'
> Defendants: 'Yes, but he never heard us say such a
> thing.'
> DM: 'If you have a clear conscience, why did you not
> appear at the preliminary hearing until after your
> names had been posted up?'
> Defendants: 'We were working far away on another
> estate.'
> DM: 'And the reason you attacked this estate is the
> one which Haronnesis stated.'
> And the District Magistrate ordered them to be tor-
> tured and said: 'Admit the truth!' but they persisted in

saying that they had not cut down the vines ...
DM: 'Make sure that these two give sufficient security
so that they present themselves to his excellency the
sub-prefect whenever he takes the matter up.'

We can almost hear the screams echoing off the page.

The state did attempt to control the use of violence
within the legal context. Anyone who pursued their legal
claims by means of force would forfeit any right to such
claims. This extended to the use of force in such matters
as debt collection where creditors were, according to a
second-century decree from Marcus Aurelius, only permitted to seize a debtor's assets once they were in
possession of a court order (*Digest* 48.7.7). Carrying
weapons was also seen as an aggravating factor in a case
such as robbery from corpses, where being armed
increased the punishment from exile to the mines to
death (*Digest* 47.12.3.7).

In the wider Roman world, though, brutality was
everywhere. The violent entertainment of the Colosseum, for example, was a hub of society. The games
needed a steady supply of criminals to satisfy this demand,
and the crimes that could see a person condemned to the
arena included murder, treason, robbery, arson or, if you
were a slave, simply running away. The best criminals
were thought to be those with powerful physiques who
knew how to fight; a lively semi-legal trade seems to have
grown up around them, with hosts buying up prime spec-
imens for their shows. The central authorities tried to put
a stop to this by insisting that the best criminals should be
sent to Rome for the games there, rather than being

traded in the provinces (*Digest* 48.19.31; Philostratus *Life of Apollonius of Tyana* 4.22).

The spectators themselves loved violence. One advert for a show even proclaims that ten bears will be killed 'cruelly'. Mere death was not enough. Punishments could be enhanced by mythological staging to increase the entertainment factor. On one occasion, a condemned criminal emerged from below the arena dressed as Orpheus. Wild animals crowded around him and, as in the myth, responded sweetly to his lyre. Wild animals were often trained for their appearance in the arena; a mosaic in North Africa depicts a hunt where members of a guild known as the Telegenii seem to have trained captured leopard cubs to attack human fighters. Something similar may have happened here: for a time, Orpheus was able to calm the beasts before him. Then, at a hidden signal from the trainer, the poor man was torn apart by a bear. The crowd loved this toying with well-known mythological plots; the violent end which everyone knew was coming just added to the fun.

Roman acceptance of violence extended to getting rid of unwanted newborn infants either by killing them directly or abandoning them. Many pre-industrial societies, lacking any effective means of contraception, have turned a blind eye to this practice. One calculation for the UK for the period 1863–87 suggests that infanticide counted for 61 per cent of all homicides. That's shocking to us, but throwing away a baby after birth was probably safer than aborting it as a foetus. One surviving letter from Egypt has an absent father telling his pregnant wife what to do if she gives birth before he returns: 'If it is a boy keep it, if it is a girl expose it' (*P. Oxy.* 4.744). But it is impossible to know how common this practice was. References to exposure are quite rare. Some archaeological sites have been found to contain large numbers of infant skeletons, but these may be related to particular kinds of establishment, such as brothels.

Despite this acceptance of infanticide and exposure, the Romans seem to have been squeamish about castration. The practice was banned by the emperor Domitian, which was odd: according to Dio, he himself entertained a fondness for a eunuch named Earinus (67.2.3). Castrated slave boys did not enter puberty. This meant that they maintained their boyish looks and, accordingly, fetched higher prices. Why? They were probably kept as a kind of pet, or because masters feared that male slaves would get female members of the household pregnant. Whatever the selling point was, it must have been persuasive: the ban on domestic production simply led to an increase in imports.

A Violent Psychology?

Today, we often talk about fear as an important factor in people's experience of crime. The Romans were no different. But fear of crime in a modern sense implies a level of anxiety that is out of proportion to the objective risk: it's a pathological state. In the Roman empire, worrying about becoming the victim of a violent assault does not seem to have been so illogical. The lack of any hard data makes speculation difficult. What is clear is that the Romans also possessed two qualitatively different kinds of fear of crime. The first was the very real fear of being

accused of a crime. The legal corpus contains references
to individuals who committed suicide after being accused
of some crime or other (*Digest* 48.21.3). The law was, for
most people, a terrifying institutional process and the
prospect of becoming caught up in it was enough to drive
some to take their own lives. The second fear was a pre-
vailing concern that an individual was about to fall into a
life of crime, not be a victim of it. Living on the bread line
probably meant that many were perpetually on the verge
of contemplating illegal means to supplement their
meagre livings, with all the negative corollaries that could
bring.

And yet, the people seemed to find the smack of firm
government reassuring. Dramatic public punishment
brought them together by reaffirming their shared values.
The crowd at the games had no pity for condemned criminals: they had earned their fate. The poet Martial
describes how one man was torn limb from limb and evis-
cerated. Even though nobody knew what crime the
condemned man had committed, the poet is adamant
that he deserved it (*On Spectacles* 9). In some societies,
such savage punishments have created a bond between
the offender and the crowd who sympathise with his terrible fate. There is little evidence for this in Rome. The
violent end of criminals served to reinforce the norms of
mainstream Roman society, which demanded a public,
physical retribution against those who dared to breach its
laws. It reassured the crowd that the social order was
stable and that its values had been upheld.

The degree of violence used also reflected the status
of the individual. Punishments for those of higher social

rank often took the form of exile; lower status individuals were whipped. The scars of corporal punishment became a potent symbol, which literally marked out those who had breached socially acceptable behaviour. It also generated significant anxiety. Beaten men were paraded about their city to exhibit their torn backs to the crowd, a profound humiliation. The fourth-century orator Libanius describes how the governor once flogged some bakers for profiteering during a corn shortage: 'I heard the sound of the lash, so dear to the common people, who were all agog at the sight of the bleeding backs' (*Oration* 1.208). Exemption from beating was associated with Roman citizenship (although this privilege ceased to have much meaning under the empire). By contrast, the scars of whip marks and brandings told people they were looking at a slave, a former slave or a criminal.

Judicial execution achieved several aims. It was seen as keeping the public safe by permanently removing the criminal from society; it deterred others from committing the same crimes and it restored society's dignity after it had been harmed by the criminal act. The Romans themselves recognised these purposes of the law. The second-century author Aulus Gellius argues that punishment existed to correct and reform, to maintain the dignity and esteem of the victim, and to deter others. The opening of the *Digest* emphasises that the law also served a positive role by encouraging virtue (1.1.1.1). The Roman legal system may have been slow to react to much violent crime but, when it did, it made an example of those convicted and ensured that this took place in the most visible way through the medium of violence, which everyone could understand. We might disapprove of its brutality but perhaps it was a pragmatic response to the limitations of the day. Fierce punishments were a way of compensating for the low chance of detection, rather in the way that a large jackpot compensates for the low chance of winning the lottery. There simply were not enough resources to do anything more than make a terrifying example of those few criminals who were apprehended.

The Violent Emperor

What then are we to make of the story of Nero mugging people in the street? We might never know if it really happened, but we can surmise that it seemed worth passing on largely because it pressed a number of the elite's most sensitive buttons. Here was an emperor who was too close to the people. Nero had fallen out with the senate and looked to his popularity among the Roman people to provide legitimacy for his regime. What better way to represent this proximity to the plebs than to portray Nero as acting like one. His actions took place in the dark and gloomy streets of night-time Rome, the last place where any respectable Roman gentleman would want to be seen. This kind of city represented all that was bad about contemporary society: a world where violence seemed endemic, where the people were out of control and where the traditional virtues that had won Rome its empire had long since disappeared. But, perhaps above all, the mugger emperor served as a metaphor for an illegitimate ruler, who deserved, like a common criminal, to be physically punished for his behaviour.

Nero's assaults on random victims reflected his violence towards the aristocracy as a whole. His personal brutality reflected his regime. The fact that the head of the legal system was breaking the law symbolised the breakdown in the proper social order under his leadership. The story can seem rather silly to us but living under Nero was a terrifying experience for many at the top of Rome's hierarchy. The image of the mugging Nero was a neat way to express all these anxieties in a simple story. I have no idea whether Nero did in fact act in this way. But, in a way, that is irrelevant. It made sense to the aristocratic readership of this text to portray Nero acting like a common crook; it was outrageous to them that someone that vulgar was in power. The fact that he did not behave like one of the elite was the real problem.

One example of a text where we do get a sense of what ordinary people thought relates to Nero's alleged involvement in starting the Great Fire of Rome in AD 64. The surviving accounts place great emphasis on the horrifying experience of the victims. Nero purportedly had henchmen, while pretending to be drunk, start various fires, and 'extraordinary frenzy laid hold of all the citizens', such that 'they ran about in different directions, as if distracted' (Dio *Roman History* 62.16–18). Tacitus in particular focuses on the fate of the crowd. There was a great crush, he says, and many were suffocated and trampled in their desperation to evade the flames, because they could see that there was no easy escape, 'owing to the narrow, twisting lanes and formless streets typical of old Rome' (Tacitus *Annals* 15.38). Many were so crazed by panic that they leapt 'into the very flames'. Did Tacitus concentrate on this because he especially cared about their fate? To a degree, perhaps, but it also seems like a way to emphasise the great suffering of the Roman people under an emperor as bad as Nero. Nero gets written up as nothing less than a violent criminal and arsonist. Tacitus's history was produced for other members of the elite, not for a reading public. The role of the people in his account is to shed light on the malpractice of high politics. We are caught up in an elite rhetorical game.

The opposite of Nero was Augustus: an emperor who established security and order. After the lawlessness of the civil wars at the end of the republic, criminal gangs were rife, probably made up of soldiers whose generals had been defeated. Augustus, Suetonius assures us, put a stop to such brigandage by posting soldiers wherever the problem existed and by banning popular clubs that were acting as fronts for organised crime. He then reformed the courts and put an end to long-running cases that were being pursued only for reasons of personal hostility (*Augustus* 32). Again, much of this may be true. But the reason why it mattered to Suetonius was that it reflected a leader who was restoring the social order and the legal system that both supported and reflected it.

Can we reconstruct anything of the reality of violent crime in Rome? The petitions are helpful in that they let us hear a voice from lower down the social scale, even if that cannot simply be treated as some kind of ancient victim statement. It certainly seems to be the case that there was a general societal disposition towards hierarchy and competition, which often found its expression in violence. Today, we tend to think it better to find a peaceful

solution to disputes and regard violence as symptomatic
of a breakdown in the process, but in Rome it often seems
that violence was considered the proper way to settle an
argument. It often took ritualised forms and could generate a powerful sense of community. In a sense, perhaps, it
played a positive social role.

Most Romans inhabited a world of fear, and violence
was as normal a part of life in the home and the neighbourhood as was wine and olive oil. Policing was minimal.
It never occurred to the government to try to do more to
protect individuals from the effects of violent crime – officials were only ever interested in violence that could
threaten the social order. The Romans coped without a
police force by turning to family to protect them against
the brutal assaults of violent criminals and, when they did
suffer violence, they often had no alternative other than
to grimace and bear it. It is, after all, hardly surprising that
a society that glorified in war and even celebrated its
martial spirit in the brutal entertainments of the games
should see nothing wrong in a daily diet of casual
violence.

Chapter II

FROM PETTY THEFT TO GRAND LARCENY

If there is one crime that gives a clear sense of everyday life in ancient Rome, it is theft. The satirist Juvenal bitterly describes Rome as a city plagued by housebreakers, pickpockets and petty thieves. Despite our doubts about him as a witness, other evidence suggests that his picture was not far wrong and that Rome was a hard place in which to keep hold of your belongings. In fact, theft seems to have been rife throughout the empire. A papyrus from Egypt describes how thieves entered a storeroom by cutting a hole through the ceiling of the room underneath. Domestic buildings in this part of the empire were generally built of wood and simple mud bricks and so walls and ceilings did not always offer much of a barrier to potential burglars. In one case someone dug through the walls of a building from the street and stole the sheep contained within. In another, the thieves removed the nails from the door of the house during the night and, as the victim complains, 'taking advantage of my absence on account of my mourning for my daughter's husband', they carried off everything (*P. Tebt.* 2.332).

These cases highlight the small-town nature of much Roman theft. It wasn't all like that. The second-century emperor Commodus (of the film *Gladiator*) is alleged to have charged wealthy senators with treason and then executed them precisely so that he could confiscate their property for the imperial treasury. Quasi-legal theft of this kind was an easy way for emperors who had no respect for their own laws to boost their incomes.

Petty theft could also be carried out by the rich. Titus Vinius, who later rose to the rank of general, besmirched his reputation by stealing a golden cup at a dinner party thrown by the emperor Claudius, an act that the historian Tacitus rather sniffily describes as 'worthy of a slave'. To make his point, Claudius invited Titus to dinner again the next day but had the servants put earthenware plates in front of him while the other guests dined off silver (Tacitus *Histories* 1.48).

A good deal of theft seems to have been carried out by people who were well known to their victims: neighbours or even family members. In this kind of crime, victims were often close to where the offence took place and so confronted the thieves, or did so later if they knew or suspected the perpetrators, with bloody consequences.

Examples of this kind of intimate theft are commonplace. One papyrus from AD 144 describes how a woman had some jewellery stolen from her house while she was away and believed that a neighbour had done it (*P. Oxy.* 10.1272). The first-century AD astrologer, Dorotheus of Sidon, gives detailed physical descriptions of thieves who are either from the household or have visited the house and 'its people know him' (*Five Books on Astrology* 5.35.76–8). He even uses his reading of the star charts to describe how some burglars gain entry by using their inside knowledge to acquire copies of the door key (5.35.137). All this happens despite the fact that, 'there is friendship between him and the people of the house and they trust him.'

Other domestic thefts resulted from marital breakdown. One jilted husband reports that his wife 'became dissatisfied with marriage to me' and left him, taking their child with her. Before she went, she helped herself to some of his property: a large cloak, a pillow, a small garment, a clothes chest, two tunics, some jars and various agricultural implements. The abandoned father complains that, even though he sends her maintenance for the child, the mother will not return his belongings. Then he hears that she has actually run off with another man, called Nilos, and has married him, so, having had enough, he fires off this petition (*P. Heid.* 13). But most theft, particularly in the cities, was probably less personal than this. The sheer size of the city of Rome meant that the average villain would have had many more opportunities than presented by a small Egyptian village and need not have preyed on neighbours.

Roman law pertaining to theft contained very different legal precepts from those of today. The Romans did not use distinct terms for theft and for burglary, which in its original Saxon meaning meant nocturnal housebreaking. But they did treat theft from a house during the night more severely than if it had occurred during the day. The Romans' primary distinction was between 'manifest' and 'non-manifest' theft, which meant whether the thief had been caught in the act or not. This largely depended on how close to the scene of the crime the thief was caught, although exactly where the line could be drawn was a matter for debate among lawyers. If you caught a thief with a stolen jug just outside your house it would count as a manifest theft, but catch him a few miles away and it would not. It was rather like trying to define what 'caught in the act' means today. Yes, if I catch the thief holding my wallet 'red-handed', a metre from me as I turn around; probably yes if I find him having a coffee further up the street; but not if he has made it home and hidden the wallet in his bedroom before the police arrive. Determining what 'caught in the act' means is further complicated by the fact that there is also a time component to this definition. Today, the punishment is the same if we catch the thief in the act or catch him a week later a thousand miles away, provided that we can prove 'beyond reasonable doubt' that he did it. Roman punishment, however, was more severe for manifest theft for the simple reason that once someone was out of sight then the degree to which they were clearly culpable declined and the Romans did not want to punish fully someone who might have been innocent.

Roman law also had a strange rite for the discovery of stolen goods, known as the 'plate and loincloth search'. The victim had to walk semi-naked through the suspect's premises while holding a plate in his hands. The point of this was that, by holding the plate, the victim was prevented from touching any evidence, or indeed planting it, in the accused's house. It may also have represented an

offering to the household gods so they might help reveal
where the stolen items had been concealed. In theory, the
victim would spot his stolen belongings and thereby
prove the case. In reality, such a procedure would only
have been useful in recovering large or living items, such
as a horse or a slave, not for coins or small valuables,
which would be far easier to hide or impossible to iden-
tify. For the most part, stolen goods were unlikely to be
recovered. One way of seeing this is in a question to the
gods contained in the *Oracles of Astrampsychus*: 'Will I find
what I have lost?' Of the possible answers, 70 per cent of
the responses were that the items would not be recovered. Only 30 per cent were positive, with a third of those
saying that such recovery would only happen after a
period of time. This distribution of possible outcomes
would have seemed sensible to whoever compiled the
responses in the oracle. There was no point giving the
impression that the stolen goods might be recovered since
that was not typical. What worked in the victim's favour
was that often, as Dorotheus warned, it was people within
the household – family members or slaves – who had perpetrated the theft and so were more likely to be found out
and the stolen items returned.

Certain kinds of theft were seen as more serious than
others and during the empire became liable to public
criminal punishment. Robbers who used violence, for
example, could be sentenced to hard labour on the public
works, either for a fixed sentence or even for life. But it
was another feature of Roman law that it did not punish
all criminals equally: it adjusted sentences according to
the perpetrator's social station. Robbers 'of superior rank'

would not face such draconian punishment but were instead temporarily demoted or sent into exile (*Digest* 47.18.1.1). It might seem strange that members of the elite indulged in theft, but it did happen: in one case a Roman knight stole money after having broken through a wall to get at it. He was banished from his home province of Africa as well as from Italy for five years (*Digest* 47.18.1.2).

Just as Roman law saw housebreaking by night as more serious than by day, so it also singled out those who carried bags when thieving as deserving of particularly harsh punishment, presumably because they were going with intent to steal as much as they could carry, rather than simply snatching an item or two opportunistically. Cattle rustling was likewise frowned upon if the perpetrators carried out the activity on a regular basis. The theft of larger animals, such as cows or horses, was also seen as a more serious offence than driving away pigs, goats or sheep. A real problem in the hills and pastures of the empire was that animals were prey to rustlers, who could easily overpower any shepherd. The Roman sensitivity about cattle theft also reflects the fact that most lawyers were wealthy, and therefore landowners, and so were constantly facing this kind of annoyance in the management of their estates. It was even illegal to wave a red flag if it frightened cattle into running off and getting stolen (*Digest* 47.2.50.4).

Those who aided and abetted theft were regarded in law as being as bad as the thieves themselves. Anyone who knowingly lent tools so they could be used to break open a door or closet, or lent a ladder for the purpose of climbing over a wall to steal something, was liable even if he had not planned the theft himself (*Digest* 47.2.55). Similarly, anyone who harboured criminals was seen as 'one of the worst classes of offenders' because they would charge the fugitives part of the stolen goods for having concealed them (*Digest* 47.16). The law did allow some leeway in the case of those who harboured members of their own family since this was more understandable and, in some cases, unavoidable.

The law tried to prevent people from helping themselves to goods from wrecked ships that washed ashore (*Digest* 47.9). But this was the kind of offence that ordinary people do not seem to have thought was morally bad, or at least they tacitly condoned it. The emperor Hadrian stated that those who owned land on the seashore were responsible for making sure that, if a ship was badly damaged or broken up, nothing was stolen from the wreck. It is also clear that as soon as a ship got into difficulties, some people would try to take goods from it – that is, those on board would try to make it to shore while also helping themselves to valuable cargo. If this is true then clearly such action was in itself likely to increase the chance of the ship being wrecked because the crew would be leaving it unmanned, abandoning it to fate. In the view of the law, taking goods from shipwrecks was simply looting – individuals taking advantage of disasters for their own benefit. It was no different from someone stealing things from a burning building, or one that had collapsed. It is no surprise that the same wealthy men who wrote the laws also tended to finance trade and objected to anyone taking advantage of their misfortune. But for the crew, and the people who lived along the coast, such wrecks provided an easy opportunity to benefit from an entrepreneur's mishap. After all, trade was known to be a high-risk business and investors could afford to take a few losses alongside the rich pickings they made when their ships docked safely. Some fishermen even tried actively to wreck ships by showing lights at night in order to trick a ship's crew into thinking they were approaching a port, when in fact they were luring them on to the rocks.

Crime Prevention

In the face of such widespread theft, Romans of all classes took a variety of measures to help protect their property. First came physical self-defence. Citizens were expected to look after themselves, their possessions and their property. To do so, they relied on a network of family members and neighbours, who acted as a kind of neighbourhood watch over each other's belongings. But such soft surveillance would never be sufficient. The Roman author Pliny the Elder, who died when he sailed close to Vesuvius in order to observe the eruption in close detail, complains how ordinary people in Rome used to keep window boxes full of flowers and plants so that they would still have a daily glimpse of rural life, but that 'countless numbers of atrocious burglaries' had compelled them to block up their windows with shutters (*Natural History* 19.59).

The cases from the astrologer Dorotheus gave us a sense of how easy it was to enter ancient houses. The Romans did develop locks, and most archaeological digs of domestic Roman sites usually yield a good crop of these devices. Many were made of wood, though, and

would not have posed much of a deterrent to a determined thief; the astrologer warns his clients that thieves
will simply break the locks. We have also seen that the
houses themselves were not that sturdy. The impressive
remains of many Roman villas that survive can blind us
to the reality that most Romans lived in buildings that
were of poor-quality construction. Dorotheus says that
burglars will gain entry after simply digging under the
walls of the house or knocking holes through them (*Five
Books on Astrology* 5.35.137).

Keys and locks were not only used for front doors.
Chests, caskets, cupboards and internal storerooms all
often had locks affixed to them. Some ring-keys have been
found, and these were probably worn by the woman of
the house as a symbol of her authority over the household and the management of its contents. A small number
of Roman padlocks survive, too, some of which have
sophisticated spring actions, but how common these were
is hard to say. The intricate manufacturing involved would
have made them expensive and so available only to those
who had quite a lot of wealth to protect in the first place.
And, as they would have been made of metal, they are
more likely to have rusted away so may have not survived
in a representative quantity. The kind of lock used on the
household chest, though, is found more widely and probably reflects its status as the standard means for a family
with valuables to keep them under lock and key.

The wealthiest members of society had to make extra
provisions to ward off burglars and ensure the safety of
their belongings. Those who owned villas would deploy
slaves as gatekeepers to make sure that undesirables were

kept out during the day and that no one tried to scale the walls or force the locked gates during the night. Dogs were widely used to guard property and were sometimes depicted in mosaics with the words *cave canem* 'beware of the dog', presumably as an extra warning to anyone thinking of entering the house uninvited. It is possible that these mosaics did not represent the kind of fierce hound that was actually on patrol but rather served as a playful image designed to amuse visitors. Perhaps it was both. Valuable items kept locked in chests might also be held in strong rooms in the centre of the house to prevent burglars simply knocking through an outside wall. The House of Menander in Pompeii, for example, has such a safe room underground, beneath the house baths, where a chest was discovered containing over a hundred pieces of fine silverware. Its owner, Quintus Poppaeus, was clearly a rich man, and the room seems to have been designed for carefully controlled access by means of a key, its walls thickened to stop thieves tunnelling into it, and placed underground to make it harder for them to tunnel under it.

Most people could not afford such strong rooms, and instead had the option of storing their valuables in a temple for safekeeping. The temple at the north end of the forum in Pompeii has a crypt that may have served as a kind of municipal strong room in the same way that the vault under the Temple of Saturn did at Rome (although that did not prevent Julius Caesar from helping himself to its contents). These temples had thick stone walls, priests and slaves on duty 24/7, and had the added protection of the gods. Any temple thief risked being struck down by divine retribution. Even so, some seem to have been prepared to take the chance. Temples were also as vulnerable to fire as the rest of the city. When the Temple of Peace burned down in AD 238, many of the richest people in Rome were, according to the historian Herodian, reduced to penury overnight, although in reality we might imagine that they also stored considerable assets in private strong rooms or held them in the form of property (*History of the Empire since the Death of Marcus Aurelius* 1.14.3). It would have made sense to spread your assets around rather than having all your wealth located in one place.

The lack of a credit-based banking system meant that all wealth existed in real assets, whether land, property, precious metals or coins. Anything that could be carried away would be, if not adequately protected. That made travelling peculiarly dangerous. There is a reference to an older Greek custom of carrying coins in the mouth to keep them safe from pickpockets and this may have continued into the Roman world. One law refers to the practice of entrusting possessions to sailors, innkeepers and the proprietors of stables (*Digest* 4.9.1.1), the idea being to reduce the number of valuables that travellers would otherwise be carrying. Of course, the law probably only existed because those sailors, innkeepers and ostlers sometimes refused to give the stuff back and, in fact, the law complains that such people were known to collude with thieves to target those travellers with fat purses.

The state recognised that it had a duty to prevent crimes such as theft. One law proclaims: 'Every good and worthy Governor should take care that the province over which he presides is peaceable and quiet.' This he will accomplish if he exerts himself to expel bad men and diligently seek them out, including those who commit acts of sacrilege, as well as robbers, kidnappers and thieves (*Digest* 1.18.13 pref.). He must 'prevent injustice, nor allow men who are honest and peace-loving to suffer injury' (Justinian *New Constitutions* 29.5). Fine intentions but the state provided limited means to deliver them. The Roman world had no police force in the modern sense, only the Nightwatch in Rome, a group that numbered somewhere between 3,500 and 7,000 men; not an insignificant force but one whose primary aim was fire prevention rather than crime-fighting.

The section of the *Digest* dealing with the duties of the prefect of the *vigiles* in Rome gives a sense of the Nightwatch's broad remit (1.15). They were to look out for arsonists, burglars, thieves, robbers and those who harboured criminals, as well as citizens who were careless with fire, since 'fires are mostly caused by the negligence of inhabitants'. It also gives a sense of what kind of burglary was most common: the most vulnerable properties seem not to have been the great villas of the rich but the blocks of flats where most people lived. These *insulae* – 'islands' – could be six or more stories high, with the quality of the flat deteriorating the higher you went. The wooden upper floors must have been very susceptible to break-ins, not least by neighbours who would know when the occupants were out. The *Digest* also describes how those who had been set as guards over these properties were often punished for the thefts. It is easy to imagine how a slave or a poor free man would be tempted to purloin something when keeping watch, but it might equally be the case that it was just easiest to blame them whenever something went missing. Finally, the *Digest* states that the head of the *vigiles* should keep an eye on individuals who look after people's clothes in the great bath houses. Having items stolen while you were relaxing in the steam room was a perennial hazard in Rome. Those who had no slave of their own to do the task would often pay others to guard their belongings. Being a bath-guard was not the best paid job in the Roman world. The temptation to steal must have been enormous.

The Victim's Choices

What could the victim of theft do? Usually, nothing. The same is true today, of course, when even if we know that the police could investigate, we may not hold out much hope of redress. In Roman times, if the victim knew the offender, he or she could seek retribution personally, probably with the help of friends or family. Naturally, dealing with bully-boy thieves would involve risks to personal safety. A less confrontational route may have been to seek some kind of private settlement whereby the thief simply agreed to return the stolen items and the victim offered to let the matter drop. In the Egyptian papyrus from AD 144, where a woman suspected her neighbour of having stolen some jewellery from her house while she was away, she asks for no more than the return of her property.

Another option, if the perpetrator was unknown, was to offer a reward. A piece of graffiti from Pompeii reflects this self-help approach in the face of petty theft: 'A copper pot went missing from my shop. Anyone who returns it to me will be given sixty-five sesterces. Twenty more will be given for information leading to the capture of the thief' (*CIL* 4.64). This may have had some success although the description is hardly detailed. It is almost as if the purpose of the notice is to advertise that the shopkeeper is doing well enough to own valuable copper pots and even has the cash to offer rewards for their safe return.

The victim could turn to the law. But rather than going to the police, a Roman victim of theft had to bring a civil case against the accused. It took money and connections to get the law to look at your case and it was up to the victims to collect the evidence. One of the characters in the ancient novel *The Golden Ass* (as Apuleius's *Metamorphoses* is traditionally translated), claims that 'the law was so humane that even the poorest man could always get redress for the encroachment of an arrogant neighbour' (9.36); the reality will have fallen short of this ideal.

Another option was to petition the city prefect or, in the provinces, the local governor. We have many examples of such petitions surviving and also many of the written responses (known as rescripts) sent by emperors and their officials. But the fact that a petition was sent did not mean that it was dealt with. One governor on a two-day visit to a town in Egypt received 1,804 petitions, an impossibly large quantity to deal with (*P. Yale* 1.61). Presumably he and his team decided which ones to reply to based on various criteria: was the petitioner important enough (of course, if he or she was that important they would not have needed to send a petition); was the case important enough in that it might have had ramifications elsewhere in the province; and was there a legal principle involved?

Even if victims did send a petition to the governor, they still had to collect their own evidence. In the case we saw earlier where someone had dug through the walls of a building and stole the sheep within, the victim searched the neighbourhood and found the animals in a temple. He showed these to a village official for corroboration before filing his petition. In another incident in Egypt, dating from AD 190, the petitioner describes how the thieves 'broke through a window which overlooks a public street and which had been blocked up with bricks, probably using a log as a battering ram'. The victim scoured the crime scene and worked out that the thieves had lowered his barley through a window, which he concluded from the traces of the rope upon the sill (*P. Oxy.* 1.69).

This claimant sounds honest enough. Others, less so. In one, a man called Hermon alleges that his fish pond has been raided and that one whole talent's worth of fish has been stolen. A talent equalled six thousand drachma, or somewhere between 2,117 and 180,000 fish, depending on what prices are used. Clearly something dodgy is going on here (*P. Oxy.* 19.2234). Why lie to the governor? It might have been a way to exaggerate the size of the claim and so make it more noticeable. Or perhaps it was a way of leaving room for negotiation in any out-of-court settlement between the victim and the accused. The very act of sending off a petition was a way of making it known that the victim was taking steps to gain redress, even if there was no real belief that the case would be heard. The victim could go to the thief, and his neighbours, and tell them that he had sent a petition. Give me my property back or else, in other words. But of course the thief might decide to take the risk and gamble that the governor would do nothing. Most of the time, he would have been right.

For the average Egyptian, petitioning the Roman governor was also not at all straightforward. For one thing, the petition had to be written in Greek, the language of government in Egypt since its conquest by Alexander the Great. For most people this meant paying a scribe to write the petition. This, incidentally, also explains the formulaic stock phrases we find in petitions. We are not hearing the authentic voice of the villagers, but rather their reported speech as written by the scribe. It was also not clear what law was being appealed to. Did law mean the imperial law – the collection of constitutions, edicts and rescripts we find in the law codes of the late empire? Or was it the Greek laws passed by the local government, often dealing with special cases, such as the Jews in Alexandria? Or was it the local custom of Egyptian society, the law of the land? In reality, all three of these legal sources could be appealed to and the governor might be persuaded by any of them. The time span involved could be enormous. One case (*P. Oxy.* 2.237) dragged on for thirty-four years, from AD 90 to 124, by which time the original litigants were all dead. Even if the petitioner were successful and managed to receive a positive response from the governor or a lower-level official, there still lay the problem of enforcement. The rescript offered a definitive legal opinion that the petitioner could then take to a local court in support of his case, but all this cost money and, even then, the local court might not enforce the outcome.

There was no sanction on the accused for non-compliance with the rescript's decision.

The Criminology of Theft in Rome

Despite all these difficulties, the petition system does tell us something about how far the law penetrated into the ordinary life of a province like Egypt. We can see a dispute process with several layers of possible escalation for the aggrieved party. From simply putting up with the loss, to face-to-face negotiation, to threats, to the sending of petitions and going to the courts, anyone with assets lived 'in the shadow of the law', in the sense that legal possibilities sat at the back of their minds. More interestingly from our point of view, the petitions also give us some very basic criminological statistics.

Of 182 petitions from the Egyptian town of Oxyrynchus, 74 (41 per cent) relate to various criminal acts, including assault, fraud, extortion and theft; while 33 (18 per cent) concerned family disputes, usually inheritance. An official archive of papyri from Tebtunis, dating from the reign of Claudius, provides a day-by-day record of every transaction drawn up for a sixteen-month period from AD 45 to 46. Of the 1,048 entries, seventy are petitions (6.7 per cent). It shows both the quantity of legal activity a local official archive had to deal with, and also that petitions were only one modest part of that business. Petitions came from many levels of society, and were never simply the preserve of the well-off. Sometimes they seem like a cry for help from those who had no other route open to them. Of the 134 found in Oxyrynchus, 39 are from women. Women often owned property, either by means of their dowry or from inheritance, but they could be vulnerable to the unscrupulous. 'I am a feeble widow', pleads one, which may be an attempt to play on the officials' heartstrings. Even if successful, though, there was little a woman could do to enforce the decisions. One papyrus from the late third century AD has a woman in dispute with her paternal uncle over her share of the inheritance from her father, who had died intestate. 'I have several times taken legal proceedings against him,' she complains, 'but he just insults me' (*P. Oxy.* 17.2133).

It is striking how often the criminal is known to the petitioner. Of the ninety-six attested complaints of theft in Roman and early Byzantine Egypt, only thirty-four were carried out by unknown perpetrators. Mostly the acts were by acquaintances and sometimes by relatives. But we cannot conclude that most theft in Roman Egypt was carried out by friends and family. There probably wasn't any point in petitioning the authorities if you had no idea who did it. They would not investigate.

Finally, of the fifty-nine surviving prefect's edicts in Roman Egypt, twenty have been found in Oxyrynchus. This suggests that the legal opinions of the province's highest official were distributed quite widely, and would have been posted up for all to see, although quite how many people could actually read them is another matter. Apart from anything else they were written in Greek, so even those who were fairly well educated might not have been able to understand them.

We need to be very careful about reading too much

into these numbers. The law and those who petitioned the legal authorities can show us the kind of problems that arose but not how often or who perpetrated them. It is also impossible to extrapolate from these fascinating provincial cases to the empire as a whole. Egypt was in many ways unique. Are there any tentative conclusions that can be reached about the incidence of theft in the Roman world? The first is that, as we shall see later, Roman historians such as Tacitus and Suetonius were more interested in high-profile political crimes than in petty theft. Their focus on the sensational gives a seriously misleading impression of the kind of day-to-day yobbery affecting ordinary people. What bothered everyday folk most was relatively minor offences such as theft, assault or inheritance disputes. The wealthy were probably less affected by these offences; after all, they had guards.

I suspect there was a higher incidence of crime in towns and cities than in the country. The growth of Rome into a million-strong metropolis presented the criminal with many opportunities. Whether it was when the streets were half-deserted on race days (when the Circus Maximus was filled with two hundred and fifty thousand cheering fans) or simply when tens of thousands every day were divesting themselves of their clothes at the baths, the city would have provided rich pickings. Most crimes are not random events but require some rudimentary planning. Rome would have rewarded that effort.

The Causes of Crime

What caused crime in ancient Rome? When criminology first became established as an academic discipline in the nineteenth century, a widespread hope existed that it would reveal what made people commit crime, leading, ultimately, to a permanent remedy. Such optimism soon evaporated; nowadays we tend to believe that all sorts of factors are involved when an individual turns to crime.

The Romans possessed their own explanations for why people turned bad. The urban environment itself was seen by many Roman writers as having a deleterious effect on people's morals. The temptations of the many bath houses and taverns and the sense of idleness that chronic underemployment created struck many contemporary writers. There may have been some truth in their observations. Day-labouring meant that many of the urban poor would have spent long periods of time standing around idling and chatting when there was no work to be had. The fourth-century historian Ammianus describes how the Roman plebs loved nothing more than discussing the finer points of chariot racing and gambling. It is easy to imagine that in such a context, many young men would have been drawn to theft if no money was forthcoming from legitimate avenues. Rome was overcrowded and its local communities were probably not as close-knit as traditional rural communities, so this too may have resulted in a higher crime rate. But we should also remember that these writers were all from the top of Roman society. There is more than a hint of an elite sneer going on here, aimed at those lazy, good-for-nothing plebs who sponged off the state and spent half their time enjoying the games. Writing was an elite pastime, which had more to do with rhetoric than the objective pursuit of the truth. Writers like Ammianus saw the world through the eyes of the rich and powerful, and it seemed natural to them to explain most crime in terms of the moral failings of the poor.

This pessimistic outlook is found also in astrological explanations. Dorotheus of Sidon contains detailed physical descriptions of thieves: 'thick is the hair on his hand,' 'fat-cheeked, narrow in the forehead' (*Five Books on Astrology* 5.35.103 & 136). These identikit images arose because it was believed that people's behaviour and what they looked like were ordained in the stars. It was a kind of ancient genetic determinism. We find a similar fatalism in the work of the Greek historian, Thucydides, who states that 'Cities and individuals alike, all are by nature disposed to do wrong, and there is no law that will prevent it.' Men have tried every kind of punishment in the attempt to deter crime, he writes, even the death penalty, but the laws are still broken (*History of the Peloponnesian War* 3.45). That said, some were more wrong than others; young men were seen as more susceptible to certain kinds of crime, such as violent assault and rape. Such criminals were naturally reformed simply by growing older.

The motivation for most theft was almost certainly poverty. One of the bandits in *The Golden Ass* describes how they are 'men whom the constraint of poverty has driven into this profession' (4.23). The poor and needy were noted for becoming shamelessly reckless, presumably because their dire situations made crime seem worth the risk. Hunger was also seen as likely to encourage theft.

The agricultural writer, Columella, describes how country slaves would claim to have sown more seed than they had actually used, and steal, shirk and fiddle the books (*On Agriculture* 1.7.1–3). Seneca warns owners to guard against 'thieving hands' (*On the Tranquil Mind* 8.8). Petty theft helped slaves to supplement their modest rations, while fixing the accounts could enable them to save more money, which could then be used to buy extra food or be put towards buying their freedom. We have seen that robbing shipwrecks provided a way for coastal dwellers to supplement their livings, although this was not recognised as an acceptable excuse by the law. The laws refer to various kinds of domestic thefts: freedmen stealing from their patron's house; slaves from their masters; and labourers from their employers. But on the whole the law was not interested in what it saw as trifling matters (*Digest* 48.19.11.1). Bad parenting at home, with the laxness of fathers being singled out for blame, was often regarded as having created moral weakness in children. Greed was also seen as a factor among the wealthy, with fraudulent attempts to rewrite wills an often-cited example.

The law did perceive a difference between crimes committed on a sudden impulse, such as men coming to blows when drunk, and acts that had been deliberately planned, such as a robbery (*Digest* 48.19.11.2). Insanity could be a valid defence, as could age for young children (*Digest* 9.2.5.2). In a similar way, popular explanations for crime might be expressed in terms of demonic possession, with people believing that individuals could come under the control of malevolent supernatural forces and be forced into committing criminal acts.

The Punishment of Theft

What kinds of punishment awaited those convicted of theft? In the earliest laws of Rome, known as 'The Twelve Tables', thieves were treated differently depending on whether or not they were caught in the act, the time of day the crime occurred and their social status. Unarmed thieves who were freeborn and were caught in the act during the day were flogged and then made the slave of the victim. Slaves, armed or not, were whipped and then hurled to their deaths from the Tarpeian Rock, a steep cliff overlooking the forum. The victim was legally permitted to kill the thief on the spot if he was caught in the act during the night or if the thief was armed during the day. However, in the case of an attempted armed theft in daytime, the victim could only kill the thief with impunity if he first shouted out a warning. The purpose of the shout is not expressly stated in the early laws but presumably was meant both to give the thief a chance to surrender and to alert neighbours (even allowing for this condition, the scope for opportunistic murder is obvious). Cases where the thief had been caught in the act were not given a full trial but simply heard by a magistrate.

By the time of the late republic and early empire, physical punishment had been abandoned for freeborn thieves, and in most cases victims were simply compensated for their loss. Typically, this would be set at a multiple of the value of the thing stolen, generally four times. Being prosecuted as a thief meant that a freeborn person lost certain legal privileges, such as being able to appear as a witness in court. Like slaves, they became liable to suffer physical punishment for any further crimes they committed.

The punishments for thieves who were slaves were always brutal. Slaves had almost no legal rights. As we have seen, if slaves appeared before a court, even as witnesses, they had to be tortured to ensure that the 'testimony' they gave was truthful. They were, in the words of one source, merely 'tools that can speak' (Varro *On Agriculture* 1.17). Those convicted of theft could be flogged or crucified, or, if they had run away, condemned either to the mines or to be thrown to the beasts in the amphitheatre. A sense of the shocking normality of domestic punishments can be gleaned from an inscription from Puteoli, near Naples, that lists the prices charged by a kind of municipal punishment service. Floggings cost four sesterces (about the price of a few loaves of bread), and included the supply of a gibbet to which to bind the slave (*AE* 1971, 88). The historian Diodorus Siculus describes how slaves in the mines were physically destroyed, forced by the lashes of their overseers to endure the most dreadful hardships (*Library of History* 5.38.1).

Leniency was also shown, however. Thieves who operated in the bath houses were supposed to be sent to the mines but sentences often had to be reduced because there were so many offenders (Paul *Opinions* 5.3.5). Those sent to the Colosseum might find themselves facing a hungry lion, a bear or a bull. Sometimes they would be given a wooden sword to prolong the entertainment; other times they would simply be tied to a stake so they could be mauled to death in full view of the crowd. Perhaps the most famous example of men being crucified for theft were the two unknown robbers who were executed alongside Jesus (in one gospel they are described in more general terms as criminals).

The severity of the law and the possibility of substantial compensation no doubt meant that many victims chose to pursue the legal route if they could. But there were many other ways to seek retribution outside the law. One method was to attack the reputation of the culprit by means of gossip or graffiti. One inscription on a wall in Pompeii states simply, 'Ampliatus Pedania is a thief' (*CIL* 4.4993). Even if literacy levels were low, this kind of graffiti put the accusation out in the public sphere where it could then be spread orally. This suggests that it was not the authorities keeping people in check but society itself. Justice became a largely local, DIY affair, and accusations of immoral behaviour were part of the armoury of sanctions people could use to force their neighbours into obeying the unwritten rules of behaviour. More direct acts of vengeance could include physical assault or even communal acts of stoning, but these all carried risks, above all of the law being brought in against the avengers. One of the problems we have in trying to assess conditions in the Roman empire as a whole is that so much of the evidence comes, like this piece of graffiti, from Pompeii. Elsewhere we do not have the splendid details and poignant reminders of the everyday lives that were being lived when Vesuvius erupted and buried the town in ash. Were these kinds of graffiti normal? Would you have seen them in every town across the vast empire or were they the peculiar scrawlings that belonged to a local, alternative literary tradition?

Stealing Yourself

It is easy to look back to the Roman experience of theft and find many similarities with the present. But there was one crime that highlights their fundamentally different attitude: self-theft. A slave was a piece of property and as such was covered by the same laws on theft as any other physical item. Slaves could be stolen by others who saw them as a valuable commodity, one that could be sold on to unsuspecting new owners (see *Digest* 48.15 on slave kidnapping). According to this logic, then, runaway slaves were effectively stealing themselves.

Runaways were a recurrent problem. Owners sought to avoid it by branding their slaves or making them wear tags. We do not possess any texts from real-life slaves explaining why they tried to flee but we can surmise that a combination of bad conditions, brutal treatment and a desire for freedom will have been the motive for most. Sometimes theft itself was a cause. Cicero complains in one of his letters about his slave Dionysius, who, entrusted with the care of his precious library, stole some of the books and then ran off to Illyricum on the Adriatic Sea (*Letters to Family* 13.77).

What is interesting is that running away would only have made sense if the slave had a reasonable chance of getting away with it. What could owners do, after all? They could use dogs in the first instance or put up 'wanted posters' to try to track them down. One poster from the village of Chenres in the area of Anthribite in Egypt gives a description of a fugitive: he has a scar on his face and 'swaggers around as if he were someone of note, chattering in a shrill voice' (*P. Oxy.* 51.3617). But presumably the slave would have been long gone before anyone read it.

In the *Oracles of Astrampsychus*, one of the questions is from a master seeking an answer to 'Will I find the fugitive?' It is heartening to find that the odds implied by the ten possible responses favour the runaway. The replies suggest that 60 per cent will not be found, 30 per cent will be, and 10 per cent only after a time. It suggests that running away often worked. Most slave owners would have lacked the resources needed to track down an individual in the vast expanse of the Roman empire. There was no police force to call on and as long as the slave managed to escape from the immediate vicinity in which he might be recognised, there was probably a reasonable possibility of starting life afresh as a free man.

Even a man with Cicero's influence was reduced to writing to friends posted abroad when he heard that runaway slaves of his were in the provinces where they were stationed. One papyrus from the governor of Egypt, sent in AD 166 to local officials, contains a long list of wanted men, some of whom were doubtless runaways, and orders the officials to look for them. A later comment has been added to the governor's copy stating that none were found (*P. Oxy.* 60.4060). It all suggests an empire where the policing was very light-touch, and where it was relatively simple for runaways to escape the law and disappear into the crowd. It also shows how the Roman world was not simply a society of 'face-to-face' communities where everyone knew one another.

For this reason the law put great emphasis on deterring those who might be tempted to aid fugitive slaves

(*Digest* 11.4.1.1). The senate decreed that anyone finding runaways had twenty days to send them back to the rightful owner or bring them before a magistrate. Soldiers and civilians alike had right of entry to private property to search for them. Magistrates could be fined a hundred gold coins if they failed to help. St Paul took great care not to fall foul of the Roman law when he came into contact with a runaway slave, Onesimus (whose name means 'Useful'). Onesimus had robbed his owner Philemon, a wealthy citizen from Colossae in Asia Minor, and had fled to Rome. He met St Paul and converted to Christianity. The best Paul could do was to send him back to his master with a letter asking Philemon to pardon him. Even slaves who had joined up to be gladiators were to be sent back to their masters if discovered, in case they had committed a serious crime that the master would want to investigate personally (probably using torture).

The fact that some people were prepared to harbour runaways is also interesting. Might it reflect some general discomfort with the practice of slavery? One story describes how a runaway happened to pass within sight of his master when a charitable man held out his cloak to stop the master from seeing his slave. For his pains, the individual was convicted of having stolen a man (Gellius *Attic Nights* 11.18.13–14). Perhaps runaways were helped by other slaves or former slaves who sympathised with their situation. Slaves were expensive and largely the preserve of the wealthy so perhaps more ordinary citizens had no particular interest in seeing a rich man's property returned. It is not obvious, though, that these ordinary people had

any qualms about watching slaves suffer brutal punishments in the arena.

Brutal indeed were the penalties meted out to captured absconding slaves. A law from the early fourth
century states that if they were captured while trying to
escape the Roman empire, runaways were either to have
a foot amputated, or be condemned to the mines, or for
that matter endure whatever punishment the magistrate
thought appropriate (*Justinian Code* 6.1.3). An earlier law
suggests that runaways should simply be returned to their
masters for punishment, unless they had been pretending
to be freeborn, in which case they should be severely punished by the magistrates.

Even if they stayed put, slaves caused problems. The
agricultural writer, Columella, gives strident warnings
about the damage slaves can do to a master's property:
they steal both the seed-corn and the harvest, rent the
oxen out to others and pocket the cash, fix the books, and
do not try to stop others from stealing either (*On Agriculture* 1.7.6–7). It may be that all of these acts were occasioned
by hunger and need. But it is also likely that there was an
element of resistance. Too fearful to risk running away,
for many slaves there was perhaps a psychological kick in
tricking their master out of a part of his revenue, however
small. Likewise, lazy slaves working in the city would try
to loaf around, enjoying the many leisure pursuits the
urban environment had to offer, effectively stealing their
labour from their master (*On Agriculture* 1.7.1–3). And why
not? Only a slave master could blame them.

Theft seems to have been a big problem in Rome –
perhaps more than it is for us. Like us, they took a range

of precautions to try to prevent it. They sought to gain redress in the courts if they could, but would also make use of a wide range of alternative strategies to enable them to recover their stolen goods and punish the thief. Over time, these civil private wrongs came to be treated as deserving of a public revenge and not just a financial compensation. The punishments the courts then meted out, especially to slaves, could be incredibly severe but the likelihood of being caught was probably low. We can see these punishments as occasional, exemplary acts designed, through their brutality, to promote maximum deterrence. But perhaps in their very shockingness they also reveal how little the state was able to offer. As we shall see later, often all the victims of theft could do was turn to the gods to try to get help in their search for justice and retribution.

Chapter III

FRAUDS, FAKES AND IMPERIAL CORRUPTION

Crime Business

Of course, it wasn't all bad. The great orator, Dio Chryso-stom (which means 'the man with the golden mouth'), gives a vivid account of the legal circus that accompanied the courts when the magistrate was in town. When the courts are in session, he says, they bring together an innumerable throng of people – litigants, jurors, lawyers, attendants, slaves, pimps, harlots and street-sellers. Shop-keepers loved it because they could jack up their prices, ordinary workers loved it because everyone had a job, all of which meant that the city grew prosperous. Somewhat tellingly, Dio likens it to when flocks of sheep make an area of land particularly fertile by dropping so much dung (*Oration* 35.15).

It wasn't cases of petty theft that kept the courts so busy. Far more commonplace was a whole range of what we might term 'white-collar' crime: non-violent offences motivated by a desire for financial gain. These were carried out not just by private individuals but also by government officials. For as we shall see, the Roman government, for all its grand talk of justice and good governance, often delegated its authority to those with far less lofty aims.

Examples of dishonesty abound. One law refers to businessmen who would fiddle the account of their proceeds from a transaction when they recorded it in the public registers in order to pay less tax (*Digest* 48.13.10). Another simple commercial fraud was to use false scales and measures in a shop (*Digest* 48.19.37). One piece of graffiti in Pompeii complains that an innkeeper is watering down his wine (*CIL* 4.3498). Many court cases dealt with land disputes. Some owners would hide boundary stones or alter the land's appearance so as to obscure where the boundary lay or they would plough land out of someone else's woodland and thereby add it to their existing fields.

The high cost of slaves (particularly once most of Rome's conquests were completed, reducing the supply of cheap captives) created many incentives for slave dealers to conceal problems with their wares. The sale of slaves was regulated by the Curule Aediles' Edict, which aimed to ensure that the prospective buyer could ascertain all the facts about a slave, and especially any weaknesses, such as an illness or a moral defect. Slave dealers were the used-car sellers of their day and would often try to cover up knock knees with long tunics or use brightly coloured clothes to conceal weak limbs or open wounds. Many slaves suffered physically from the long process of transit to the marketplace and dealers were known to use various kinds of make-up to conceal the effects. They would apply resin from the terebinth tree to relax the skin and conceal weight loss. Depilatories made of blood, gall and tuna liver were used to remove the facial hair of adolescent males in order to make them look younger and more attractive. Other frauds included using dye to add colour to the pale cheeks of a sick slave. A potential buyer was advised to ask questions to find out about the slave's true character and physical well-being. The law governing the purchase of slaves advises that, if buying a female slave, the purchaser should make sure the dealer declares that she is capable of bearing children, if she has ever given birth to still-born infants, and whether she menstruates regularly. Sellers were also legally obliged to reveal to prospective buyers whether a slave had ever tried to kill himself and if he was healthy. It was not always clear what healthy meant. One case asks whether a slave is healthy if he has had his tongue cut out (the answer is that he is not; *Digest* 21.1.8).

The quantity of money involved in the supply of grain, the staple food for most, meant that it attracted parasites and predators. Offences against the imperial corn dole, handed out to a quarter of a million male citizens in Rome, were considered so important that a slave could make an accusation against his owner if he suspected him of committing a fraud. A woman could also bring a charge even when she had no personal interest in the case. People were especially alert to any signs that the wealthy were hoarding grain and other goods to drive up prices. An angry crowd in Rome in the fourth century burned down the consul Symmachus's house when he said he would rather use his wine for quenching lime-kilns than sell it at the then current rock-bottom prices (Ammianus *Histories* 27.3.3–4). The creativity of criminals meant that a catch-all term was established, whereby any novel offence was designated *stellionatus* (cheating) and could be punished as the magistrate deemed appropriate (*Digest* 47.20).

Coins were issued in vast numbers. This was a handy way for emperors to disseminate propaganda messages about themselves and their regime. One coin of Caligula shows him proudly wearing laurel leaves while on the other side his three sisters stand dressed as representations of Security, Harmony and Good Fortune. Given rumours that the emperor had committed incest with his sisters, it is hard to know what people would have made of such images. Many certainly tried to make forgeries of them. Using simple casts or coin stamps, they would use base metal that they would then cover with silver plate so it looked like the real thing. Sometimes the coins have spelling mistakes or show the wrong emperor, but how closely do you look at your change? Other tricks known to fraudsters included clipping bits from the edges of coins (in the first century AD the denarius had a 95 per cent silver content). Or silver would be scraped or shaved off from the surface of the coin (*Digest* 48.10.8–9). To some extent we can imagine that most people saw this as a victimless crime. The quantities involved would not have resulted in any significant increase in the money supply and nobody understood how inflation worked in any case. Most people's concern would have centred on being given one of these duds and not being able to pass it on, but again most people probably did not examine their coins closely enough for this to be a problem.

Interest rates charged on loans were limited to 12 per cent per annum but anyone who needed the money badly enough was in no position to complain to the authorities. It was also easy to bypass the limits by using non-monetary loans, such as grain, with one example revealing a rate of 50 per cent (*P. Tebt.* 110). Usury was found among all groups. A poem by Commodianus, probably written in the third century AD, complains about Christian creditors charging a rate of 24 per cent and then seeking to gain heavenly credit by donating alms to the very poor they have created. Not surprisingly, some debtors ran away to escape their liabilities. This made lending itself an anxiety-inducing business. The later Christian source, Gregory of Nyssa, describes in his *Against Usury* how a moneylender would keep himself informed about his debtors' whereabouts and movements and, if he heard bad reports about one of them, who had perhaps fallen into destitution or run off, the moneylender would sit 'with folded hands', groan 'continuously', and 'weep much'. One law describes a con trick whereby someone recommends a man called Titus to a moneylender, but then actually introduces him to another man, also called Titus. The second Titus would then run off with the money leaving the lender with no idea where it had gone (*Digest* 47.2.68.4).

Crime Families

One of the most important financial issues in the Roman world was inheritance. This was the easiest and probably the most common way to acquire money. Some made fortunes in business or as soldiers, but most families made sure that their wealth was carefully handed down from one generation to the next. Low life expectancy often interfered with this transmission process. In the *Oracles of Astrampsychus*, of the ten possible replies to the question, 'Will I inherit from my mother?', three are, 'No, she'll bury you.' This meant that legacy-hunting was a lively occupation for some, who preyed especially on the childless in the hope of securing a generous bequest. Another of the questions to the oracle asks, 'Will I receive an inheritance from someone?', and 80 per cent of the replies are positive. But the importance of inheritance meant that it was never quite that simple, with the answers hinting at various possible legal difficulties: 'You won't be sole heir', 'You won't receive all of it', 'You'll suffer a great financial loss', or 'After another trial'. The large sums of money involved also meant that fraud was a risk. A text from Egypt, dated 24 January AD 211, contains a petition from Tanomieus to the centurion Crenuleius Quintilianus. In it he complains that his children have been made joint heirs in a will but that the executor has sold off part of the estate to benefit others (*BGU* 1.98). A decade earlier, in Tebtunis, Heraclia complains that her appropriately named husband, Hermes, had run off with all the money her parents had left her in their will (*P. Tebt.* 334).

A common form of fraud was to open a will surreptitiously and tamper with it before resealing the document with either the real seal or a fake copy. This could be done when the testator was alive or dead but clearly the risks of being discovered were greater if he or she were still living. The emperor Claudius issued an edict against those who, while legally writing the will of another person or adding a codicil to it, would simply write in a legacy to themselves (*Digest* 48.10.15 pref.). This might seem too brazen to work, but in a world of limited literacy it would have been common for people to ask others to write their wills for them. Or a person may have had poor vision and, with no spectacles to help, was unable to read the additions. Or someone could go to a lawyer who simply defrauded them.

Another way of dealing with a will that was feared to contain unwelcome clauses was to steal the document and destroy it. Fiddling with official documents was not limited to wills. The laws banned individuals from trying to defraud others by means of changing registers, decrees, petitions, public records, witness statements, loans and letters (Paul *Opinions* 5.25). Another illegal use of documentation involved lawyers or agents revealing the contents to their client's adversaries, presumably in return for a bribe.

It is impossible to tell how frequently such things occurred, but the threat was deemed to be sufficient for the emperor Nero to have introduced a new form of protection against forgery. It was decreed that public or private documents should first be signed by witnesses, then they should be perforated along half of one margin, through which holes a cord should be passed three times. The documents should then be closed with a wax seal impressed upon the cord so that it would be impossible for anyone to break into them without leaving some trace of having done so. Any documents not protected in this way no longer had any legal force (Suetonius *Nero* 17). With regard to wills, an extra safeguard was set in place which meant that when presented to witnesses, the first two pages should contain only the name of the testator in order that they should not be able to see any of the provisions contained in the will. It was also decreed that anyone who wrote a will for another could not include a legacy for himself, and that lawyers should charge a fixed fee for the service because so many had been levying unreasonable sums (plus ça change).

How effective such prohibitions were further down the social ladder is hard to say. By definition wills were largely the preserve of the wealthier sections of society. Even so, documents survive that concern quite modest assets. There is also a ridiculous spoof known as the Piglet's Will which claims to be the last will and testament of a pig about to be butchered for a dinner. 'To my father Lardy Pig,' it says,

I bequeath 30 pecks of acorns, and to my mother, the Old Sow, I leave 40 pecks of wheat, and to my sister Gruntress, whose wedding I shall be unable to attend, I give 30 pecks of barley. And of my organs I leave my bristles to the cobblers, my thick skull to the fighters, my ears to the deaf, my tongue to the pleaders and gossipers, my innards to the sausage-makers, my thighs to the stuffing-makers, my loins to the women, my bladder to the boys, my tail to the girls, my muscles to the gays, my heels to the runners and hunters, and my claws to the robbers.

It finishes with the necessary seven witnesses, who in this case are pigs, all of whom have feeble pig-related word plays for names (translated something like 'Bacony signed, Pork-scratching signed ...). It is *Carry-On*-esque, but St Jerome later describes how people would shake with laughter when they heard it. Perhaps part of the fun was that wills belonged to another world, the world of the rich. But more likely, it seems to me, the audience recognised the simple legal phraseology from documents they had encountered from time to time in their own lives.

Governmental Graft

Ordinary people certainly seem to have been just as capable of fraud as wealthy Romans. An Aesop fable tells the story of how Zeus once directed Hermes to give false-hood to all craftsmen and the extra leftover to tanners, and therefore 'craftsmen have all been liars ever since and tanners most of all' (103). Other fables warn that neigh-bours are not to be trusted in case they steal things (166). During the fun of the games, some spectators would try to grab more than their share of the food permits that were sometimes handed round (Martial *Epigrams* 1.11 & 26). And a typical strategy of beggars was to pretend that they had broken legs or were blind (Martial *Epigrams* 12.57; Philostratus *Life of Apollonius of Tyana* 4.10).

Those at the top of Roman society were certainly not immune from temptation. Judges could be influenced by friendship to award their decisions in favour of one side or the other. This seems corrupt to us, but in many ways patronage was the driving force of the Roman world and it would be strange if it had not also permeated the legal system. The very process of a legal case was likened by one former lawyer to an aggressive act of robbery. Firmicus Maternus, who lived in the first half of the fourth century AD, started out as an advocate before turning to astrology. His book on the subject contains an outline of his reasons for quitting the law:

> Those like myself who work on legal defences become involved in quarrelsome contests and dog-eat-dog confrontations. From these disputes I have gained nothing but a daily accumulation of danger and an enormous burden of ill-will. I have constantly found myself opposing aggressive characters – either those who delight in stirring up trouble, or those who try to exploit strangers from motivations of greed, or who terrify miserable men with fear of the courts.

Firmicus concludes that he has 'deserted the law to avoid being enmeshed in ever increasing plots and dangers' and has 'given up the occupation of stealing or, more accurately, banditry' (*Eight Books of Astrology* Bk 4 preface).

Governors were meant to ensure that the judicial system was not the plaything of the rich and powerful. The emperors decreed that governors were honour-bound to make sure the powerful did not harm the humble nor pursued them through the courts by means of false accusations. But other laws make it clear that the courts were open to abuse. Litigants might produce false witnesses or put forward fake documents in support of their case (*Digest* 1.18.6). They might bribe the judge or bribe witnesses not to appear.

Plenty of examples also survive of officials abusing their power. They might pretend to hold a higher position than was in fact the case (Paul *Opinions* 5.25), or force people of limited means to hand over their only slave or lamp (the text is unclear) or small supply of furniture with the false claim that it is being requisitioned for use by the army (*Digest* 1.18.6.5). Judges could elect to execute, torture, whip or put in chains a citizen, contrary to the law (Paul *Opinions* 5.26). In fact, provincial governors seem to have become almost synonymous with corruption. Juvenal sourly reminds an ambitious politician that when, 'you finally get that provincial governorship try and set some limit on your anger, restrain your greed, feel some compassion for the poor locals' (*Satires* 8.87–91).

Sometimes poor governance was the result of incompetence and inefficiency rather than malevolence. When Pliny the Younger was appointed as governor of Bithynia-Pontus under the emperor Trajan, he found individuals who had been sentenced to the mines or to be thrown to the wild beasts in the arena working as public slaves (*Letters* 10.31–2). One law states that if a judge forgets to set a term when sending a convict to the mines the sentence should default to ten years (*Digest* 48.19.23). Another law admits that appeals are frequently needed to correct the injustice or ignorance of judges (49.1.1 pref.). Judges were not legal specialists and received no prior training, although they did have advisers to consult, who may have included a lawyer. As amateurs they were highly likely to make basic legal errors in interpretation or sentencing. We have an interesting example of this from Aulus Gellius, who gives an account of his own incompetence as a judge. He describes how a claimant appeared before him demanding money from another. He had no documentary evidence or witnesses of the debt but, it was clear to Gellius, he was a 'thoroughly good man, whose integrity was proven and well-known, and who led a blameless life'. By contrast, his opponent was shown to be a liar and a cheat. But he was backed up by lawyers, a bunch of 'noisy advocates' who demanded that the usual documentary evidence be produced. Unsure of what to do, Gellius asked some friends in the legal profession for advice. They said the advocates were correct and that the claim should be dismissed. But, Gellius says, 'when I contemplated the men, one full of honesty, the other thoroughly shameful and degraded ... I could not by any means be argued into an acquittal.' Instead he ordered the case to be postponed and turned to a philosopher for advice. The philosopher agreed that he should find in favour of the honest man. But Gellius was worried that, as a young man, he would acquire a bad reputation if he passed judgement on the grounds of character rather than from evidence. So, still unwilling to find in favour of a bad man, a man who lived 'a most shameful and degraded life', he swore that the case was unclear to him and so passed the matter on to another judge (*Attic Nights* 14.2.4–11).

This is a fascinating case because it can be read in different ways. It could be interpreted to show that judges were more interested in litigants' moral character than in the facts of the case. This would inevitably have resulted in their favouring those of higher status or those with whom they had some personal connection. Gellius tries to resist this urge and stick to the facts, but does he record the case in order to show how much better he was than the average judge? Or the case could be read as saying the very opposite. Everyone involved, from claimants to lawyers to the judge, knew that evidence was required for any decision. No doubt a judge's assessments of character might nudge the decision one way or the other (as it still does today), but Roman law, in this view, was fundamentally concerned with the facts.

Judges had wide discretionary powers, which made the outcome of a case hard to predict. The personal nature of the legal process therefore also meant that litigants would try to see what they could get away with. One interesting document that sheds light on how governors were perceived is the *Interpretation of Dreams* by Artemidorus. Written in the second century AD, this text is a handbook on how to interpret hundreds of different dreams, and it features characters and events from all areas of Roman life. The interpretations work by establishing mental equivalences between different people and things, and judges and governors do not come off well. To dream of a pure, translucent river flowing gently was good for slaves and defendants in a law case because 'rivers are like masters and judges since they do whatever they like, on a whim, and do not provide any explanation' (2.27). Flooded rivers signify senseless judges because of their violence and their great roar. Artemidorus seems to have it in for the whole legal process. Dreaming of fighting as a gladiator indicates becoming involved in a court case, where weapons signify the documents, while to dream of courts, judges and lawyers prophesies disturbances, bad tempers and untimely expenditure (2.29 & 32). For someone already involved in a court case, it was good to dream of walking on the sea as this meant that he would win because he was superior to the judge, 'since the sea resembles a judge because it treats some well and some badly' (3.16). In a similar vein, to dream of carrying out contemptuous acts is a bad omen, except for those who are capable of governing, because 'nothing prevents governors from feeling contempt for their subjects' (4.44).

We get a similar view of gubernatorial malfeasance in various stories of high-profile corruption. According to Suetonius, when governing Hispania Tarraconensis (now in modern Spain) the future emperor Galba ran the province in a 'variable and inconsistent manner'. At first he was vigorous and energetic, and inclined to be overly severe in his judgements. When a dishonest moneylender was brought before him he ordered his hands to be cut off and then had them nailed to the man's table from where he operated in the forum. When a man poisoned a child under his protection, from whom he stood to inherit if he died, Galba sentenced him to be crucified. When the man protested that he was a Roman citizen and so could not be executed in such a cruel way, Galba had a taller white cross set up for him as a 'special' honour (Suetonius *Galba* 9). Is this a reasonably accurate description of what life was like in the provinces? Surely not. Or is it an extreme anecdote relayed by Suetonius because he thought it revealed something particular about Galba? Possibly, but it also gives a strong sense of how powerful the governor of a province was.

It is certainly not unique. The most famous example of a governor abusing his position is that of Verres, prosecuted in 70 BC by Cicero for his mismanagement of Sicily. In venomous prose, Cicero describes the former governor's many dreadful acts against Roman citizens and allies alike, and his wicked acts against both gods and men. He accuses him of illegally expropriating four hundred thousand sesterces (*Against Verres* 1.56), and of using slaves to extort cash from the rich. At the time when Spartacus was causing chaos on the Italian mainland, Verres was alleged to have arrested certain important slaves belonging to wealthy landowners and charging them with plotting to join Spartacus's revolt. After sentencing the slaves to death, he would hint to their owners that he could be persuaded to pardon them in return for a hefty bribe. Sometimes it was claimed that he would even accuse non-existent slaves of conspiring to rebel and then charge the landowners with having concealed them. When the owners, unsurprisingly, were unable to produce the slaves Verres would throw them into prison until they paid a penalty.

This was in the days of the republic when it is possible that higher standards of public office were expected. By the time of the empire, it is easy to get the impression that governors could do what they wanted. The historian Dio Cassius records how, during the reign of Augustus, the Gauls suffered greatly at the hands of their procurator, Licinus. Dio says there had been a premonition of this when a sixty-foot-long sea monster, which, apart from its head, resembled a woman, was washed ashore. When nature itself went awry, particularly anything that suggested women getting out of their proper place, then dire troubles must surely follow. A Gaul himself and a former slave of Julius Caesar, Licinus had risen rapidly in the imperial household after receiving his freedom. To maximise the revenues he raised from his countrymen, he made them pay their tribute by the month but then declared that there were fourteen months in each year. The locals complained to Augustus, who claimed to be unaware of the extortion and pretended not to believe other accusations against Licinus. Licinus feared the worst so invited the emperor to his lavish house and showed him the many treasures within. He then claimed to have gathered it all on purpose, for the benefit of the emperor himself and for the Roman people, so that the Gauls should not be inspired, by having such wealth, to revolt. Licinus was in this way saved by pretending that he had sapped the strength of the barbarians in order to serve Augustus (Dio *Roman History* 54.21).

In some ways the story serves to paint a picture of unchecked official corruption in the provinces. But it also demonstrates that victims could lodge a complaint with the emperor. In this case, if Licinus had not forestalled him, Augustus would have acted to restrain his abuse. One act of corruption prevalent under Augustus concerned his habit of giving people cash rewards. Obviously, the emperor would not hand over the money himself (like the Queen, he didn't carry any) but would leave that to other officials. For their trouble, these officials were in the habit of helping themselves to a large cut. When

Augustus's successor, Tiberius, learned of this he changed the practice so that the recipients got their money on the spot (Dio *Roman History* 57.10). Dio praises Tiberius because he made these payments out of regular imperial revenues rather than obtaining funds from the confiscated estates of the condemned, or from other deceitful methods. Again, the picture is of a regime in which it was easy for officials to be on the make, but that such malpractice, should it come to light, would be stopped. Why did Dio choose to relate this tale? Was it to show that imperial administration was haphazard? More likely it was intended to show that the emperor Tiberius was, at first, not without scruple, at least compared to how he turned out.

The attitude of emperors can perhaps best be summed up by another story concerning Tiberius. When the governor of Egypt, Aemilius Rectus, once sent him more money than was stipulated, the emperor sent back to him the message: 'I want my sheep shorn, not skinned' (Dio *Roman History* 57.10.5; Suetonius *Tiberius* 32). The emperors delegated considerable powers to their governors and officials and, while it was tacitly accepted that there would be substantial opportunities for financial gain, it was also understood that there had to be some limits. The government did little to root out malpractices, however, and was largely reactive whenever they came to light. In other words, it did not want to pursue its own supporters, but had to be seen to clamp down on the worst excesses.

Now, we need to be very careful here. These colourful anecdotes were selected by Roman writers because of the vividness they brought to what might otherwise have been a dry historical narrative (just as I'm using them here). They cannot simply be regarded as evidence of how Rome administered its empire. In truth, as the empire matured there appear to have been increasing limits set on how governors exercised their powers, either because Roman citizenship became more widespread or because the emperor kept a closer eye on what his representatives were up to. Pliny the Younger's letters to the emperor from his time as governor offer a very different picture. Here we have a diligent and thoughtful official who is keen never to do anything that might be interpreted as overstepping his jurisdiction. 'I beg you, Sir,' he says in one letter to Trajan, 'that you will give me the guidance of your advice. I am unsure about whether I ought to use public slaves or soldiers to guard the prisons.' This is a trifling matter that cannot have needed imperial input, but Trajan replies, telling Pliny not to waste good soldiers guarding prisons (*Letters* 10.19 & 20). We get the feeling here that Pliny is trying hard to emphasise his good sense and his utter loyalty: the emperor need have no worries that Pliny is ever going to do anything risky. But when he polished up his imperial correspondence for publication, Pliny was also doing his best to show how much better a governor he was than the average. Still, even an average governor's behaviour would probably have ranked well ahead of the kind of venal cruelty displayed in many historical anecdotes.

The same is true if we look at some of the treatment meted out by governors and judges. Read Roman law books and you can almost hear the crack of the whip coming off the page. As the section of the *Digest* dealing

with torture says, 'It is customary for torture to be applied
for the purpose of detecting crime.' This was especially
true in more serious cases: 'All persons, without exception, shall be tortured in a case of high treason, if their
testimony is necessary, and circumstances demand it'
(*Digest* 48.18). That is to say nothing of criminals punished
by being worked to death in the mines or torn apart by
wild animals in the arena. It is easy to look at these cata-
logues of brutality and see a system that gave judges a
licence in cruelty. But, while it is certainly true that Roman
law had a very harsh side, it is not the case that judges
could do whatever they wanted. Indeed, the laws precisely set down the rules for sentencing. The section of
the *Digest* dealing with punishments details what consti-
tutes an offence – whether acts such as theft or murder,
verbal statements such as insults, written acts such as
forgery, or persuasion, as in the case of conspiracy (*Digest*
48.19.16). These four types of crime were to be considered
under seven different headings: the cause, the person, the
place, the time, the quality, the quantity, and the result.
The cause might consist of the blows in an assault, which
might, for example, be permissible if given by a master to
one of his slaves (but not to someone else's slave). The
person relates to the status of the accuser and accused,
such as whether the individual concerned is a freedman,
a woman or a minor, all of which should be taken into
account in sentencing. Place determines whether the act,
such as theft, is regarded as theft or, if from a temple, is in
fact sacrilege and therefore deserving of far greater punishment because it risked offending the gods. Time
distinguishes a slave who has gone missing for a short

period from one who has run away, or determines whether a housebreaker has committed a worse offence by carrying out his theft at night. The quality of a crime represents the assessment of how dreadful it was, with manifest theft being seen as worse than non-manifest, or a violent argument between neighbours being perceived as less serious than highway robbery. Quantity assesses the magnitude of the crime: was only one sheep stolen or an entire flock? In making a judgement, the judge needed to take into account whether the crime was committed by accident or design. Some crimes might also be punished more severely in certain regions, as for example in the grain-exporting province of Africa where crop burning received a heavy sentence, or in areas near gold and silver mines where coin counterfeiters were singled out for an enhanced penalty. Banditry was taken seriously in most places. Clearly not every judge would have followed these guidelines meticulously but, as the case of Gellius suggests, some did take their responsibilities seriously and the punishments they handed out were far from arbitrary.

Mind the Gap: Ideals and Practicalities

Unsurprisingly, there seems to have been a gap between the imperial ideal of law and justice on the one hand and the ability of the system to deliver it on the other. The ideal was expressed in such texts as the formulaic statements at the start of petitions: 'Since your ingrained justice, my lord prefect, is extended to all men, I too, having been wronged, have recourse to you, begging for redress' (*P. Oxy* 17.2131, dated AD 207). In reality, bringing a case took time, money and familiarity with the legal system. The system was plagued by inefficiencies, such as a lack of judicial training, the limited number of personnel allocated to it, and the huge quantity of cases and petitions. Getting a hearing was no easy task, requiring a dogged determination on the part of the claimant.

If a case reached court, the lack of appropriate training could prove particularly problematic. In some cases it is clear that nobody knows what the law actually says and the judge simply uses his discretion. Knowing what the law said was not as simple as it might sound. The great codified collections the Romans produced date from the late empire when, as we shall see, there was a drive to improve legal efficiency and increase the power of the centralised bureaucracy. In the earlier empire, the law consisted of an ever-expanding collection of legal opinions, imperial decrees and rescripts, and precedents. There was no easy way to access all these documents. Judges, lawyers and litigants had to make do with what they could find. Often these laws were contradictory and so the judge had to decide which legal principle to accept. The extent to which a judge carried out his job diligently and sought to ascertain what the law said may even have reduced the number of cases he could hear. Accuracy in some cases simply denied the opportunity for justice to others.

Other practical problems with delivering justice involved the bias of courts towards those with whom they had connections. As a character says in Petronius's novel, the *Satyricon*, when weighing up whether to go to court: 'nobody knows us in this place and nobody will believe what we say' (14). We can imagine that magistrates will have known the important men in a locality and been reluctant to find against them. What's more, Roman society could be cut-throat and the law was often used as a weapon. One section of the *Digest* deals with people who have been paid to bring vexatious charges against innocent people in order to make their lives difficult (3.6). We find many references to false charges being laid, suggesting that some Romans were perfectly prepared to lie in the pursuit of legal victory. This was a risky business as detection could bring down a judge's wrath, but when so much relied upon the reputation of the witness it is easy to see why many thought they could get away with it. I'm sure we can all think of politicians today who have lied under oath, so the Romans were not obviously worse in this respect. Wealthy Romans were always likely to have had the upper-hand in legal disputes. As Plutarch says in his biography of the Greek law-giver, Solon, 'These decrees of yours are like spiders' webs … they'll tie up anyone weak who gets caught in them but they'll be pulled to bits by the rich and powerful' (5). And the decisions of the courts themselves were sometimes driven by political expediency. So, when a plague during the reign of Marcus Aurelius produced a shortfall in available manpower for the games, Christians were persecuted to increase the flow of convicts condemned to be thrown to the beasts.

Why did such a gap exist between the ideal of justice and the reality? In the first place, there is clearly always a difference between the pure ideal of justice and the

workings of a system designed to deliver it in practice –
some degree of shortfall must be expected. The
practicality of the Roman system, whereby judges were
expected to use a kind of common sense to interpret the
laws, can give the appearance of arbitrariness. Yet in this
regard, the Roman empire's justice system does not seem
to have been materially worse than existed in many other
pre-industrial societies. In practice, the aims of the Roman
system were limited by the size of the available resources.
The primary objective was to maintain social order, which
it achieved both by punishing miscreants and by providing a means for private individuals to settle their disputes.
The state's greatest interest was in those citizens who had
the biggest stake in society: the rich and powerful. It was
important that they had a way of settling their differences, since they had the capacity to destabilise society. By
going through the courts, these individuals were at least
keeping their personal conflicts contained within a state-
sponsored framework. The alternative would have been
private vendetta.

There was never any hope of universal access; that
would simply have resulted in an unlimited supply of
cases. The difficulty and cost of the system was a way of
cutting down the queues while at the same time creating
preferential access for the wealthy and well-connected.
Again, the government wanted those at the top of society
to be broadly content. Everyone else mattered less.

This in reality is what seems to have happened, as far
as we can tell from the documents from Roman Egypt.
The courts were used mainly by those of high and
middling economic status, with most cases reserved for

high-value transactions, especially those relating to property.

Why did the emperors set up an ideal only for its short-comings to be publicly exposed? The answer depends on the role that we see law playing in society. If law existed solely to deliver justice then, yes, the gap seems startlingly wide. But the law did other things. Above all, it served a ceremonial function that cemented power relationships within Roman society. Law was part of the public image of the imperial system. It helped to establish an ideal of authority which was majestic, rational and beneficent. It legitimised the unequal social relationship between the emperor and his subjects. The very layout of the court-room, with the space hierarchically arranged, and with the progress controlled by means of ritualistic procedure, combined with the arcane judicial language, all served to generate an aura of permanence and legitimacy. It was, after all, the fiercely unequal social order that the courts sought to maintain. In doing this, they assured the people that these laws reflected the consensus view of acceptable behaviour, a consensus which itself reflected the will of the gods and their support for the Roman state.

Popular Justice

How did ordinary Romans feel about this gap between the rhetoric and the reality? When Cicero became gover-nor of Cilicia, now in mainland Turkey, in 51 BC, he writes that his arrival had been keenly awaited. The region had suffered from appalling mismanagement under Roman hands. Much public property had been embezzled, which had left the towns financially weak. Taxes were high: 'Everywhere I heard the same tale,' he says; 'people could not pay the poll-tax.' The locals had been forced to sell their assets and every town was full of groans and lamentations: 'everyone is tired of life.' In short, people were looking to him to bring back good government. And according to Cicero, they were not disappointed. He wouldn't even accept hay from them for his horses. As a result, he was greeted everywhere by throngs of people who rushed out from farms, villages and towns to meet him. As he put it, 'On my mere arrival, the justice, purity and mercy of Cicero gave them a new lease of life' (*Letters to Atticus* 5.16).

Cicero's account is obviously partial to the Cicero camp, but it's interesting that he assumes a sense of natural justice on the part of the governed. We find a similar sense of natural right, independent of the law, at work in proverbs such as 'let Attius be the same as Tettius', that is, let there be equal rights for all (Roman male citizens, that is), and in many traditional fables, such as the one where the ploughman says to the wolf, 'you good-for-nothing, I wish you would forget your thieving life of crime and turn to farming' (Aesop 38).

If most inhabitants of the empire shared this sense of natural justice, how did they feel when they saw the imperial system fail to live up to its own grand claims? Did it erode whatever faith they might have had in the system and in the legitimacy of the social order? Or did they have such low expectations that they thought nothing of it? Did it make them think that the powerful had scant respect for the law and that nothing could be done about it? Many scholars have a broadly optimistic view about people's attitudes towards the law, arguing that there was little opposition to particular laws or to Roman law in general, and that it satisfied most people most of the time. Lack of resistance need not, though, have resulted from social satisfaction, but could have been a matter of obedience to the law out of self-interest or fear. We might also add that 'satisfaction' is a slippery term. If expectations are low, it takes little to satisfy them.

I think we can challenge this optimistic view. The law and, for that matter, the emperor, were not regarded with automatic, unquestioning reverence. But it was dangerous to attack these imperial institutions openly, so people couched any ambivalence or hostility they felt in anonymous and indirect terms. The fable of the swallow and the snake tells the story of a swallow who hatches her brood in a courthouse. A snake comes along and eats them and the mother grieves bitterly. Another swallow tries to comfort her by saying that she is not the only one to have lost children. 'I'm not lamenting so much for my children,' she replies, 'as because I've been wronged here in this place where those who are wronged find help' (Aesop 227). And in another fable (155), a wolf sees a lamb drinking from a river and decides to find a plausible reason for making a meal of him. As the moral states, 'those who are set on doing wrong are not deterred even by a legal argument.' In such popular stories, we get a sense of how distant a force the law could be, and how wary people were of those in authority over them. (Which is not to say that they didn't make jokes. In the only surviving ancient joke book, the *Laughter-Lover*, an over-educated type who was involved in a lawsuit was told that the fairest judgements were those in Hades, so he hanged himself (109).)

There was also outright hostility. The *Acts of the Pagan Martyrs* is a collection of fragmentary documents that recount opposition from members of the Greek-speaking community in Alexandria, mainly from the first two centuries AD. They probably never formed a coherent collection and are called martyr texts because they read very like accounts of Christian martyrs. And so we find dramatic representations of brave individuals standing up to the oppressive Roman regime, such as the man who complains to Maximus the prefect, 'if a beggar in poor clothing petitions you, you confiscate his property along with that of his wife and friends' (*P. Oxy.* 3.471).

People could also make their dissatisfaction with emperors known by rioting, which sometimes targeted imperial images. In tax riots, the crowd hurled insults at imperial pictures or pulled down imperial statues, smashed them, hit them and smeared them with dung. When the emperor Domitian died, Suetonius says that the people were indifferent, but his statues were pulled down and senators delighted in hacking at them as if they were real (*Domitian* 23). The emperor's statue was also a place of refuge to which slaves could run if looking for sanctuary from a brutal master (a magistrate would then hear the slave's complaint and, if upheld, the slave would be sold to another master). One story tells how a woman manipulated this allowance to make her views known to a senator. She followed the aristocrat and hurled abuse at him but did so while holding a picture of the emperor for protection (Tacitus *Annals* 3.36).

The evidence suggests that ordinary people were capable of expressing disapproval of their superiors. They did not simply believe everything they were told. The reason the surviving evidence is so biased is simple: most texts come from members of the highly literate ruling class who naturally supported the status quo. Speaking the truth to a dictator is no easy task and for the most part people simply lied and feigned happiness. We might reasonably conclude from the fate of Domitian's statues that he was unpopular. Yet when he was alive there is no evidence of people expressing such hostility. The ordinary folk flattered him just as everyone else did.

Most people were understandably wary of those in power. Some, like the hare in the fable, might even have 'prayed for this day always, when even the strong would fear the weak' (Babrius *Fables* 102). But outright resistance was dangerous because it risked bringing down the might of Rome on your head. As the philosopher and former slave Epictetus warns, 'If a soldier seizes your donkey, let it go. Don't resist and don't grumble. If you do, you will be beaten and you will still lose your donkey' (*Discourses*. 4.1.79). We should also remember that for most inhabitants of the empire, living under its rule was not a question of choice. Roman military power struck down any serious opposition. The Jews, for example, became far more resigned to their fate after their defeats in the revolts of the first and early second centuries: 'You go into the country and you meet a bailiff; you come back to town and bump into a tax-collector; you go home and find your sons and daughters starving' (Simeon ben Laish, B Sanhedrin 98, 6). Privately, Rabbis even used to call Rome the 'evil empire'.

But should these isolated pieces of evidence affect our moral assessment of Rome as a whole? Does it provide a false picture of a moral turpitude at the core of Roman government? There is plenty of counter-evidence which attests to people believing in the system. In the late second century, during the reign of Commodus, a group of peasants on one of the emperor's North African estates got fed up with being forced by some nearby soldiers to do unpaid work for them. So they wrote to Commodus and complained. 'Help us!' they cried. 'We are weak peasants who are sustaining our lives by the work of our hands and are confronted by your agents'(*CIL* 8.10570). They claimed that the local officials were bribed to ignore their complaints, probably hoping that accusations of bribery would not go down well with the emperor. They were right. Commodus replied asserting their rights, which they commemorated in a public inscription in his honour. But there was a twist in their message to the emperor. They asked him to confirm what they already knew to be the truth of their situation, and asked him to defend their rights as free peasants. But, as they made clear, if he did not, then they would refuse to pay their taxes and would run away and 'become fugitives from your imperial estate'. As they also made clear, they were not a group of hot-headed radicals. They had been born and bred on the estate and, like their ancestors before them, had worked faithfully for their owner and 'kept faith with the imperial account'. Put simply, these were the honest poor who put up with a lot, but they had reached the end of their tether. If the emperor did not put things right then they would simply stop buying into the system.

What to make of all this? The historian Agathias wrote in the late empire about how, after an earthquake,

> The ideals to which people constantly pay lip-service but rarely put into practice were then eagerly pursued. Everyone suddenly became just in his dealings towards his neighbour, so much so that even magistrates gave up all thoughts of personal gain and began to administer justice in accordance with the laws and those who were influential in some other way lived quietly and peacefully, refraining from the most shameful abuses and leading generally virtuous lives.
> (*Histories* 5.5)

But such good behaviour only lasted for a short time, so long as the terror was fresh in people's minds.

While this is probably an exaggerated view, aimed at producing an image of imperial decay, it tells us something of the resignation that most probably felt. Law was largely the preserve of the wealthy, dealing for the most part with property disputes. We cannot therefore see it as something used and respected by all Romans. Nor can we assume that it enjoyed widespread legitimacy. The law played a major role in trying to persuade common people that the social order was just, divinely constituted and natural, and that they should therefore acquiesce to it. But the poor and middling sorts did not simply believe and obey. Nor did they simply resist or oppose. Like the British with the weather, they got on with it as best they could.

Chapter IV

THE POLITICS OF TERROR

The senator fumbled in the inner fold of his toga: 'How much do you want?' Leaning out from the shadows where he lurked, another toga-draped arm held out a scroll. 'This stuff is red-hot. It will blow your mind, senator.' A small bag of gold coinage exchanged hands and the two men scurried apart. The senator walked quickly through the dingy, twisted streets of Rome, pushing aside the grasping hands of beggars, and made straight for the private room in his villa on the slope of the Esquiline hill. Panting, he pulled out the scroll and placed it on his desk. A bead of sweat dropped from his forehead onto the table as he slid his tremulous hand under the wax seal, which broke with a gentle crack. The senator rolled out the document and leant forward to read it, his nose almost touching the desk as he struggled to make sense of the text in the candlelight. Yes, it was the genuine stuff. Pure Veiento.

During Nero's reign a senator named Fabricius Veiento had written all kinds of libellous stories and lampoons about other senators and priests, which he called his 'Last

Will and Testament'. The emperor was not amused and had Veiento exiled and his books burned. But banning and burning just made them all the more desirable, and Tacitus describes how people were desperate to get hold of this risqué material, none of which survives, unfortunately (*Annals* 14.50). Living under an emperor meant that the news was restricted and people never really knew what was going on. Here was their chance to hear all about the crimes and vices of the aristocracy. Once Nero had been assassinated, though, Veiento returned and became a favourite of the emperors Vespasian and Domitian. Now that he was part of the establishment again, people lost interest in his salacious tales. Why would anyone believe the rumours spread about by a successful politician?

Rumour flourished under the empire. Anonymous and off-the-record gossip was the only way for people to say what they really thought about an emperor; and it was the only way for people to discuss ways of changing the regime. Even then they had to be very careful as criticisms could easily be relayed to the authorities. Actual plots had to be carried out with the utmost care. This was treason and we shall see in this chapter how a Roman emperor took no crime more seriously: after all, if he failed to prevent a plot, he could soon be dead. Just as Romulus and Remus had fought for control of the founding mission of Rome, so high politics in the Roman empire was always a matter of life and death. The Romans were fascinated by this ongoing political struggle. Contemporary historians, such as Suetonius and Tacitus, crammed their narratives with detailed accounts of the intricate plots of particular reigns and of the terrible fates that awaited their perpetrators. Caligula provided perhaps the worst examples of Rome's brutality. Never too squeamish to inflict the most savage punishments – when there was a shortage of food for the wild beasts he had them thrown criminals, whom he lined up for selection, choosing 'from baldy to baldy' – the emperor reportedly enjoyed dining while watching people being sawn in two.

The crime of treason sat at the heart of how the Roman imperial political system operated. Intimidation and terror tactics were an important part of how a Roman emperor went about getting things done and controlling those beneath him, using cruelty against those who might dare to oppose or plot against him. Spying and trumped-up charges were all part of his armoury. But when we read such dreadful tales in Roman historians' accounts, we are left with the impression of the arbitrary, illegal actions of an autocracy, not of a legitimate response by a threatened political leadership. Tacitus explains that he wrote his *Histories* because the period, from the civil war after Nero's death to the assassination of Domitian, was one of tyranny (1.2). When bad emperors took control, then high birth, wealth, or even the refusal or acceptance of office could all give grounds for political accusations. Things were so bad, Tacitus claims, that virtue caused the surest ruin. The emperors offered huge rewards to informers to keep track of those they feared. Priesthoods, consulships and secret influence at court all awaited those who betrayed their peers and in doing so generated havoc everywhere. Everyone hated and feared these spies in equal measure.

Tacitus portrays the reign of a bad emperor as no better than a reign of terror. Legality is presented as being no different from the possession of power. In many ways, Roman law can be seen as representing the interests of those at the top, in particular the propertied class. But when we look at the political crime of treason, we can see that simply lumping the Roman aristocracy into one single, undifferentiated bunch does not do service to the sometimes incredible level of competition within that social group. Even if they did share a broad class interest, each individual also wanted the best possible position within that hierarchy.

The actions of an emperor can in that sense be understood as the reasonable response of a leader who sits atop a rolling maul of competing aristocrats. It must have been terrifying having constantly to keep an eye out for the potential assassin or the loyal servant-turned-traitor. Terror became a means by which to keep everyone else on the back foot. Partly it was about rooting out actual plots; partly about acting in an almost random way, so that nobody could anticipate one's next move; and partly it was about making the potential rewards seem not worth running the terrible risk of discovery. Overall, in the ongoing political struggle of life at the top in Rome, terror kept the initiative on the emperor's side.

Emperors were right to fear conspiracies. Caligula, Nero, Domitian, Commodus – to name but a few of the long list of murdered emperors (or those rumoured to be) – all succumbed to plots. It is perhaps not surprising that our surviving sources dwell on the fate of these less-than-perfect rulers. But accusations of treason also gave the emperor another great political opportunity: the chance to grant clemency. The successful emperor could never rely solely on terror if he was to generate any genuine loyalty. He needed to show a wider range of emotional responses that could highlight his ability to rise above the violence of the political scrum. What better way of doing this than to pardon those who had plotted against him. Sometimes this clemency might seem rather inclement to us. Often it meant giving the accused the opportunity to open their veins or fall on their sword in return for their family being allowed to keep hold of their status and wealth. But in the Roman world, where family money acted as the bedrock of success, such an opportunity could be regarded as generous indeed.

Types of Treason

For a Roman emperor, the words of Louis XIV of France would have rung true: 'L'état, c'est moi' (I am the state.) Technically, though, the first emperor, Augustus, had set himself up as *princeps civitatis*, meaning 'leading citizen'. The public image that he and his supporters had created meant that the emperor had to be seen to be just a normal citizen. He had to go along with this claim in his public image, even if it did not reflect the reality of his true position of power. Such simplicity was, of course, more than a little undermined by the emperor's claim to divinity (though such status was only achieved at death after a vote by the senate). But one of the key components of the imperial imagery established by Augustus, and followed by his successors, was that his power did not rest simply on brute force. Rather it reflected his authority, his *auctoritas*. In other words, the emperor was emperor because he deserved to be emperor. Augustus's high status reflected his moral standing and it had been granted to him by the senate and the Roman people because he was the best man for the job.

Since the image of the Roman emperor as good was so fundamental to the legitimacy of his rule, anything that threatened to undermine that image was harmful. Treason became the crime of wounding the emperor's majesty (*crimen laesae maiestatis*) and, as such, did not consist only of plots and attempted assassinations. Anything that was perceived as rude or insulting constituted a harmful attack on the imperial image. Of course, it was the emperor himself and his officials who decided exactly what counted as insulting behaviour. So treason came to encompass a wide range of actions, effectively allowing the emperor great freedom to destroy any real or imagined opposition. Some of these charges are alleged by contemporary historians to have been completely trumped-up.

The section of the *Digest* dealing with treason gives a comprehensive list of possible crimes (48.4). It begins by noting that the crime is committed not so much against the emperor as against the Roman people. As far as the emperor was concerned, he stood as the embodiment of the Roman people and their wishes, so to hurt one was to hurt the other. Giving information to the enemy or inciting soldiers to rebel seems an unproblematic definition of treason. Men who threaten the security of the state by gathering in armed groups and occupying public places also represents a fairly clear-cut case. Cases where 'gatherings have been called together for sedition' might seem clear but could easily be applied to any crowd, irrespective of the nature of their discussion. Any gathering in public or private therefore ran the risk of being interpreted as a political event and so threatening to the state. The authorities certainly seemed to have feared crowds. They were thought to cause violence and fires, to attack officials, and even to prevent bodies from being buried (*Digest* 48.6). Partly these types of concern resulted from the same desire to maintain order that we find in all states. But it also reflected the very light level of policing within most of the empire. A few soldiers might be able to keep a lid on isolated acts of individual violent crime but they could not deal with major outbreaks of communal violence. Riots could quickly get out of control and, if they did not dissipate of their own accord, would require the intervention of the army to stamp them out.

The importance of image to the imperial regime meant that even insulting a statue could be interpreted as an act of treason. The law was careful to state that anyone who threw a stone and accidentally hit a statue of the emperor was not guilty of treason, but you can imagine the fear you would feel if you were seen to have done such a thing. People got so paranoid about dealing with the imperial image that emperors in the second century had to say it was permissible to sell imperial statues (so long as they were not consecrated in temples) (*Digest* 48.4.1.5). Tacitus records a case where someone was acquitted for melting down a silver imperial statuette (*Annals* 3.70). Caracalla convicted those who urinated near his statues, interpreting such acts personally. (He was right to be suspicious, as the people of Rome did indeed tear down his statues when he died; *Lives of the Later Caesars* Caracalla 5.7.) And it was not just statues. Any defacement of a picture of the emperor could be perceived as treason, as could verbal attacks. A later law, from AD 392, makes clear that the emperors did forgive a man for engaging in such abuse if he was drunk or insane, but the law also states that the emperors wanted to know exactly what had been said before they granted such clemency (*Justinian Code* 9.7.1).

One problem was that magistrates were loath to pass up any opportunity to underline their loyalty to the regime by dealing harshly with anyone accused of offending the imperial image. One law urges judges to take into account the accused's previous conduct and to decide whether his offence was merely a slip of the tongue. Rash people, it says, should sometimes be excused in the way that lunatics are. After all, what could be more insane than to criticise the emperors when their rule was so perfect (*Digest* 48.4.7.3)? Instead, the law states the importance of discovering accomplices involved in an act of treason, as a means of gauging the seriousness of the threat (Paul *Opinions* 5.29.2). In order to help achieve this aim, Augustus circumvented the restriction against torturing slaves to give evidence against their masters by first compelling their masters to sell them to him. He was then at liberty to torture them as he pleased in order to ascertain the truth of what their former masters were really planning (Dio *Roman History* 55.5).

The Sword of Damocles

When Cicero wanted to illustrate the unhappiness that power brings, he told the story of Damocles, a sycophantic courtier to King Dionysius II of Syracuse in Sicily. Sucking up to his ruler, Damocles exclaimed how lucky Dionysius was to have such wealth and power. In response, the king switched places with Damocles so that Damocles could experience first-hand what it was like to be king. He had Damocles sit on the throne with a sword hung over his head, held only by a single hair from a horse's tail. Very quickly Damocles was begging to be released from the swap because he realised that great power brings fear and danger (*Tusculan Disputations* 5.21).

Living in such an atmosphere generated a whole range of imperial insecurities. First came the fear of assassination. Towards the end of AD 182 or early 183, the emperor Commodus was sitting in the imperial box, watching the games in the Colosseum, when a friend, Claudius Pompeianus Quintianus, walked up to him briskly. Pompeianus had been engaged to the daughter of the emperor's sister, Lucilla. Allegedly he had affairs with both daughter and mother, but in spite, or perhaps because, of this he had become friends with Commodus and used to attend banquets with him and accompany him in what one source calls 'youthful escapades'. But instead of a friendly greeting, Pompeianus pulled out a sword and cried, 'The senate sends you this dagger.' It took so long for him to get the words out that the imperial bodyguard had time to react and Commodus was able to escape unharmed. Many others were later implicated in the plot (Dio *Roman History* 73.4). Some of the contemporary sources suggest the assassination attempt had been planned by members of the emperor's family, his eldest sister, Lucilla, being portrayed as its main driver. She was exiled and later killed, but her children were spared. Whether Pompeianus was actually revealing the truth about the assassination attempt – that it had been planned with widespread senatorial support – is impossible to say. But it would hardly be surprising if Commodus had taken his words at face value and it is hardly surprising that his relationship with the senate continued to deteriorate. Commodus faced a series of plots during his reign and the effect seems to have been to make him feel increasingly vulnerable and adopt a more dictatorial attitude towards his enemies. Filled with fear and unable to trust those around him, Commodus largely withdrew from public affairs. He was certainly not the first or last Roman emperor to have reacted in this way to the anxiety of holding imperial office. It was what Rome's second emperor, Tiberius, had done a century and a half before when he retreated to his villa on the isle of Capri.

Pompeianus's attempt to kill Commodus also reveals how such plots often involved those who were dearest to the emperor. Family often provided potential rivals, and so we find that dynastic fears dominated many imperial accusations of treason. Nero, for example, executed Antonia, the daughter of Claudius, because she refused to marry him (he charged her with an attempt at revolution). The historian Suetonius says that Nero treated all others who were in any way connected with him by blood or by marriage in the same way. Among them was the young Aulus Plautius, with whom Nero's mother had reputedly had an affair. The liaison appears to have inspired Aulus to believe that he might be in with a shot at the throne. The emperor allegedly sexually assaulted him before his death, saying, 'Let my mother come and kiss my successor now.' Nero had a stepson, Rufrius Crispinus, from his wife Poppaea's previous marriage. After her death (said to have been caused by Nero, who supposedly kicked her in the stomach when pregnant), he had the boy drowned by the child's own slaves while he was fishing, because Nero had heard that the boy used to enjoy playing at being emperor. He even banished his nanny's son, Tuscus, who, when on official business in Egypt, had had the temerity to use some baths that had been specially built for Nero when he had visited the province (Suetonius *Nero* 35).

Suetonius accuses Nero of violating these close relationships but, in a way, all such relationships were polluted by the power an emperor held. It was impossible to be emperor and not be suspicious of your close advisers and family members. Nero may have been more paranoid than most, or he might have faced more threats, but all emperors had to deal with the likelihood that some of their closest advisers and family members would at some time try to murder them.

Emperors could also use the charge of treason to manage those close to them and to generate extra revenue for the state's coffers. Nero is accused of abusing treason charges in this way. Suetonius records that the emperor was down to his last denarius, with scarcely enough money to pay the army, which was a dangerous position for an emperor to be in. As well as issuing creative financial laws, such as one decreeing that any freedman bearing a name in any way connected to the emperor should bequeath him five-sixths of his estate, Nero also stated that informers should be encouraged to bring charges of treason against people so that he could confiscate their property (Suetonius *Nero* 32). Likewise Domitian is alleged to have spent so prodigiously that he turned to treason laws to raise revenue. The property of the living and the dead was seized everywhere on any charge brought by any accuser (Suetonius *Domitian* 12). As Pliny says, the treasury was enriched by the charges of treason, 'the unique and only way of incriminating men who had committed no crime' (*Panegyric* 42).

Pliny's comments come in his *Panegyric* to the emperor Trajan, who succeeded Domitian after the brief interregnum of Nerva. Pliny praises Trajan for having stopped relying on informers and for treating citizens and senators as friends not slaves. Should we believe this claim? It is easy to be cynical and dismiss it as the brown-nosing of an ambitious courtier. Or to say that such flattery is all Pliny could produce given that he had to deliver the speech in the presence of the emperor himself – what other option did he have? But I think it is probably accurate to infer from Pliny's statements, and from the histories of Suetonius and Tacitus, which were written at roughly the same time, that there had been at least a shift in emphasis in the imperial style of government. Nero and Domitian had fallen out with the senatorial class and had used the law as a means of managing and controlling these powerful and potentially threatening individuals. The conflict was itself then reflected in the bad write-up later given by high-ranking historians. Pliny's gushing account of Trajan may be exaggerated but Trajan was, at least in the historical record, a good emperor if not 'the best' as he was called (*optimus princeps*). He ruled alongside the aristocracy, not over them. Look at his actions with regard to his close friend, Licinius Sura. Some people complained that Sura held too much influence over the emperor, raising the concern that he might be ambitious to become emperor himself. Trajan proved Sura's loyalty by turning up uninvited at his house and, having dismissed his bodyguard, ordering Sura's barber to shave him with his razor (Dio *Roman History* 68.15).

When relations between the senate and the emperor broke down, it could only result in mutual fear and suspicion. A classic case involved the emperor Commodus. Commodus was hunting animals in the Colosseum when he fired a bladed arrow that decapitated an ostrich. Taking the bird's severed head, the emperor held it up in front of the senators in the first two rows of seats and raised his bloody sword in his other hand. The historian Dio says that the senators stifled their laughter by chewing on laurel leaves taken from the wreaths on their heads, but I don't think he is fooling anyone. Commodus had recently executed a large number of high-ranking Romans, from members of his own family, to six former consuls and their entire families, to current consuls and proconsuls and innumerable others. If you ask me, the senators were terrified.

In such an atmosphere of panic and paranoia, it is easy to see how trust could completely break down. This could be exploited by the ambitious and the unscrupulous to their advantage. An imperial freedman, called Graptus, played on Nero's peculiar suspicion of Cornelius Sulla. Sulla was dim but Nero assumed that this was an astute act performed by a man of keen intelligence who could see the perils associated with being seen to be smart. Nero was in the habit of going down at night to the Milvian Bridge area of the capital, where there were taverns and prostitutes galore, and Graptus claimed that Sulla had arranged for the emperor to be ambushed on his way back from there on the Flaminian Way. There was no evidence and the accused was too stupid to think up such a plan let alone execute it. But, just to be sure, Nero had him safely exiled to the city of Massilia, modern Marseille (Tacitus *Annals* 13.47). This kind of arbitrary injustice mattered to upper-class writers. Tacitus served as a senator, rising to consul, as did Pliny, who also became a provincial governor. Suetonius worked on the staff of both Trajan and Hadrian. These were the kinds of men who would suffer directly if the relationship between the elite and the emperor broke down. That is why they put so much emphasis on it in their writings.

How far have these ancient writers coloured our own views? The histories of Tacitus and Suetonius have formed the basis for so much modern writing about ancient Rome that it is impossible to escape their influence. Robert Graves's novel, *I, Claudius*, the fictional biography of the emperor of that name, was heavily based on these ancient texts and widely perpetuated the image of the imperial household as little better than a nest of vipers. It is a view found repeatedly promulgated in more recent popular images of Roman politics, whether it is the father-murdering Commodus of the film *Gladiator* or the endlessly conniving imperial family of the HBO *Rome* series. Can we put aside these impressions and form an impartial assessment of Roman political life or are we hopelessly condemned to see ancient events through the politically savvy eyes of their contemporary recorders?

Freedom Fighters?

So far we have concentrated on the treasonable acts of the elite. But we also find evidence of ordinary people opposing the ruling class. Egypt had a long tradition of resisting foreign rule, having been conquered previously by the Greeks under Alexander the Great and then ruled by his successors, the Ptolemies. One third-century papyrus prophesies, 'it will go badly for the rich. Their arrogance will be cast down and their goods confiscated and delivered over to another ... And the poor will be exalted and the rich humbled' (*P. Oxy.* 31.2554). The *Sibylline Oracles* (not to be confused with the official Sibylline books consulted at times of crisis) looked forward to a time when the 'unclean' and 'lamentable' city of revelry, Rome, would be destroyed by those over whom it currently held sway. Rome would be 'reduced to ashes' and its young men and women would be sold off into slavery just as those whom it had conquered had been (see 5.386–433; 5.155–78; 3.356). In these texts, Nero himself became the embodiment of Roman wickedness. While it is easy to dismiss these writings as very rare acts of provincial defiance, they do at least show that it was not just the Roman elite who thought about the justice or otherwise of imperial rule. Even ordinary people were able to imagine a time when the social order could be completely overturned.

It is impossible to know how common such sentiments were among those who were governed by Rome. Not surprisingly only a few such texts survive. Writing them was dangerous and, in any case, required literacy. We get perhaps a better sense of how people questioned the legitimacy and efficiency of the regime by looking at what they did rather than what they said (which we don't know) or wrote or had written about them. And perhaps the best example we have of actions that can be interpreted as critical in some way of the system is rioting. One reason for this is that we actually have some evidence. We saw earlier that treason could encompass all kinds of public gatherings. The authorities were interested in such collective acts because they had the potential to destabilise the system, albeit only temporarily, and cause considerable amounts of damage. The sources are not interested in how many rioters died or in the details of what they were demanding, only in their possible political ramifications. But at least we have details of collective actions by ordinary people that the literary elite thought worthy of recording in their histories.

The most common reason for riots was shortage of food. The historian Ammianus calls food the 'usual' cause (*Histories* 21.12.24). Often it was not so much a real shortage as the fear of one, for example because the grain ships had not arrived from North Africa. Technically such riots could have been interpreted as treasonable but, in fact, we find emperors and governors broadly tolerating them.

The reason was that riots of this kind did not have any politically subversive purpose. If anything, they were aimed at establishing a dialogue with the authorities. If the fear of food running short was growing, then the best way for the people to make sure their voice was heard was to shout out loud and back this up with physical violence. It would be wrong to see this as mindless hooliganism. Overall, the aim of the crowd seems to have been to re-establish the normal political arrangement whereby the government made sure there was a ready supply of afford-able food in return for popular support. It was a kind of conservative rioting that sought to restore order.

The fact that the people needed to work so hard to have their voice heard is telling. The authorities had no interest in their day-to-day problems but they did have an interest in issues that might affect public order.

Of course, we can see these occasions as times when the elite were trying to wriggle out of what was expected of them. The wealthy would be condemned for deserting the city when grain and oil ran short (Symmachus *Letters* 6.18) – this kind of behaviour smacked of them looking after their own backs and not caring about the fate of ordinary citizens. This would have been a dangerous stance for an emperor to adopt. He justified his rule in part by reference to his benevolent patronage of the people, so it would have undermined his popular legiti-macy to walk away when times got tough. When there was rioting in the provinces, the emperor would often try to force local elites into calming the situation down, thereby reinforcing his public image as a distant but benign ruler.

Not all riots had such politically conservative aims. Ammianus notes that riots were about both 'serious and trivial things' (*Histories* 15.7.2). One law refers to groups of young men who misbehaved in the spectacles and started up disruptive chants among the crowd (*Digest* 48.19.28.3). We saw earlier how the fight between the people of Nuceria and those of Pompeii, where many died, arose out of a 'trifling incident' at a gladiatorial show (Tacitus *Annals* 14.17). This kind of riot was likely to be treated more harshly by the authorities because it lacked any greater purpose. Pompeii was banned from holding games for ten years (although the ban was lifted, or simply ignored, soon afterwards).

The games offered a good opportunity for the crowd to express political opinions. During the reign of Septimius Severus, the crowd complained about the ongoing civil war by clapping in unison and chanting, 'How long will we wage war?', but then they seem to have got bored with that and shouted 'That's enough' and turned their attention back to the races (Dio *Roman History* 75.4.4). Perhaps they knew better than to push it too far.

In many ways, the games replaced the popular assemblies of the republican period by providing an occasion for the rulers and ruled to meet in a spirit of festival fun, where it was acceptable for people to give voice to their opinions. These expressions of dissent were not the norm, though. They are examples gleaned from upper-class male histories written for other upper-class men, in which the people feature only as walk-on parts in the narrative of high politics. But these examples do show how the people were, on occasion, capable of adopting a critical stance to the regime. And in order to do so, ordinary citizens must have been alert to the occasions when the shortfall between imperial rhetoric and what was delivered was at its most extreme – no doubt, generally speaking, people expected some gap between rhetoric and reality. The risks of vocal or violent complaint were also so great that people mainly grumbled in private. But when an emperor or his officials were patently failing to deliver the social fundamentals of food and justice then the risk of confrontation became worth running.

One source that provides an interesting sense of how politically powerful the crowd could be is the Acts of the Apostles. The text recounts the twelve disciples and Paul preaching the gospel across the East and then in Rome after Jesus's death. His message led to a breakdown of public order in six different places. In Thessalonica, Paul and his followers were described as 'These people who have been turning the world upside down', who are all 'acting contrary to the decrees of the emperor, saying that there is another king named Jesus' (17:6). At one point, the disciples Peter and John were taken before the temple leaders and told to keep quiet because they were stirring things up. Paul caused riots in Ephesus because his message threatened the local religious centre of Artemis and the livelihoods associated with that cult. The Ephesians rushed to the theatre and spent two hours shouting, 'Great is Artemis of the Ephesians' (19:23–41). And he upset some of the locals at Philippi by driving out a spirit from a slave girl that was thought to allow her to predict the future. Her owners, aggrieved at losing their cash cow, took Paul before the magistrates and accused

him of 'throwing our city into an uproar'. The crowd
joined in the attack against Paul and the magistrates
ordered him to be stripped and beaten.

Paul was, in fact, whipped on several occasions despite
being a Roman citizen and so supposedly immune from
such punishment – although the magistrates in Philippi
apologised once they found this out. Local leadership in
the provinces always feared unrest because it risked pro-
voking a military response from Rome. Of course, the
Acts probably do not describe a normal period in Roman
provincial life, but the text does give a sense of how
crowds of ordinary people could become politically
involved and how the local leadership was always keen to
keep them quiet. The politics of the crowd, though, was
a mix of both the radical and the conservative. In other
words, they were like crowds everywhere. If we were
hoping to discover evidence that Rome's masses were
ultra radical then we are going to be disappointed.

It is difficult to say how often protest led to violence.
The seeming readiness of Romans to turn violent in personal confrontations might suggest that they would have
been just as quick to do so collectively. In the sources, a
high percentage of popular protests end in riot, but they
have probably only been recorded because they were
extreme cases. It is certainly clear that at times of stress
people had no qualms about attacking even the emperor.
During a grain shortage, Claudius was surrounded in the
forum by an angry mob who hurled insults at him and
pelted him with rock-hard crusts of bread. He was lucky
to escape back to the imperial palace on the Palatine by a
back door (Suetonius *Claudius* 18).

The same text also states how much effort Claudius then put into trying to source grain for the city's population. It is also clear that the crowd were not out to harm him – they would have thrown stones and used weapons if so. It was like throwing eggs at a politician. Hitting the emperor with bits of mouldy bread served to shame him into doing his duty by his people. Similar examples concern the future emperors Vespasian, who was bombarded with turnips when governor of Africa, for reasons the text does not make clear, and Vitellius, who was once pelted with manure.

The sources show how intolerant the emperor could be of opposition. The town of Puteoli once saw a face-off between its governing officials and the populace, the one complaining about the violence of the crowd, the other of the rapaciousness of the leading citizens and magistrates. Tacitus describes these as quarrels that had reached the point of stone-throwing and threats of arson, so it was not yet a full-blown breakdown in public order. The emperor sent in a cohort of the praetorian guard whose presence alone terrified the people into backing down, helped, as Tacitus dryly notes, by 'a few executions'. Tacitus calls this a return to 'concord' among the town's inhabitants: 'armed suppression of political dissent' might be a more accurate description (*Annals* 13.48).

Of course, sending in the troops risked losing public support. Often emperors seem to have been keen to balance the demands of maintaining order with giving the people what they wanted. Blaming incompetent officials was one way out of the impasse. The third-century emperor Gallus once refused to help the city of Antioch when famine threatened. Instead he just pinned it on the governor of Syria, Theophilus, whom the people then kicked to death (Ammianus *Histories* 14.7.5–6). Often there was nothing these governors could do. In the same period, a prefect of Rome, Tertullus, was faced with an angry crowd during a failure in food supplies. He resorted to showing the mob his two young sons, saying that they too would starve unless the winds changed to allow the grain ships to dock. It was a desperate strategy but it worked. The people took pity on the children, quietened down, realised they were all in the same boat, and prayed for the seas to grow calm, which they obligingly did (Ammianus *Histories* 19.10).

Fear the Crowd

The inclusion of incidents of violent popular protest in the narratives of Roman historians shows how politically important such events were perceived to be. It also reflects something of the fear that the ruling elite felt when surrounded, like Claudius, by a sea of hostile people. The senators, equestrians and governing classes of the empire numbered a couple of hundred thousand in a population of sixty or seventy million. Sitting atop this volatile mass could be a profoundly unnerving experience. This is why we find such a sense of unease in the surviving record about any kind of public gathering. There was always a concern that such meetings would generate violence. The fierce laws concerning sedition tried to counter any pressure from below: those who 'stir up the people' are to be, according to their rank, crucified, thrown to the wild beasts or exiled to an island (Paul *Opinions* 5.22).

We should not overestimate the ability of the army to suppress the populace. The Roman army was small given the size of the population and the land mass of the empire, and it existed primarily to keep enemies out rather than keep the lid on domestic pressures. Calling in the troops was always the last resort. As Tacitus records a conservative senator saying in the case of the murdered Pedanius Secundus, 'You will not restrain the scum of the earth except by terror' (*Annals* 14.44).

The emperors relied on public support to lend their regimes legitimacy, but this latent fear of the power of the people created a parallel sense of contempt among the upper classes. Laws refer to the *faex populi* – the shit of the people – and in one case prescribes the death penalty for those 'thrown by poverty into plebeian vileness and muck' (*Theodosian Code* 9.42.5). According to the dream interpreter, Artemidorus, to dream of sleeping on a manure heap was good for the rich as it indicated forthcoming public office: in other words ruling the people was the equivalent of sitting atop a dunghill. It is noticeable that this contempt is often reserved for the urban mass. In the late republic, Cicero also refers to the *faex populi* and to the plebs as the city's sewage water (*Letters to Atticus* 1.19). Juvenal complains that it is the oriental influence that has degraded Rome with its foul-smelling and funny-sounding foreigners and their customs: 'For years now the Syrian Orontes has poured its sewerage into our native Tiber' (*Satires* 3.62–4). I dare say there was an element of truth in this: ordinary people in Rome must have stunk given the lack of hygiene, cramped living conditions, a poor sewerage system and having to work manually in a hot climate. But the abuse hardly fits with any notion of concord between the different classes of Roman society.

The authorities made periodic efforts to clamp down on and control popular gatherings. These measures affected not just overtly political meetings but gatherings of all kind, as any occasion when individuals came together was seen as being vulnerable to conspiracy. Exemptions tell us a lot about how the emperors viewed such events. Augustus, for example, permitted Jews to assemble in synagogues because, unlike assemblies of ordinary citizens, they were perceived as an expression of piety that did not threaten to end in disorder (Philo *Embassy to Gaius* 311–12). Regulations sometimes banned popular organisations, known as *collegia*, which existed as burial clubs to help people save for a proper funeral, but also assumed certain social functions, such as holding regular dinners for their members. A surviving list of rules from a club in Lanuvium, near Rome, lists club regulations, such as how much wine and food a chairman should arrange for each dinner. It states that members who disrupt these dinners by changing seat or becoming abusive will be fined on a sliding scale according to the severity of the misconduct (*CIL* 14.2112). It hardly seems a hotbed of potential revolution. The joining fee alone, one hundred sesterces for the club in Lanuvium, enough to feed a family for a couple of months, would have restricted membership to the well-to-do. But what to us seem like utterly harmless institutions faced restrictions because the authorities felt unease about what might go in within these meetings. So it was forbidden to join more than one club at a time. And slaves could only join with their master's permission (*Digest* 47.22).

An exchange of correspondence between the emperor Trajan and Pliny, when he was governor of Bithynia, reveals just how sensitive emperors could be about clubs. Pliny writes to his boss saying that an extensive fire has struck the city of Nicomedia and done a great deal of damage to public and private buildings alike. He blames the ordinary people for letting the blaze spread so quickly because they stood around like 'lazy and immobile spectators'. He also notes that there was no fire-fighting equipment and so suggests setting up a fire brigade, like the vigiles in Rome, of no more than 150 men. Pliny is at pains to emphasise that he will make sure that only suitable people are appointed and that the club is not used for any other purpose than that for which it was established. It is striking that an important man, a provincial governor no less, should feel the need to consult the emperor about what seems such an insignificant matter, but he did so because he knew emperors could be very touchy about these issues. And he was right because Trajan promptly replied with a firm 'no', pointing out that several other cities in the region had been troubled by these clubs. 'Whatever name we give them,' he concludes, 'and for whatever purpose they meet, when men come together for the same purpose they will quickly become political clubs.' As for the risk of fire, the emperor says property owners should extinguish the fires themselves (Pliny *Letters* 10.33–4). In another exchange between the two men, Trajan reluctantly grants permission for a charitable club to be established in the city of Amisus, which enjoyed the privilege of making its own laws. Even then he is worried that the proceeds will be put towards rioting rather than helping the poor, and he emphasises that in all other cities, 'I would have all clubs of this kind banned' (10.93–4). For Trajan, the risk of sedition justified continued close control.

Controlling Rumour and Sedition

Treason (*maiestas*), as we have seen, covered more than violent acts against the state. It included also words and insults that might bruise the imperial ego. We have several examples of people not being afraid to mock emperors: jokes about Augustus being allegedly illegitimate, or the young Julius Caesar as the recipient sexual partner in a homosexual relationship (Macrobius *Saturnalia* 2.4.20; Suetonius *Julius* 49). The piss-pots that stood outside fullers' shops, because they used urine in processing wool, were called 'Vespasians' because that emperor had introduced an unpopular tax on them (Suetonius *Vespasian* 23). These kinds of jokes only went so far. Little more than teasing, they served to emphasise the emperor's generosity and tolerant nature. But what they also do is to underline how important chat and rumour were in ordinary life. Most people were illiterate and relied instead on oral sources to find out the news and to get information.

Popular rumours often concerned the alleged hoarding of food by the wealthy during times of shortage. There was probably some truth in them: after all, it would have made sense in a period of poor food supplies, and must have been particularly galling for the poor when they were short of food.

Rumour was a way to pressure the powerful into helping by getting them to release food for the general populace. Sometimes rumour concerned an even more immediate matter of life or death. During the Great Fire in Rome, people ran about asking 'where is the fire?', 'how did it happen?', and 'what started it?' This was a very different set of questions from those asked by later elite historians, who were concerned more about the damage caused to public property (see Dio 62.16–18). The ordinary people of Rome wanted to know who or what was responsible, reflecting a desire for simple justice and accountability, and they wanted to know exactly where it had spread, so that they could escape. Popular discussions were not expressed in letters or formal histories, but in gossip, common knowledge and half-whispered questions, all of which served to spread the news about what was really happening.

The emperors themselves were often the focus of rumour. Emperors were so central to the political life of Rome that stories about what they were up to spread quickly. Rumour-mongering of this kind might have been harmless but it also allowed alternative versions of events to be discussed and passed around. Perhaps these stories served to form bonds between the teller and the listener, a way for them to share the terrifying and frustrating business of being ruled by an autocrat. All kinds of exaggerated tales could be told, many of which will have contradicted the emperor's official image, and some of which later found their way into the formal histories of men like Tacitus and Suetonius. So we find stories that 'reveal' how wantonly cruel Caligula was, or how mad Nero was, or how paranoid Domitian was.

The main problem with treasonable tales such as these was that they were impossible to police. In the *Acts of the Pagan Martyrs*, we find an account of an interrogation of someone named Appian by the emperor Commodus regarding rumours that have circulated about the price of wheat:

Appian: 'People are sending their wheat to other cities and profiteering by selling it at four times the price.'
Emperor: 'Who is making all this money?'
App.: 'It is the emperor himself who is benefiting.'
Emp.: 'Are you certain?'
App.: 'No, but that is what we have heard.'
Emp.: 'You ought not to have circulated the story without being certain of it. Executioner!'

As he is being led away, Appian asks an onlooker, 'Have you nothing to say at my being led to execution?' and the despairing reply comes, 'Who can we speak to if there is no one who will listen?' The emperor then recalls Appian and, making a point, says:

Emp.: 'Now you know who you are speaking to, don't you?'
App.: 'Yes I do, to a tyrant.'
Emp.: 'No, to an emperor.'

But Appian is having none of it. He insists that Commodus's father, Marcus Aurelius, was fit to be an emperor because he was wise, parsimonious and good. 'But you,' he says to Commodus's face, 'have precisely the opposite qualities: you are tyrannical, dishonest and cruel.'

It makes for great reading but this slanging match could not have been the norm. Nor could this confrontational approach suppress the widespread use of rumour to criticise the emperor. But the emperors did try to control verbal opposition, and used agents to spy on people in the provinces. Ammianus describes how an agent was at a dinner party in Spain when, as it was growing dark, the slaves brought in the candles with the traditional saying 'Let us conquer', meaning the darkness. The agent interpreted this as a political statement of intent to overthrow the emperor and had the household reported (*Histories* 16.8.9). Clearly he was trying to ingratiate himself with the emperor by being seen to get results, but the fact that the agent's version of events was accepted gives an indication of just how sensitive emperors could be, with the result that a noble family was destroyed. And in Rome, we are told how reckless men could be trapped by soldiers in the following manner. A soldier in civilian clothing sits down in a tavern and begins to vilify the emperor. 'Then,' says Epictetus, 'as if you had received from him a pledge of good faith just because he began the abuse, you too say what's on your mind – and the next moment you are handcuffed and led away' (*Discourses* 4.13.5).

Some emperors were notorious for relying on informers, *delatores*, to sniff out any hint of treason, and Domitian used household slaves to find out what was going on in private behind closed doors. Slaves were ubiquitous in the households of the rich and powerful and they functioned as a kind of CCTV on all the comings and goings within. Juvenal complains about how slaves went around gossiping about their masters. 'Do you really believe a rich man's secrets can ever stay hidden?' he asks (*Satires* 9.102–19). He calls it extracting revenge by rumour because in reality there was little the master could do about it. Probably all emperors used agents to some extent to act as their eyes and ears, and the rewards for the successful informer were significant. They received a share of the confiscated property of the accused in the event of a guilty verdict. The problem with this practice was, of course, that it encouraged all kinds of false accusations or, as with the slaves and the candles, over-interpretations of the facts. Informers were driven not only by greed, but by personal enmity against those whom they accused, and by desire for political promotion. Perhaps some had a profound sense of duty to their emperor and thought they were doing their best by him.

Tacitus provides us with a creepy account of one of these informers. He describes how the senior official in Bithynia, Marcellus, found himself accused of treason by one of his staff, a quaestor called Caepio Crispinus. This was during the early part of the reign of Augustus's successor, Tiberius, a man who seems to have been far less comfortable in the role and was the first to make heavy use of informers. Caepio came from a poor background and an unknown family. But he was hugely ambitious. He wheedled his way into the emperor's trust by giving him private reports about what senators were up to behind his back. He was well paid in return and acquired a great fortune from his spying. The nobles despised him at first. Then they feared him. Caepio brought his accusation before the senate, where he alleged that Marcellus had gone around telling sinister stories about the emperor's character. The fact that the stories he was alleged to have told corresponded to the truth made the accusation even more believable. One of Caepio's cronies added that Marcellus had placed a statue of himself on higher ground than those of the emperors, while a statue of Augustus had had its head hacked off to be replaced with a likeness of Tiberius. The emperor was so angry he shouted out that he would vote guilty. All the senators felt obliged to follow his example but, Tacitus notes, a few traces of dying liberty still remained and Gnaeus Piso asked, with fake simplicity, 'Will you vote first or last, Caesar? If first, I shall have something to follow, if last, I am worried I might inadvertently find myself on the other side.' Tiberius backed down and voted for acquittal on the counts of treason (*Annals* 1.74).

As there was no public prosecutor, the system relied on an individual to bring an accusation and, as there was no penalty for bringing a failed case unless it could be proved to be false or malicious, this was a lucrative business for informers. Emperors who felt less than secure had no interest in discouraging these accusations and so a poisonous atmosphere could quickly develop. The concentration of all legal and judicial power in the person of the emperor meant that such a situation could easily arise unless the emperor took action to prevent it. Later in Tiberius's reign, a man accused by an informer of treason took his own life before the trial was completed in an effort to save his family's assets and standing. It was pro-posed that the informer's reward should be forfeited because the defendant had not been found guilty. The resolution was about to be accepted when the emperor intervened. He complained that the country would fall into chaos if informers, the 'custodians of the constitu-tion', were removed from public life. Thus, concludes Tacitus, a breed invented for the ruin of the state was encouraged all the more (*Annals* 4.30).

But Tacitus would say that. He was a senator who had nothing but contempt for these pushy careerists from the lower classes. From the emperor's point of view, it was clear that plenty of plots did take place among the aristoc-racy and these needed to be rooted out. It was also a kind of management tactic, whereby the leader played off those beneath him against each other. What better way to keep subordinates too scared to plot than to have them police one another? The key was striking a balance. Too heavy a reliance on this tactic created a culture of terror, where blackmail must have thrived. But perhaps too little would simply have ended in assassination. Trajan gave a clear lead on how the emperor should be seen to treat anonymous accusations. When Pliny asked for advice about those anonymously accused of being Christians, the emperor replied that such cases should not result in prosecution. Not only would it introduce a very danger-ous precedent, but 'it is quite foreign to the spirit of the age'. Whether Trajan took such an attitude if an informer went to him with hard evidence of a plot is another matter (Pliny *Letters* 10.97).

The Use of Clemency

Emperors faced real limits on the extent to which they could police the opinions of those beneath them. They also faced the threat of being damned by posterity. When Tacitus and Suetonius wrote about the dreadful examples of previous dynasties they were in some sense praising their own emperor, Trajan, for his just rule. But there was also an implied threat. If the emperor did not behave as a good emperor was expected to, and indeed claimed to, then he could expect to receive a damning report in the histories written about his reign. So what, we might object. But you only have to look at the great imperial buildings of Rome to see how much emperors cared about their image when alive, about the survival of the dynasty, and about their legacy in history. By writing histories full of the actions, good or otherwise, of past emperors, the elite historians of Rome were effectively trying to hold their own emperors to account. It was a weapon of the weak, to be sure, and it clearly did not always work, but it does show how those ruled by the emperor were not completely powerless.

What better way for an emperor to deal with these limitations on his behaviour than by making a virtue out of a necessity and emphasising his clemency? It meant not trying to enforce the unenforceable, while delivering something of the promises of imperial propaganda by helping to create an atmosphere of decency and responsible government. Ammianus describes how the fourth-century emperor, Julian, let a rapist off with exile, and when the girl's parents complained that the perpetrator had been banished and not executed, the emperor merely replied, 'The law may criticise my clemency, but it is right for an emperor who has a very merciful disposition to rise above the law' (*Histories* 16.5.12). Exile instead of the death penalty itself served as a way of demonstrating clemency to those of high status.

This spirit of strategic mercy seeped down to the emperor's officials. One second-century edict, from the governor of Egypt, Sempronius Liberalis, grants amnesty to those ordinary people who had fled their homes after riots, presumably fearing they would be arrested, or those who had run away because they were too poor to pay their taxes: 'I urge you all to come back to your proper home and to obtain the first and greatest fruit of prosperity.' If they do return, the edict continues, 'let them know they will experience the emperor's favour and kindness and that he forbids any judicial enquiry against them'. Yes, this was an act of mercy but there was no real alternative. The government needed people to pay their taxes and could do little to hunt them down if they chose to abandon the settled regions of the Nile and head for the wilderness. No wonder the emperor would be grateful if they heeded his request.

Augustus, as ever, set the example of how leniency should be exercised by an emperor. He spared many who had opposed him and even promoted them to high office. In one instance, two plebs, Junius Novatus and Cassius Patavinus, had offended the emperor. One had circulated a scurrilous letter libelling him while the other had brazenly declared at a large dinner party that he would happily kill him. But Augustus merely fined one and exiled the other (thereby putting him a safe distance away in case he should really have wanted to carry out his wish). When the future emperor Tiberius complained to Augustus that someone was vilifying him, the emperor replied that he should not take idle talk too seriously, rather that, 'We must be content if we can stop anyone from harming us' (Suetonius *Augustus* 51). Not words that Tiberius took to heart. But other emperors did and it became common for them to grant pardons on holidays, or to use them to mark special occasions or to celebrate successes (*Digest* 48.16.8). Such leniency may have allowed a few criminals off the hook, but those who faced punishment only ever represented an exemplary group chosen to act as a deterrent to others. By pardoning some of them, the emperors created the same effect. The spirit of the law was maintained even though the miscreant was let off, while the ideal of benevolent imperial justice was prominently enacted for all to see. Needless to say, such clemency always contained with it the implicit threat that next time you might not be so lucky. Mercy was always coloured with a hint of malice.

What Did People Really Think of the Emperor?

How do we square the various opinions of the emperor that we have encountered? Was he regarded as a benign father figure or, in private at least, as a despotic dictator? If we took much of the evidence at face value we would conclude, as most historians have, that the people loved their sovereign. In festivals and ceremonies, in processions at the games, people chanted out their support. They put up pictures of the emperor in their shops. There was no escape from the imperial image: on coins, in the form of statues (by the fourth century Rome had 4,000 bronze statues of emperors, to say nothing of stone ones), and badly painted pictures, which are described as 'sitting on money-changers' tables, in stalls, in shops, hanging in the eaves, in entrance halls, in windows, in fact everywhere' (Fronto *Letter to Caesar* 4.12). Laws had to be passed to restrain the excessive adulation of the imperial image at the games (*Theodosian Code* 15.4.1). It was even claimed that people loved paying their taxes to the emperors (Aelius Aristides *Panegyric on Rome* 65–7).

I think we can be sceptical about these views. For one thing, most people in the empire were probably not very interested in, or bothered by, the emperor; they were too busy struggling to survive. We have also seen ample evidence that people of all social levels were capable of expressing critical opinions of their emperor. And we have plenty of evidence that emperors knew that people were saying things behind their backs, and that some rulers tried to stop this. In a way, the ubiquitous imperial image is reminiscent of a modern totalitarian regime. I remember being in Libya when Gaddafi was in power. His picture was everywhere and nobody had a bad word to say about him. That obviously all changed. The same thing appears to have happened in Rome when emperors such as Domitian and Commodus were assassinated. In the case of Commodus, in the first session of the senate held after his death, it was decreed that his memory should be erased from record. His statue in the senate house was thrown down and replaced with one symbolising freedom. It was not the case that Roman emperors controlled a state with anything like the centralising control of a modern totalitarian regime but they were terrifying enough to stop most public dissent. But silence did not mean consensus and the Roman people could complain vociferously when they saw an emperor failing to live up to his claims.

It is, of course, wrong to think that there was one single, unified public opinion about the emperor. All Romans had their axes to grind. Some, like Tacitus, criticised rulers who abused their powers, especially in their dealings with senators. Others judged the emperor in accordance with the price of grain. Some saw him as a protector; others abused that image by using it as a cover to insult the upper classes (Tacitus *Annals* 3.36). Still others, like the evangelist Luke, treated so-called imperial justice with a mixture of fear and contempt:

> When you go with your accuser before a magistrate, on the way make an effort to settle the case, or you might be dragged before the judge, and the judge will hand you over to the officer, and the officer throw you in prison. I tell you, you will never get out until you have paid every last penny. (Luke 12:58)

For him, as was no doubt the case for many provincials, the law was part of their colonial relationship with Rome.

Popular opinion was flexible, necessarily so. Most of the time the populace doubtless vigorously supported the regime. On occasions, they might voice complaints in the acceptable arena of the games. More infrequently they might resort to violence to express discontent. On the rare times when a regime fell, they might have the opportunity to vent their feelings more openly. But you never knew who would come to power next. Within three years of Commodus's death, for example, Septimius Severus was in control and keen to forge links with the previous Antonine dynasty. He criticised the senate for its hypocrisy in its attacks on Commodus, whose body was transferred to Hadrian's mausoleum, now the Castel Sant'Angelo on the banks of the river Tiber, as a sign of his being restored to a place of honour. Similarly, after the death of Augustus, people 'arranged their expressions so as not to seem too happy at his death or too upset at the new beginning, combining tears with joy, lamentation with flattery' (Tacitus *Annals* 1.7.1). There was a real need to be a good dissembler.

Speaking truth to power is always difficult and even more so when dealing with an autocrat, so individuals of all social levels were careful to tell the emperor what he wanted to hear. As astute emperors knew, power breeds flatterers and sycophants. In public, especially, people had to be seen to support the regime, and, at the very least, an individual would need to be deferential to the rhetoric of imperial government. They had to watch the mood of the emperor and react accordingly. Keeping the emperor sweet could bring great advantages: money and political advancement for the elite and food and entertainment for the ordinary people. By contrast, his wrath could bring down charges of treason and its dreadful punishments. Outright opposition was dangerous. A public loss of face would always demand a parallel public retribution. And so, when we read most of the written accounts and letters of the emperor's subjects, we find that all is harmony and contentment – on the surface.

Chapter V

CRIMES AGAINST THE GODS

Tiberius did not come out well in the last chapter. As we saw, he increasingly abused the laws relating to treason by relying on informers to prosecute for profit. Yet in his early days as emperor, he seemed to be following in the footsteps of his illustrious predecessor Augustus. Tacitus recounts how Tiberius rejected the first tentative charges brought by spies. Two mid-ranking Roman equestrians, Falanius and Rubrius, were accused of allowing a homosexual actor to take part in religious rites held in honour of the now deified Augustus, of violating his divine memory by perjury, and of selling a statue of the dead emperor as part of the contents of a house. Tiberius was not bothered by the supposed disrespecting of the imperial cult and image. He wrote to the consuls in charge of investigating the case that the senate had not granted Augustus the honour of a place in heaven so it could be used to destroy his fellow Romans. He said his own mother had regularly allowed the actor Cassius to take part in the games celebrating the memory of Augustus, that statues of all the gods counted as property in a house sale, and that when it came to perjury, if Rubrius had taken a god's name in vain then it was up to the god to exact retribution (Tacitus *Annals* 1.73). If Tiberius had carried on like this he might have got a far better press later on.

Religion and crime sit uneasily in the Western world. Blasphemy laws are rarely if ever enforced and only amid controversy if so. But in the Roman world, religion sat at the heart of how people understood all crime, as well as its prevention and punishment. Any act which offended the gods risked damaging the *pax deorum*, the 'peace of the gods', the divine support for the Roman people that was believed to have allowed them to conquer so great an empire in return for appropriate worship and offerings. The maintenance of this divine support was a priority of any Roman emperor. But, as Romulus had shown at the outset, Romans were perfectly prepared to use religion to further their political ends.

Types of Religious Crime

The importance of preventing any crime in the religious sphere meant that the Romans assigned jurisdiction over such offences to the highest priest, the Pontifex Maximus. It was his task to prosecute offences against the chastity of Vestal Virgins and the violation of oaths, both of which counted as being *nefas*, contrary to divine law. Originally, the priest's duties had included the upkeep of the wooden bridge across the river Tiber, which was reflected in the meaning of his name: 'Supreme Bridge-builder'. By the time of the empire, the bridge-building duties had become purely metaphorical, ensuring that proper contact was maintained between men and the gods. The Pontifex Maximus acted as judge in any religious dispute and he set the laws regarding the correct observance of religious rites. It was also his job to investigate whether magistrates and priests had carried out their religious duties in line with sacred law. They had the power to punish offenders according to the severity of the offence. In matters of religion, they themselves were not liable to prosecution or punishment, nor were they accountable to the senate or the Roman people.

The Pontifex Maximus was also responsible for selecting the Vestal Virgins, who symbolised the maintenance of Roman piety. Vestals could receive guests during the day but no man could enter their temple at night. A Vestal was required to remain unmarried for a minimum of thirty years, during which time she devoted her energies to offering sacrifices and performing the other rites laid down by holy law. At the end of this term, Vestals were free to marry but many chose to live as virgins in the temple for their entire lives.

Despite this oversight of correct religious practice we have evidence of a range of religious offences. Stealing from temples was seen as the worst of these. We saw earlier that, since the Roman world lacked banks, the wealthy often used temples to store their valuables, entrusting them to the protection of the gods. Temples themselves also had their own wealth donated to them by worshippers. An inner sanctum of a stone-built temple, often protected by a caste of priests, offered a significant level of asset protection. Nevertheless, burglars came up with inventive means of circumventing them. In one story, a young man from an illustrious family arranged for a chest to be placed in a temple. After the temple was closed, he climbed out of the box and stole many items, which he took back inside the chest with him. The manner of the discovery of his deception is not recorded, but discovered he was and deported to an island (*Digest* 48.13.12).

We get a clear idea of how seriously temple theft was taken by laws that rank it alongside murder in gravity (for example *Digest* 7.1.22.6). The creative youngster above was lucky in that his high status saved him from the usual fate that awaited nocturnal temple-robbers: being thrown to the wild beasts. Thieves who broke in during the day faced exile or, if not of high status, were condemned to the mines. Clemency was sometimes shown even in cases of this most shocking of crimes. One law states that even though those guilty of sacrilege are often thrown to wild beasts, burned alive, or hanged, these severest penalties should be restricted to those who have broken in as part of an armed gang. Individuals who have merely stolen a low-value item from a temple should be exiled to an island or sent to the mines according to their status (*Digest* 48.13.7).

Temple theft was a highly emotive crime that violated what should have been the most sacred places and in doing so threatened both the assets of the rich and the relationship of the Romans as a whole with their gods. It is no surprise, then, to find the most notorious emperors engaging in such disgraceful activities. Nero is said to have stripped many temples of their gifts and melted down gold and silver images and statues of the gods (Suetonius

Nero 32). Similarly, one of the infamous boy-emperor Elagabal's worst crimes in Roman eyes was to have forced a Vestal Virgin to marry him, thereby violating her holy chastity (*Lives of the Later Caesars* Elagabal 6). Whether these things actually happened is a moot point. Either way, it was the kind of dreadful crime that a bad emperor was thought likely to have carried out.

Despoiling tombs also crops up in the law codes as an offence (*Digest* 47.12). Three types of attack are listed. First, there are those which demolish a tomb. The best-quality tombs, lining such roads as the Via Appia outside Rome, were built with high-quality stone and faced with marble, which made them attractive to those looking for knock-off building materials. Legal texts also refer to statues being taken, again the motivation being to put them to other use or to sell them. The law explicitly states that the tombs of enemies of Rome are not perceived as religious places and so could be freely plundered for stone. Obviously it is possible for some of these attacks to have been motivated by a desire for vengeance. Numbers of tombs in Pompeii, for example, are defaced with graffiti which may have been targeted at the dead individual by an enemy. A worse form of this crime was when thieves despoiled the dead bodies interred in the tombs, when carrying arms was considered an aggravating factor. It is interesting that some felt the need to go armed. The tombs of the wealthiest would have been protected by slaves posted as guards in order to protect the bodies within and any valuable items buried with them.

Some reckless individuals tried to cheat the gods by failing to deliver on promises made to them when looking for divine help. In one inscription from Phrygia and Lydia in modern Turkey, it is said that Diogenes 'made a vow for the ox', presumably hoping that Zeus, the god invoked, would help his sick ox recover. But, as the inscription goes on, when the animal did indeed recover Diogenes thought he could get away with not making whatever votive offering he had originally promised. He was to pay a terrible price for this double-crossing of the divine, or rather his daughter did, for she was 'punished in her eyes' (*TAM* 5.1.509).

Religion against Crime

Many of the questions contained in the *Oracles of Astrampsychus* relate to the difficulties of dealing with the law. 'Am I safe from prosecution?', 'Will I obtain the petition?', 'Will I defeat my opponent in the trial?' All these questions highlight the anxieties generated by involvement with the Roman legal system and the fact that people felt the need to turn to the gods for reassurance and advice. Another question, 'Will I be safe if informed against?' also gives a good idea of how the law was perceived to operate: among the responses are the statements, 'through your friends' and 'after appeal'. It was never enough to have the evidence on your side. The successful claimant needed perseverance and a network of social contacts to help him pursue his case through the courts.

The problems involved in taking a legal route to gaining redress meant that many crime victims followed alternative religious avenues to try to gain satisfaction and revenge. Magic in particular seems to have offered a readily available means of solving and avenging crime. In one fourth-century curse, the victim of theft cries, 'may the thief's eye be struck as hard as I strike the eye with this hammer and may it become inflamed' (*Greek Magical Papyri* 5.70–95). Clearly, hitting an image of an eye with a hammer and imagining it as being the real eye of the thief could give vent to the feelings of frustration and powerlessness induced by the theft. But it also reflected a very real belief that such magic could work. Pliny the Elder claims, 'there is nobody who does not fear being spellbound by curse tablets' (*Natural History* 28.19). People wore amulets to ward off the threat of crime. Pliny recommends wearing the right foot of a chameleon tied to the left arm by hyena skin as a powerful protection against robbery and other terrors of the night (28.115). Carrying a vulture's heart about one's person was thought to provide protection against bandits (29.77).

Curse tablets survive in their hundreds (more than 1,500 in all) and were written on a variety of surfaces but especially lead. Lead was cheap and, as one formula suggests, could always be 'borrowed' from the lead pipes of the water system. Lead, with its cold heaviness, was redolent of the underworld.

Despite their popularity, these curses, *defixiones*, were illegal, partly because they threatened to injure others, and were believed capable of doing so, but also because they represented a kind of alternative religious power that was somehow not quite acceptable. They cover the whole gamut of human issues, from sex, love and marriage to crime, health and chariot racing. Many are found buried in tombs or written on gravestones; depositing a curse in this manner was a way to gain access to the gods of the underworld. The language is often starkly violent. One curse on the horses of a rival chariot team urges the spirits to 'Bind every limb, every sinew, the shoulders, the wrists … torture their thoughts their minds' (see J. G. Gager: 62–4). It may be that the language is borrowed from the hostile legalese employed within courtrooms and was thought to be more effective as a result. It certainly suggests that people felt such aggressive language was the best way to try to sort things out between rivals, a kind of Roman version of a Twitter war, with which it shares massive overreaction to what were often small offences suffered in rubbing shoulders with others during the routine of daily life. This spirit of exaggerated overstatement also extended to love spells, where the target was imagined to be afflicted with an overwhelming passion for the person casting the spell. In one, from fifth-century upper Egypt, the curser urges that his amorous target will not be able to sleep at night: 'Don't let her eat, drink, sleep, or joke or laugh, but make her rush out of her house, abandon her father, mother, brothers and sisters, until she comes to me, Theon, loving me, wanting me with a divine, unceasing and wild love' (Gager: 102–106).

The curses were not only used instead of legal routes but were also deployed as a complementary tactic to help in a trial. In south-west Gaul, a coin dated to AD 172 in the reign of Marcus Aurelius was found alongside a dead puppy and a curse tablet. The text denounces two characters, Lentinus and Tasgillus, and urges that they die and go to meet the gods of the underworld, Pluto and Persephone. It turns out that the curser is involved in a legal battle with the pair. 'Just as this puppy harmed no one,' the curse goes on, 'so may they harm no one and may they not be able to win this lawsuit.' The puppy may not have been killed specially for the procedure but the text suggests that its death was part of the curse, so we have to suppose that it was: 'just as this puppy is on its back and is unable to rise, so neither may they; they are pierced through, just as this is', referring to the curse being nailed to a table (Gager: 143–4).

The city of Bath in the west of England, already a place well known for its waters in Roman times, has yielded up a particularly interesting crop of curse tablets. Thrown into the waters to access the underground deities believed to lurk within the well, about 130 have so far been recovered. The tablets are highly formulaic and many were probably bought from a professional spell-writer. The text usually describes the offence in detail. Many seek the recovery of stolen property, which was a perennial problem at bath houses, as we saw earlier. Missing items include jewellery, money, household goods and, above all, clothes. One example states: 'The person who stole my bronze vessel is utterly cursed. I give him to the temple of Sulis, whether woman or man, boy or girl, and let him who has done this spill his own blood into the vessel itself' (Gager: 194–5) The plea clearly reflects the powerlessness of most victims to do anything practical about their plight. No one in authority was going to be interested in a missing pot. But it does also give a clear sense of the injustice felt at this action. The victim wanted his pot back. Realising that he was unlikely to get it, he demanded vengeance. He wants more than simply a return of the pot or some compensation. The victim wants blood. A common tactic to try to achieve this was to transfer the ownership of the stolen item over to the god. Steal a pot from a local and the thief has nothing to worry about. Steal a pot from a god and he is in trouble. The curses establish a kind of legal arrangement between the victim and the deity whereby the god gets offerings, the victims get their goods returned and the felons are punished. The degree of punishment is completely out of kilter with the scale of the offence but even that goes to show how strongly the victim felt. His demand for punishment over and above the return of the item also shows clearly how ordinary people generally saw these petty thefts as crimes, whatever the law itself said. As one curse found in the amphitheatre at Caerleon, in Wales, said, 'Nemesis, I give you this cloak and these shoes. May the person who has taken them not redeem them except with his own life and blood' (Gager: 197–8).

The British curses are very similar to others from all over the empire. There seems to have existed something of a *lingua magica*, a language of the underworld that everyone recognised. Full of weird phrases, the ancient equivalent of abracadabra, magical spells mixed up everyday objects and senses with strange textures and things to subvert the experience of the ordinary world. They share the same aggressive verbal violence of the modern internet troll. One from second-century Sicily says on one side of the piece of lead, 'I put a spell on Valeria Arsinoe, the criminal, sickness, the bitch, putrefaction.' On the reverse it reads, 'the bitch, the dung worm, the criminal, and useless Arsinoe' (Gager: 214–5). Charming. Again there is a feeling of the misogyny found in modern trolling, which aims fierce abuse at any woman who appears to be getting 'above her station'. Another, from North Africa, expresses a profound sense of powerlessness in the face of a life dominated by malevolent forces, malevolently directed: 'Here lies Ennia Fructuosa' a wife of 'great modesty and unusual loyalty'. She married at fifteen and died at twenty-eight but 'she did not receive the kind of death she deserved – cursed by spells; she long lay mute so that her life was rather torn from her by violence than given back to nature.' Fructuosa's husband, Aelius, a tribune in the Third Legion, set up the inscription so that 'either the infernal gods or heavenly deities will punish this wicked crime' (Gager: 246).

Curses like these let us see how people thought of crime as an act that the gods themselves would have disapproved of and sought to punish. It also shows how much people believed that magic could help them deal with it. Crime was never just a private matter, and by referring the matter to the gods, the whole affair was in some sense brought out into the open.

The aggression involved in the imagined physical assaults is considerable. One tablet from the first century BC in Rome promises an offering to Cerberus, the multi-headed dog of the underworld, if he attacks the spell's target, Plotius. It begins by asking for the victim to suffer fevers then lists the body parts he wants the dog to target: the head, forehead, eyebrows, and eyelids. The curser, Proserpina Salvia, then 'gives' to Cerberus the target's 'sacred organ' so he cannot urinate, then his arse, anus and thighs, all the way down to his heels, toes and toenails. The motivation for this savage supernatural assault was straightforward revenge for an earlier curse by Plotius: 'just as he has written a spell and commissioned it against me so I consign Plotius over to you … Let him perish miserably.' There is no sense of divine justice here, just a desire to harness the power of the gods in a vicious personal vendetta (Gager: 240–42).

The magic was itself symptomatic of a society where local bitterness and bad blood often dominated social interactions. One lead curse tablet from near Carthage gives a flavour of this competitive, mocking and envious society. The victim Maslik has lost some money (presumably by theft but it could have been in a business venture) but he has been ridiculed by another man called Emashtart. 'I, Maslik, make Emashtart melt, the place where he lives and all his belongings, because he has rejoiced at my expense about the money that I have completely lost. May everyone who rejoices at my expense about the loss of my money, become like this lead which is now being melted.' Poor Maslik. Not only has he lost his money but people are openly laughing at him. No friendly neighbourliness here; everyone is out to get whatever they can.

Magic in this context often did no more than help people keep harm at bay, acting as a sort of passive barrier set up to keep the hostile actions of others away. One all-purpose defensive spell from Pontus, in modern Turkey, reads, 'Drive away the curse from Rouphina; and if someone does me an injustice, send the curse back against him. And don't let poison harm me' (Gager: 225–6). It takes us into the psychology of the curser. Rouphina seems almost paranoid, assuming the likelihood of someone being out to curse her is great enough that she takes the trouble to make a prophylactic counter-curse. Of course, we do not know the full story here and it may be that she had good reason to be fearful. Even so, it is interesting that she assumes her attacker would use supernatural means and it seems to have generated in her a high level of anxiety. The fear of physical attack in the form of poison is almost an afterthought – it is the supernatural forces of the spell that most terrify her.

This was a world where approximately 85 per cent of the population worked in agriculture. It was the annual round of the harvest that primarily generated wealth and there was little long-term growth in production. This meant that people tended to see life as a zero-sum game. They did well only to the extent that someone else did badly. Equally, if a neighbour did well, by definition it meant that there was less to go round for everyone else. People seem to have automatically suspected that an individual's success was the result of cheating by using illegal means like magic, which acted as a kind of theft in that it took an unfair share of economic output via unjust means. There is a good example of this outlook from a small community in North Africa. A newly freed slave called Chresimus (his name meant 'Useful') started to generate much bigger harvests from his smallholding than did his neighbours with far larger farms. As a result, he became extremely unpopular and people accused him of using sorcery to steal their crops. During his trial he brought all his farm equipment into the forum along with his slaves. His tools were well kept and sharp, while his slaves were all healthy and well looked after. 'Here is my

magic,' he declared. 'The invisible ingredient is my work
and the sweat I've poured early in the morning till late at
night.' He was unanimously acquitted (Pliny the Elder
Natural History 18.8.41–3).

Some jokey graffiti in Pompeii suggest that people
were able to see the funny side of cursing. One curser
warns those who shit in his doorway: 'Beware of the
curse. If you look down on this curse, may you have an
angry Jupiter for an enemy.' Obviously it is, in part, meant
seriously but it also seems to be a joke. Another scrawl
even goes so far as to threaten one of the gods with violent
assault: 'Let everyone in love come and see. I want to
break Venus' ribs with clubs and cripple the goddess' loins.
If she can strike through my soft chest, then why can't I
smash her head with a club?' (*CIL* 4.7716 & 1824). Again it
is clearly meant as a joke but it uses the same kind of
aggressive language found in curses in order to generate
its effect. There was no fear that the goddess would punish
such hubris. It was a shared joke among those afflicted by
love. People were also capable of spotting charlatans. In
one of the jokes of the *Laughter-Lover*, an astrologer casts
the horoscope of a sick boy, promises his mother he will
live a long time, and then demands his fee. She says that
she will give it to him tomorrow. 'But what happens if he
dies in the night?' he replies. People were probably too
wary of being conned in their everyday lives to blindly
accept every claim made by some religious quack.

But we would be wrong to infer from this that people
did not somehow believe in the supernatural forces
appealed to in curses. Numbers of confessional inscriptions from second- and third-century Lydia and Phrygia,

in what is now Turkey, show how deep-seated was the belief in the power of the gods. In these texts, people who think they have been targeted by magic, because they have suffered the kind of illness or misfortune often requested in curse tablets, set up tablets of their own proclaiming their innocence. In one, a woman called Antigone makes a dedication to Demeter declaring that she had not put a curse on a certain Asclepides or ever contemplated doing anything evil to him. The rebuttal then becomes quite specific. She says, 'Nor have I called a woman to the temple, offering her a mina and a half to remove him from among the living' (Gager: 189). In other words, Antigone has been accused of paying a woman to kill her husband, presumably by poisoning. If she is lying, she says she herself will be struck by a fever, and an unmerciful goddess Demeter will make her suffer great torments. It is easy to imagine how rumours and suspicions would arise if a husband suddenly grew sick. Accusations of witchcraft were easy to make and may simply have reflected other pre-existing social tensions between the accuser and the accused. Mud sticks and the suspected offender would have had to go to considerable lengths to try to publicly quell the rumours circulating against her.

But another undated inscription emphasises that making false accusations would itself bring risks. A man called Hermogenes, son of Glukon, and Nitonis, son of Philogenos, admit to having slandered Artemidoros with respect to the theft of wine, a charge to which Artemidoros responds by setting up a tablet affirming his innocence and, probably, asking the god to punish those responsible for spreading the rumour. The god duly responds and Hermogenes suffers in some unspecified manner. Hermogenes, in turn, tries to put a line under the matter by setting up his own inscription in order to placate the god of the temple and to promise publicly that he will from now on extol all the gods (Gager: 176).

In another, a woman called Tatia tries to assert her innocence when suspected of having placed a curse on her son-in-law, Loukoundos, who had become insane. She had suffered various personal misfortunes, which she attributes to others having cast spells against her, and responds by setting up a sceptre in the temple and placing a number of counter-curses in order to protect herself (Gager: 246–8). But, as the text makes clear, the gods send her punishment in the form of an injury to her son, Socrates, who drops a vine sickle on his foot. Tatia's descendants (presumably she had since died) therefore remove her sceptre and curses from the temple and now 'constantly propitiate the gods and praise them, having affirmed in this inscription the power of the gods'. Clearly, accusations of serious family misconduct could persist for generations and meant that younger family members felt the need to appease the gods for the sins of their forefathers.

Some openly confessed their guilt. In one inscription, a man admits that he had stolen a cloak and, as a consequence, the god was vexed with him. After some time, he therefore brought the cloak to the god and openly confessed his guilt. The god ordered him to sell the article of clothing and to use the money to publicise the god's power in a stone inscription (Gager: 176). It is interesting how the thief himself believes utterly in the power of the god to track him down and punish him for his offence. Not much use for the victim, who did not get his cloak · back, but a warning to all about the risk of divine retribution for an apparently petty theft. We tend to imagine that religion had little use either as a deterrent against crime or in solving it, but it did do something to help. Fear of a divine reaction may have shaped people's behaviour, both inhibiting them from committing crime in the first instance and then prompting them to return stolen items later. Illness and misfortune, common enough occurrences in the ancient world, would play on criminals' minds, nudging them to keep on the path of righteousness.

Unacceptable Religion

One notable feature of these confession texts is that the action all takes place in the local temple. Curses and other religious practices, which we would probably label as magic, here sat side by side with mainstream religion. Yet not all forms of religion were tolerated, and religious crimes could be punished with the greatest cruelty.

A Vestal Virgin who lapsed and had sex was dressed in burial clothes and carried, while still alive, in a kind of mock funeral procession. Accompanied by her family and friends, the Vestal was taken on a funeral bier to the Colline Gate where she was interred in an underground cell and left to die. The Romans were largely tolerant of the religious customs they encountered in the provinces but they banned the Druids in Gaul partly because they were thought to participate in human sacrifices. Druidism also represented a local religious tradition that allowed those subject to Rome to express themselves in a way that the Romans found hard to understand or interpret. In one example, a female druid used the local dialect to predict forthcoming doom for the Romans in the local language (*Lives of the Later Caesars* Alexander Severus 60.6). The Romans also disapproved of circumcision, seeing it as a Jewish practice. The degree of this disapproval is reflected in the fact that Romans who carried it out on themselves, their family or their slaves were liable to confiscation of property and exile for life. Doctors who performed the procedure faced execution. Jews themselves were permitted to continue the practice but were banned from circumcising their gentile slaves (*Digest* 48.8.11).

Scapegoating had long formed part of traditional Roman practice. Each year on 14 March, on Maurius Veturius day (Old Mars Day), a man dressed in animal skins was led in procession through the streets of Rome before being beaten with white sticks and driven out of the city. Old Mars represented the old year but the approach shows how it was part of the Romans' traditional psychological make-up to transpose problems to individuals and then outlaw them. The Romans were no worse than many people in doing this. (Today, many arguments against immigration focus on the alleged problems it creates rather than on the many economic and cultural benefits.) But it also happened only occasionally. Most of the time, the Romans were broadly tolerant of other belief systems and incorporated many new religious

customs into Roman society alongside their many conquests. It was only when certain practices were thought
to be threatening the *pax deorum* that a communal
response was thought necessary.

In such a world-view, all misfortune could itself be
interpreted as evidence of other wrongdoing. Crimes
were not seen as self-contained acts but rather as assaults
on the entire fabric of the community with potentially
widespread harmful effects. Unfaithful Vestals, for
example, were often discovered when the sacred eternal
flame, which burned in the Temple of Vesta, unexpect-
edly went out. This much-feared event was read as an
omen of imminent disaster. It would itself be seen as a
sign from the goddess that one of her ministers had been
unfaithful and was therefore threatening to bring harm
on the state. The answer was simple: find out which Vestal
was the guilty party and so eradicate the cause of the
divine offence and the threat to the community stem-
ming from it. So a Vestal was duly buried alive, various
supplicatory rites were held to appease the goddess and
the *pax deorum* was re-established.

Roman politics had always involved religion as a core
element and it could be used to pursue political goals. We
can see how it was put to unacceptable use in the death of
Germanicus, the adopted son of Tiberius, who died at the
age of nineteen (Tacitus *Annals* 2.69). Suffering from a
virulent sickness, Germanicus believed that his political
rival Piso had poisoned him. An investigation of the room
where Germanicus was resting found human remains,
spells, curses and lead tablets with his name inscribed on
them. Here was religion being used improperly, risking

the communal health of the empire for personal advancement. If emperors believed such means were being employed against them then the response could be vigorous. Those who consulted religious mediums about the life expectancy of the emperor or the safety of the state could be punished by death (Paul *Opinions* 5.21.3). The same law also states that slaves who consulted a soothsayer with reference to the life of their master should be crucified.

Emperors felt genuine anxiety about the power of such prophecies and their capacity to stir up trouble. Predictions of doom were quite common and astrologers faced frequent bans from emperors including Augustus, Tiberius, Nero, Vitellius, Vespasian and Domitian. Tiberius was so spooked by a popular prophecy of the coming end of the empire that he had various spurious Sibylline oracles destroyed (Dio *Roman History* 57.18). Augustus, also according to Dio, claimed not to care about such matters and even made public the aspect of the stars at the time of his own birth so that any astrologer could read his future. But, as Suetonius points out, he still banned the practice. At a much lower political level, an inscription on the base of a statue erected in the first century AD in central Italy thanks Jupiter for having miraculously saved the members of the city council after their names had been cursed on tombs by an unknown public slave. We can only guess what motivated the slave to do this but it generated a strong, public response against this use of the supernatural for political purposes.

Magic was often singled out as being illegal. Those who were 'addicted to the art of magic' were to be thrown to wild beasts or crucified. Magicians themselves would be burned alive. Nobody was permitted to possess books on the art of magic and when they were discovered, the books were to be publicly burned. Both the practice of magic and the knowledge were decreed to be unacceptable (Paul *Opinions* 5.23.17–18). Yet, as has been clear throughout this chapter, magic seems to have been widely used in the Roman world, often alongside more mainstream religious worship. In such a context, it is very hard to define exactly what constituted magic. It was no more related to personal aims than other pagan practices and many of the acts themselves could also occur within a temple context. Perhaps when the Romans called something magic it was simply a way of describing religious practices which they deemed to be especially unacceptable. In that sense, magic seems to have been just one man's view of unauthorised, unacceptable religion, a view that usually only came to the fore when traditional religious morality seemed to be under threat.

The Persecution of Christians

It seemed perfectly reasonable to ascribe positive outcomes in human affairs to divine will. Similarly, misfortune was understood as a scourge sent by the gods to punish Rome for any social or political acts that had hurt divine sensibilities. Persecution of any religious groups whose behaviour was perceived to be upsetting the gods was a natural corollary of these attitudes. The Christians have gone down in history as the most prominent example but many other individuals, such as magicians, astrologers,

Dionysus worshippers, Manichees and, later, Christian heretics, all suffered at the hands of the Roman state at certain times. Even so, dramatic persecution was not the norm. Rome's pagan religion represented a broad set of practices, which lacked the centralised orthodoxy of later Christianity, so there was no intrinsic drive to stamp out religious difference or innovation. It was usually only when the community felt actively threatened, often because it had suffered a disaster of some kind, that persecution followed. The numbers involved were generally fairly small, as the state lacked the capacity to persecute in a systematic way. It was a simple form of scapegoating that was designed to be a powerful symbolic reaffirmation of traditional morality rather than to eradicate alternative religion entirely.

Most of the time, Roman officials were happy to let local leaders police themselves and their religions. The Jews were granted various exemptions on account of the antiquity of their faith. In the Acts of the Apostles, when the disciples are stirring things up in the east, Gallio, the Proconsul of Achaia washes his hands of the matter by saying, 'If you Jews were making a complaint about some misdemeanour or serious crime, it would be reasonable for me to listen to you. But since it involves questions about words and names and your own law, settle the matter yourselves. I do not wish to be a judge of these matters' (18:14–15). It was when politics intervened that alternative religions risked being seen as subversive. The Jews often got into trouble with the Romans because they quarrelled with the Greeks who inhabited many of the same cities. When this resulted in riots or otherwise threatened good order then the Romans were perfectly prepared to abandon the traditional policy of religious toleration. The Great Fire of Rome in AD 64, for instance, found an emperor with a major disaster on his hands, one, moreover, that he was accused of starting for his own benefit. What better way to shift the blame than to find a scapegoat in the form of the strange new sect known as the Christians (Tacitus *Annals* 15.44)?

The problem for Christians was that, as a group, they were seen to embrace criminality. It was a movement born out of the rebellious province of Judaea. It appealed to many low down the social scale because of its optimistic message of an imminent, just new order, and recognised the worth of all human beings in a world where the existing hierarchy deprived many people of any value at all. Christianity offered a vision of an alternative social order. The Christians claimed that there was not a needy person among them, 'for as many owned lands or houses sold them', and the proceeds were then distributed to each according to need (Acts 4:32–4). It offered a world-turned-upside-down view of the future, where there was equality instead of hierarchy, charity in place of greed, and celibacy not sex. In its early days, at least, this seemed to be a radical movement aimed at the underdog.

By concentrating on mutualism between the brothers and sisters of the church, Christianity rejected the core institutions of the Roman world: the social order, the family, the importance of patronage. Many Christians also steadfastly refused to sacrifice to the emperor. This did not necessarily represent an act of open resistance.

Sacrificing to the emperor contradicted their religious beliefs and by making them do so the Romans were forcing them into dissent. For the Romans, the Christian refusal to honour the emperor merely completed their view of Christians as a group who rejected society outright. Sometimes this perception was the result of a literalist Roman interpretation of the Christian message: as Justin complains, 'Hearing that we expect a kingdom, you really conclude that it must be a kingdom in the human sense'(*Apology* 1.11.1). But many Christians also went out of their way to become martyrs in a full-blown assault on Roman norms and authority. Significantly, these acts were often located in the empire's amphitheatres, where the values of Roman imperial society were so clearly on display.

The number of such martyrs was relatively small but their deaths helped unite a group in opposition to the Roman state. The Roman authorities were largely indifferent. Most of the time, the Romans refused to give the would-be martyrs what they wanted. One fictional governor has a Christian brought before him but, 'being aware of his lunacy and that he would welcome death for the fame he would get from it, let him go because he was not worth punishing' (Lucian *Peregrinus* 11–14). If they did make the arena, the accounts of their executions are often highly exaggerated, written to inspire the next generation of Christians. The fanciful account of the martyrdom of Polycarp in AD 155 describes how the Romans tried to burn the saint by laying him on logs and brushwood. The flames bellied out 'like a ship's sail in the wind' and surrounded the martyr's body like a wall. But Polycarp remained within this fire-wall, not burning but rather 'baking like bread' and giving off a delightful smell 'like incense or some other costly perfume' (*The Martyrdom of Polycarp* 15).

For the Christians, of course, it was the Romans who were the criminals. The convert Athenagoras the Athenian, writing in the second half of the second century AD, wrote a plea to the emperor Marcus Aurelius complaining that the Christians were being singled out for persecution, contrary to both custom and law. In the Roman empire, he says, different peoples have different customs and laws and no one is hindered from following these, however ridiculous they may seem. People are free to offer whatever sacrifices and celebrate whatever mysteries they please. This is good for the peace and tranquillity of the empire, he says, because it is necessary for each man to worship the gods he prefers, in order that through fear of the deity, men may be kept from wrongdoing. Not believing in any god is what should be considered impious and wicked because such atheists have no moral compass at all. Athenagoras flatters the emperor, saying how much he admires his mildness and gentleness, his benevolent disposition and intelligence, thanks to which the empire enjoys a profound peace. So why was he persecuting the Christians? Why does the emperor not care about them, he asks. Christians are pious and have done no wrong and pose no threat to the state but the emperor is allowing them to be harassed, plundered and persecuted. It is completely unjust and contrary to all law and reason for Christians to be slaughtered at the instigation of false accusers. He claims that the victims have learned the hard way that there is no point turning to the law for redress, rather they turn the other cheek and accept whatever injustices are directed at them.

Athenagoras is at pains to stress his loyalty to the emperor and that the difference between the Christians and Romans is purely a religious matter that could easily be sorted out if the emperor so wished. Other Christians took a far more pessimistic view of the Roman state and wrote vitriolic attacks against it. Writers like the third-century Christian Commodian identified Nero with the Antichrist. On Nero's return, Commodian says, as a precursor to the second coming of Christ, the Roman judges will be made to issue edicts throughout the empire to compel Christians to abandon their faith. They shall be made to worship idols and, if they refuse, they shall die in the spectacles. Blood shall flow everywhere and fear will prevail. Nero will carry on the persecution for three and one-half years, but then a fatal revenge shall be exacted for his crimes. Rome, its emperor and its people will be handed over to God for justice and Roman rule will come to an end (*Instructions* 40).

Other apocalyptic literature also looked forward to the end of Rome, when justice would be restored and revenge taken upon the Romans. The *Sibylline Oracles* we saw above prophesy a time when 'implacable wrath shall fall upon the men of Latium'. At that point in the future, 'law and justice shall come from the starry heaven' and there will be an end to lawlessness. There will be no more poverty and a whole list of criminal activities will cease: murder, violence, theft by night and every ill. Rome will have to pay back all the wealth it stole from Asia in tribute, and Romans will serve as slaves not masters (3.45–62, 350–55, 356–80; 5.155–78, 386–433). This burning sense of indignation and thirst for vengeance often linked the Roman regime with the defiled and corrupt body of the prostitute, as in the biblical identification of the whore of Babylon with Rome (Revelation 2:13; 6:9–10, 12–18; 19:2).

Not all Christians were so radical. Indeed, the shrill resistance to Roman laws found in martyr texts and apocalyptic literature is relatively rare. Most Christians tried, like Athenagoras, to come to an accommodation with their Roman masters as St Paul had urged them to do when he said that slaves should serve their masters with all their heart. At the end of the second century AD, the Christian Tertullian went further and wrote in glowing terms about the quality of life under Roman rule. The world, he says, is obviously becoming better cultivated and more fully populated. Commerce is thriving, and 'everywhere are houses, and inhabitants, and settled government, and civilised life'. And he calls for Christians to 'pray for the emperors, for their ministers and those in authority, for the preservation of society and for peace' (*Apology* 39). Much of what might be termed everyday Christianity seems to have shared Tertullian's far more relaxed attitude towards Roman religious practices than accounts of martyr acts would have us believe.

But the high-profile acts of martyrs in the arena did leave a lasting impression on the Roman mind. It meant that people were quick to link Christianity as a whole with its more radical wing, in the same way that radical groups of Islamists affect how Islam as a whole is often

perceived in the West. The crowds in the empire's amphitheatres were shocked by this public rejection of their
values. It is also striking just how conservative these
crowds could be. In martyr accounts, we find descriptions
of ordinary Romans demanding that Christians suffer the
worst punishments. When Polycarp was martyred, the
crowd were vitriolic in their contempt for him. Once the
herald had announced that he was a self-confessed Christian the whole crowd cried out with great fury. Here was
someone who sought to overthrow their gods and who
had been teaching people not to worship them. Not to
punish such a man severely would have risked offending
the gods. The spectators themselves shouted out for the
governor to set a lion on Polycarp. But the governor
replied that this would be illegal because the wild beast
hunts were now finished. So they demanded that he be
burned alive. When the governor approved this punishment, the crowd actually went out and gathered wood for
the bonfire. And when the funeral pyre had been built,
the crowd surrounded Polycarp in order to nail him to it.

The stubborn refusal of some Christians to recant,
even when faced with the full rigour of the law, infuriated
many Romans. Origen describes how Roman judges
could get very angry when torture victims refused to give
in (*Against Celsus* 8.44). Their refusal symbolised their
intransigent opposition to the Roman way of life. The
Romans responded by doing everything they could to
punish this deeply offensive behaviour. They even left
Christian bodies unburied in the belief that this would
deny them their hoped for physical resurrection. The
whole process of the punishment of Christians in the

arena, from being ripped apart by beasts to being burned alive or left to rot, was designed to destroy all physical traces of these social outlaws.

Crime served both sides of this religious argument. Both Christians and pagans believed that the other could be defined by their dreadful crimes. Each side also used these crimes to justify their own stereotypical views of the other. The periodic Roman persecution of Christians made an example of these religious extremists and reasserted traditional religious values. Conversely, tales of martyrdom became a powerful weapon in the armoury of the Christian missionary. Every convert now knew that the Roman state and its legal apparatus could never be fully trusted. Pagan–Christian relations grew ever frostier.

Are we in any position to judge Rome's actions against the Christians? The majority in the Western world come from a Christian tradition even if they are not practising and have imbibed something of the biblical view of the Romans as the brutal executioners of Christ. For all Rome's achievements, achievements which the later Western world has respected greatly, this act of religious persecution has left an indelible stain on Rome's record. As epic films such as *Quo Vadis* have suggested, Rome in this view was a great power but one lacking in any higher moral purpose. It took the Christians to bring meaning to the ancient world. But modern views of martyrdom have also changed. The line between martyr and terrorist has always depended on the political stance of the viewer and, since the attacks of 9/11, perhaps we have all become even more wary of those who claim to be using violence in the pursuit of spiritual goals.

Chapter VI

SEX, DRINK AND GLUTTONY: CRIMES AGAINST MORALITY

In AD 218, with the emperor Caracalla murdered, a grand-mother in the imperial household, Julia Maesa, successfully engineered a palace coup to have her fourteen-year-old grandson Elagabal placed on the throne. All-powerful all of a sudden, this adolescent felt liberated from Rome's conservative social constraints. He is reputed to have loved to dress as a woman and to have wanted to castrate himself. He had a series of male lovers, lavishing favours on them, and allegedly even selected candidates for high office according to the size of their penises. The Roman world was not ready for this sexual free spirit, and in AD 222 the same grandmother had him assassinated.

In the eyes of his Roman biographer, Elagabal was but the latest in a long line of sex-offending emperors, from Caligula, who allegedly committed incest with his sisters, to Tiberius, who supposedly kept an apartment that had been specially adapted for carrying out extreme sex acts. It is all too easy to form the strong impression from the lurid way in which Roman writers described these emperors that this kind of sexual inventiveness was normal in the Roman world. This impression was fuelled by later Christian writers, who liked to draw a hard-and-fast divide between their own emphasis on the moral benefits of chastity and the supposed lasciviousness of their pagan predecessors. It is an image that has been perpetuated in modern popular culture, with films such as *Gladiator* portraying the emperor Commodus as bent on committing incest with his sister. Yet these stories were passed down, not because the Romans thought we would like to read about them, but because *they* did. As recounted earlier, one version of the foundation of Rome held that the shepherd Faustulus's wife was actually a prostitute. The Romans seem to have had a fascination with finding out about each other's secret vices. This was not because they were morally degraded, as they are often portrayed, but because the Romans actually had strong views about sexual behaviour of all kinds. This chapter will explore some of these attitudes. Sexual exploitation certainly seems to have existed in at least as serious a way as it does today, with prostitution, rape and sexual abuse all widespread, but the perception of what constituted sex crime differed markedly.

What will also become clear is that Roman attitudes can only be understood within the framework of a wider sense of morality, which informed their attitudes towards a variety of what they saw as anti-social acts. Whether it was drinking warm wine or eating cooked meats in taverns, Roman law expressed a disdain for any personal pleasure that was taken in a manner that was deemed unpalatable. But the law was made by the upper classes.

Some of it seems completely pointless, while other aspects overlook the worst kind of abuse. Looked at together, we can see how the law expressed the morality of the dominant elite but did not necessarily reflect what ordinary Romans thought about such matters.

Sex Crime

Roman law saw rape as a public crime, a criminal offence for which perpetrators could face a public retribution. Rape covered not only assaults of women but also those against men or children. The woman was not blamed for being a victim but it is a sign of the weak position of wives that the law had to specify that the husband of a victim of rape could not prosecute her for having committed adultery (48.5.14.7). Rape is listed in the law codes as the unacceptable abuse of force (*vis*), which included abuse of office, sedition, public disturbance, armed robbery, as well as physical and sexual assault. In part, this reflected the Roman view of rape as being a particularly vicious assault on the integrity of the individual, as it is today. But it also expressed the view of a world dominated by the male head of the household, whose honour was damaged by any injury done to those under his protection. It was also a matter of hard cash. Daughters had to be provided with a dowry when they married and a girl who had been raped was likely to need a much larger cash incentive to make her an attractive catch for a suitor. Rape, then, ranked alongside other violent attacks on core Roman institutions because it threatened to undermine the whole basis of marriage and the civil society that rested upon it.

Ideas about what constituted acceptable behaviour by a woman were, needless to say, established by senior male members of the family. Myths from early Roman history helped to reinforce this image of the chaste woman. Lucretia was held up as a shining beacon of honourable female behaviour when, after she was raped by one of the early kings of Rome, reported what had happened to her to an assembly of the senior men of her family, then pulled out a sword and killed herself (Valerius Maximus *Memorable Deeds and Sayings* 6.1).

Many women were not in a position even to complain about rape. It was legal and acceptable to take advantage of slaves for sex: this kind of abuse was commonplace. The philosopher emperor Marcus Aurelius was proud of himself for resisting the temptations posed by two of his beautiful slaves, which suggests that most masters would not have held back. Unwanted slave pregnancies were sufficiently common to joke about. In one from the ancient joke book, the *Laughter-Lover*, a father tells his too-clever-by-half son, who has got a slave girl pregnant, to kill the baby when it is born. The son replies, 'First murder your own children and then tell me to kill mine' (57). We have no real way of knowing how slaves felt about these rapes. Is it possible that some were pleased to have received the master's attentions and perhaps some kind of gift or better treatment as a result? There is a hint of resentment in the novel, the *Satyricon* (57), when a freedman says that he bought the freedom of the slave woman who was his de facto wife (slaves could not legally marry), 'so that no one could put his filthy hands on her breast'. One of Valerius Maximus's historical tales concerns a young man,

Titus Veturius, who fell into financial ruin and sold himself into debt-bondage to a man called Plotius (*Memorable Deeds and Sayings* 1.9). Plotius made sexual advances on Titus and when he refused to submit, flogged him like a slave. In the story Titus complained to the consuls, who ordered Plotius to be thrown into gaol, because they wanted to ensure that a Roman's honour was protected whatever financial condition he might find himself in. Titus was not a slave but perhaps the tale reveals that a Roman audience would assume that no man would want to submit to the predatory sexual advances of a master. But it also shows that they only cared if the victim was a Roman citizen. What slaves thought was irrelevant.

Victimless Crime

What is clear from the above is that the Roman state was not interested in the act of rape or sexual assault per se. What mattered was the legal status of both the assailant and the victim. The law aimed to protect the honour that each individual possessed according to their social status. If a victim had no standing in the community, as a slave did not, then he or she had no reputation to maintain. The law was fundamentally concerned with actions that were inappropriate to an individual's position in society. But more than that, the law reflected a concern about the impact such unacceptable behaviour would have on the wider community. If a slave was beaten, so what? If a senator was assaulted, the entire community was under threat. Roman law, therefore, reveals a strong interest in actions which might seem harmless to us but that to them were perceived as posing a threat to society's morals. Fundamentally this was about maintaining the support of the gods: Romans behaving badly risked losing divine support. What we see as victimless crime, from the Roman point of view, risked bringing disaster down on everyone's head.

The Roman state had a long tradition of enacting what are called sumptuary laws – laws made for the purpose of limiting or preventing expenditure on certain items of personal consumption. The second-century AD writer, Aulus Gellius, notes that they were introduced to maintain the frugality of the early Romans (*Attic Nights* 2.24). One of the earliest of these was a decree of the senate concerning the Megalensian games, which ordered all the leading citizens to swear an oath before the consuls that they would not spend on dinner more than one hundred and twenty asses (the as was a small denomination coin) in addition to vegetables, bread and wine, nor would they serve any foreign wine, nor use more than one hundred pounds' weight of silverware at the table. What is clear is how the measures were originally aimed at the Roman elite. The fear was that society would rot from the top down if these leaders were corrupted. It also shows the high level of concern about the weakening effect of anything perceived to be over-consumption. The Romans' tough self-discipline, which served them so well on the battlefield, risked being softened by exposure to too much luxury. And, of course, it highlights how different from ours was the Roman notion of luxury. I doubt we would see a glass of foreign wine and some silverware as posing a huge threat to our moral health. It is possible the emphasis on the foreignness of the wine also contains a hint of

economic protectionism, trying to ensure that the
Romans bought Roman goods – but such aims coincided
with larger moral aims so closely that perhaps they did
not need to be articulated separately.

The problem for the Romans was that, as they grew
more successful and their empire larger, so did the wealth
at their disposal. Tribute and other profits flowed into the
city of Rome, allowing the wealthy to spend liberally on
private entertainment. The law tried to act as an anchor
on this steady rise in luxury. The Licinian law, probably
passed in 103 BC, limited the financial outlay on designated
holiday feasts, while permitting larger sums for weddings.
It allowed for a fixed weight of dried meat and other pre-
served products to be served but permitted unlimited use
of anything grown in the earth, on a vine or in an orchard.
Morally acceptable food was that produced naturally
from the ground and eaten fresh, rather than anything
salted, or, indeed, meat. Meat was a valuable commodity,
best reserved as an offering to the gods. But, as Gellius
sadly notes, these laws were soon forgotten and many
wealthy men were gormandising and 'recklessly pouring
their family fortune into an abyss of banquets'. Finally, he
lists the Julian law of the emperor Augustus, which
limited expenditure on dining to two hundred sesterces
on a working day, three hundred on holidays, and a thousand at weddings and banquets, and another edict that
increased the holiday limit from three hundred to two
thousand, which itself says something of the high level of
dinner-party inflation. The thinking behind this increase,
he says, was that it was better to put some kind of limit
on luxury than to allow it to increase uncontrollably. We

might more cynically suggest that the laws were having no effect, and that consumption rose regardless of what was on the statute book.

Sumptuary laws attempted to regulate more than just the consumption of food and wine. In the aftermath of the crushing defeat at Cannae in 216 BC, when the Romans lost fifty thousand men in a single day and found themselves facing defeat at the hands of Carthage and its brilliant general, Hannibal, one of the Roman responses was an attempt to place legal limits on the amount of jewellery a woman could wear, what colour clothing she could dress in, and how far she could travel in a horse-drawn carriage. The Oppian law, as it was known, stood for twenty years. Then, in 195 BC, Rome having defeated Carthage and become even richer, with the added inflows of tribute from the many provinces formerly in the possession of her opponent, it was proposed to repeal the law. It probably seemed irrelevant to many now that the fighting was over and, with the Roman aristocracy never having had it so good, the limits seemed positively draconian. Livy gives a long account of the great public debate generated by the proposed abolition of the law (*History of Rome* 34.1–8). The very length of the description underlines how important these laws concerning luxury were in the Roman mind. But the two sides of the debate also give us an insight into wider Roman psychology. At heart, the Romans found themselves in a completely contradictory position: hooked on frugality, addicted to wealth.

What is also clear is that when Roman men failed to win on the battlefield, the natural response was to blame the women back home. It was as if the women of the household were somehow at fault for having softened their male offspring by wearing too much finery. Again, we see a direct relationship in the Roman mind between personal consumption and military prowess. And while the law was aimed primarily at the elite (it limited the wearing of gold jewellery, the use of that most expensive colour purple, and travel by means of expensive horse-drawn transport), the entire Roman people seemed to have held strong views about the issue and crowded into the Capitol to hear the debate. Women came out in numbers to voice their strong support for the law's repeal. They filled the streets, imploring men on their way to the forum to overturn the regulation now that Rome was doing so well. Every day more and more women came into the city from the surrounding towns and villages until they even summoned up the courage to press the consuls and other officers of the state with their demands.

One of the consuls was the hawkish Cato the Elder, who naturally had little truck with this band of female protesters. If only Roman husbands had better control of their wives, he argued, there would not now be this trouble with the whole sex. Now women were even entering the forum and interfering in the world of male politics. This was a breach of traditional roles and Cato was out-raged: 'What sort of behaviour is this, running out in public, filling the streets, and speaking to other women's husbands?' In Cato's mind, we find a clear link expressed between luxury and religion. He complains how many people admire the decorations of Greek culture and ridi-cule the earthenware images of the Roman gods that stand at the entrances of their temples. 'For my part,' he says, 'I prefer these gods' – that is, the gods who won Rome its empire. There was another problem with luxury: it was like a disease that could never be sated. The more that individuals indulged in personal pleasure the more they would want it. It was, Cato argued, like a wild beast.

Cato was a traditionalist and a reactionary. He could see no benefit in Rome changing its all too successful ways. But his voice sat at the extremes of the debate. More moderate speakers argued that now Rome was victorious there was no need for a law passed in the depths of despair following a massive defeat. Austerity had been the buzzword then, when everyone was trying to save money to help the war effort. It had been right for Rome's women to shoulder their share of the burden and not to waste money on decorative items and pleasure. But now it was only right for Roman women to reap the rewards of victory. The crowd of women continued to protest and hammered on the doors of the homes of those who had spoken against the proposed repeal. The women won. The Oppian law was annulled.

Roman laws on luxury reflected a range of moral concerns: fear of a loss of military prowess, fear that luxury was an addiction, and fear that lavish expenditure would erode the family fortunes of Rome's aristocratic class. The laws represented an attempt at self-regulation by Rome's elite to prevent luxury from corrupting the ruling class and so undermining the social order. But, as the Oppian law shows, all Romans had a strong interest in these matters. This was perhaps partly the result of rising real wealth in Roman society, with more people finding themselves brought into the scope of the expenditure limits of the laws. But we also find increasing worry from the Roman state about the behaviour of the lower classes in certain areas. Bars in particular became a focus of elite concern at what ordinary Romans were now getting up to in their free time.

Dens of Iniquity

Taverns featured prominently in the daily life of the people of Rome. These places served as mini leisure centres and, since most people did not have access to cooking facilities, as places to get hot food. Cold food and wine, which was usually mixed with hot water, were also served. This centrality to daily life is seen in Pompeii, where something like 140 bars have been found (although it is often impossible to tell for sure when a bar is actually a bar and not a shop). Their popularity is also reflected in the numerous names the Romans had for these places: *taberna, popina, ganeum, caupona, hospitium, deversorium*. Often they offered other entertainments, including music, prostitution and gambling. They were frequented by all levels of society, including slaves, but often came in for elite condemnation, suggesting that they were seen as primarily a destination for ordinary folk.

Upper-class Romans just did not understand taverns. Where ordinary people found food and entertainment, the elite saw gross immoralities. Taverns appeared as dens of all kinds of vice: heavy drinking, gambling, fighting, prostitution, all combined with the risk of sedition. In Apuleius's novel, *The Golden Ass*, one character,

Thrasyllus, a young man of wealth and high birth, is given to the pleasures of the tavern. He spends his time in whoring and daytime drinking and therefore falls into the evil company of thieves. Before long, he commits a murder (8.1). A simple drink in a bar was, from an elite perspective, the first step on a slippery slope leading to ruin.

Drinking alcohol was a central feature of upper-class parties but the manner in which it was done mattered. A late second-century AD Christian writer, Clement of Alexandria, reflects something of this contempt for lower-class practice in his description of how a good Christian should be careful not to drink like a heavy drinker: 'drink without contortions of the face and do not greedily grasp the cup, nor before drinking roll your eyes in an unseemly way … do not drain the cup in one go, or splash it all over your chin and clothes … do not make gurgling noises by downing it in one.' The refined drinker, by contrast, will do so slowly, taking small sips in an orderly fashion (*Christ the Educator* 2.2.31).

Gambling on games of chance took place in most bars even though it was illegal. It was also permitted for small stakes at dinner parties and during the holiday period of the Saturnalia. This official scrupulousness is puzzling. Romans of all social levels seem to have enjoyed gambling, and the emperor Claudius was even said to have written a handbook on the subject. But when it occurred in a popular context such as a bar, it seemed to pose a greater moral threat to society. This hostility was reflected partly in simple sneering. One snobbish Roman writer even complained about the nasty snorting noises that you would hear late at night in a Roman bar – the noises that came from a combination of snotty noses and intense concentration on the board game in question. Gambling seems to have been a common source of conflict and the laws concerning gambling are full of references to assault and the use of violence (*Digest* 11.5). But the authorities also reflected social animosity by issuing laws to attempt to limit what was going on in bars, beyond the banning of gambling.

Various emperors issued sumptuary laws concerning what could be sold in taverns. Tiberius banned the sale of pastries, Claudius banned cooked meats and hot water (which would have been mixed with wine). Even though Nero is alleged to have spent practically his whole life in bars he forbade the sale of anything boiled except vegetables and pea soup (no meat, in other words). Vespasian allowed nothing cooked to be sold in bars except pulses. It might be possible to see some level of economic justification for these bans, but the main driver was surely the fear that, in the big, imperial city of Rome, it was not just the upper classes who were now enjoying luxury. And just as the Oppian law had sought to restrain women's personal consumption, so laws against taverns and gambling attempted to set limits on what was considered appropriate for an average Roman pleb to consume.

There seems to have been a mismatch between elite aims and how ordinary Romans experienced their bars. The decorations of the walls of the standard, slightly seedy bars of Pompeii show typical scenes of bar life. These focus on the pleasures of drink – we see groups of men sitting around bar tables, ordering another round from the waitress – we see flirtation (and more) going on between customers and barmaids, and we see a good deal of gambling. To be fair, the wall paintings do depict men fighting about dice games, and the law-makers probably were right to see this as part and parcel of bar culture. In the paintings from one Pompeian bar (the Bar of Salvius, now in the Archaeological Museum at Naples), the final scene in a series shows a couple of gamblers having a row over the game, and the landlord threatening to throw his customers out. In a speech bubble coming out of the landlord's mouth, he is saying (as landlords always have said) 'Look, if you want a fight, guys, get outside.' But the fights can also be seen as a reflection of the intense rivalry that existed among local groups of ordinary Romans of broadly equal status. A lot of the fun of gambling came from going head to head with a social rival in a heated contest where status could be won. And there was a kind of group camaraderie. The historian Ammianus claimed that, in Rome, only those friendships forged by gambling were intimate, whereas all others were rather cool (*Histories* 28.4.21). Another issue that contributed towards anti-tavern legislation was their association with gossip and rumour. We have seen that any popular gathering was viewed by the elite as politically suspect. The people standing round the bar came to represent, quite literally, a counter-culture, which posed a threat to the social order.

But for all this legislation, there seems to have been little real effort to enforce it. The vocal and legal attacks of the elite on taverns, the foods they served, and the entertainments they offered, were largely a way of letting off moral steam. Fulminating about these new kinds of urban institution reflected some level of elite anxiety about their lack of control over the mass population of the huge city that Rome had become. But the authorities lacked the resources to enforce this legislative regime in any other than an exemplary way. The sheer number of bars suggests that whatever little they did had no effect. Instead, we can see the hostility in elite sources, both legal and literary, reflecting their unease at this alternative culture operating so freely around them.

Female Crime

It might seem odd to treat female crime in a chapter on moral crime. But Roman male conceptions of women were so bound up in the language of morality that it makes it impossible to discern from their representations of female offences what the underlying reality actually was. The portrayal of female crime, and the understanding of it, was strongly influenced by these perceptions of what women were considered capable of doing. In the modern Western world, about three-quarters of those convicted of serious crimes are men; women tend to commit more minor offences, such as petty theft. It is impossible to produce any reliable data for Rome, but the sources give the strong impression that Roman women were far more likely to be victims of crime than perpetrators, and such crimes as they did commit were generally small-scale.

Roman women may have committed less crime because their families kept a closer eye on them than they did their boys. They may also have faced greater pressure to be good. If a woman wanted to succeed in the role society expected of her, that of being a mother and a home-maker, then she needed to ensure that her reputation was unsullied. Being a good daughter, being chosen as a wife by a man with prospects, bringing up children properly, all required women to follow a far more tightly controlled and limited set of behaviours than men. In the same way, some argue that the increase in female crime in the modern world reflects a lower level of social control of girls and women than was the case a generation or two ago.

Women were therefore largely excluded from the criminal legal process for the simple reason that it was not thought to be relevant to them. Public law was an occasion for public dispute, a skill which upper-class boys had learned as the mainstay of their education. If a woman did need recourse to the criminal law, it was assumed that a male member of her family would act on her behalf – in fact, women were not usually permitted to accuse anyone in a criminal case unless the usual male representatives had died (*Digest* 48.2.1). Women were able to make a criminal accusation, but only if avenging a wrong done to the significant men in their life. They could not act as witnesses to formal legal acts or represent others in court. This did not mean that they had no rights in private law. In many ways, Roman women did not do badly compared with other pre-industrial societies: they could own property, they could inherit and make contracts, they could bring civil actions and, on the downside, be held liable for crimes. But from the Roman legal standpoint, criminal law dealt with major public actions of community-wide importance and these were thought to exclude female participation almost entirely.

But Roman women were involved in a variety of legal situations. Often these revolved around a breach of expectations of appropriate domestic behaviour. The fictitious cases of the law schools give interesting insights into how male authors perceived women. In one ridiculously contrived example, a man who thinks he is the son of a female citizen catches his 'mother' red-handed committing adultery and kills her with a spear. Trying to stop him, she tells him that he is not her legal son. But, having killed her, he is sold into slavery as punishment for being a foreigner who has passed himself off as a citizen. The mother's father, that is his 'grandfather', then buys him and, as his master, leads him off to crucifixion as revenge for killing his daughter (Calpurnius Flaccus 23).

Legal niceties aside, the case emphasises how many identity issues filled the male mind. A Roman man was never fully sure what his womenfolk were doing and could never know with complete certainty that his children were really his and had not been sired by one of the household slaves. In another case of uncertain identity (Calpurnius Flaccus 2), a baby boy of white parents is born black. The mother is accused of adultery by the husband. Her defence is that the discolouration is the result of an injury to the baby, such as sunburn or bruising. The prosecution argues that it is clear what the mother has been up to. A real case from Roman Egypt tells of a woman called Pesouris who had picked up an exposed baby boy from the rubbish dump and given him to a wet nurse called Saraeus, who already had a son of her own. One of the two babies then died. Pesouris claimed that the survivor was the foundling she had picked up, but Saraeus insisted the child was her own. In the end, the judge decided that the child looked like Saraeus and allowed her to keep it (*P. Oxy.* 1.37). The first, fictional, case serves as a model for the kind of uncertainties that pervaded the domestic life of men: how did you know who you were and who you could trust, and how could you control your women? The message comes across loud and clear: strict punishment must be enforced to maintain male authority.

The burden of poverty probably hit the ordinary women of the Roman empire hardest. They were expected to feed and care for their families. Widowhood was commonplace as a result of high mortality combined with later marriage for men, and was synonymous with dire need. It may be that many of these women turned to crime such as petty theft in order to survive. But opportunities for paid work also existed. Female jobs generally arose in the domestic sphere, such as making or mending clothes, or in the low-paid service sector, such as working in taverns. Barmaids are often assumed in our sources to be working as prostitutes. Whether they really were is hard to say and the view may just have reflected an amalgam of two possible moral contagions: wine and women.

It is impossible to know how many women worked as prostitutes. The second-century orator and philosopher, Dio Chrysostom, gives the impression that they were everywhere. He talks of their dirty booths being openly set up in every part of the city, even outside the magistrates' offices, in the forum and next to temples (*Oration* 7.133–52). Obviously he has a moral point to make, but it is likely that prostitution was a common form of female economic activity. It could be argued that prostitution offered many poorer Roman women some degree of relative freedom compared with the semi-slavery of domestic work, even if most did it only out of direst need. Male attitudes towards their own use of prostitutes certainly seem to have been very relaxed, and even temples, such as the one at Corinth, would sometimes act as brothels (Strabo *Geography* 8.6.20).

Male attitudes were far less relaxed when it came to the effect it saw prostitution as having on the women themselves. Prostitutes had their legal status lowered by the inflicting of *infamia*, which meant that they were deprived of some of the protections of the state and could suffer physical punishments. It was a fate shared by pimps, gladiators, actors and other entertainers: anyone, that is, who was working to pleasure others. In a classic piece of male hypocrisy, it was seen as acceptable for men to buy sex from prostitutes but shameful that the prostitutes themselves earned a living from it. As Dio Chrysostom says in his oration on the matter, 'all the world condemns such business as shameful'. The prostitute represented the nadir of a female fall from grace; she was the very opposite of the ideal woman. Instead of domestic, passive, respectable and virtuous, the female prostitute was public, immoral and active. She suffered the legal punishment of losing her female status and was compelled to adopt an inverted male lifestyle by wearing the toga as a symbol of her active, public role. It is tempting to read other murkier rationales into this. Did Roman men make female prostitutes dress as men because they found that more sexually appealing? Are we seeing a sublimation of homosexual urges here? Or could it be that, since only males of status could wear the toga, Roman men got a thrill out of screwing other 'citizens'?

Prostitution did receive some limited legal attention. Slaves could be sold with the proviso that they could not be prostituted. Money paid to a prostitute, like gambling debts, could not be recovered. But the main focus of male writings about prostitution was aimed at limiting what was seen as a moral menace. The assumption seems to have been that, once a woman had lost the respect of society, she had started on a slippery slope that would see her sink to ever lower depths. Prostitution could also be presented as posing a broad social threat through its ability to corrupt its male customers. Dio claims that when prostitution is so freely available, men will grow weary of the pleasure offered by female prostitutes and turn to young men, thereby corrupting 'the youth who will very soon be magistrates and judges and generals'. Perceived as a source of moral contagion, the prostitute acted as a mirror of the health of society as a whole and the greater the number of women who were prostitutes, the greater the likelihood that society would suffer.

The paternally dominated family did bring some benefits to women. By holding up an ideal of virtuous womanhood it gave the men an added incentive to protect their wives and daughters from sexual exploitation, if only to protect their own reputations. In that sense, women were also seen as the victims of moral crime, when bad men seduced them away from the path of domestic virtue. Even then, their seduction simply acted as an indication of the inherent weakness of women. They were thought to need men to keep them on the straight and narrow. Many, perhaps most, women were also fully socialised into their dependent position. Gossip and chat served to maintain a woman's reputation in the family group and denigrate those seen as falling short of expected norms of behaviour. Family pressure from mothers, aunts and grandmothers could compel a girl to follow the unwritten rules. The poet Ovid gives an indication of how strong this public opprobrium could be. He describes how some girls got rid of unwanted pregnancies by means of abortions and often died as a result. As one such girl was carried to the funeral pyre, the onlookers cried out, 'She deserved it!' (*The Loves* 2.14).

The ideal of womanhood established that women should be less likely to commit crime. More naturally chaste, more committed to private virtue, requiring male control because of their weakness, women were portrayed as having less need to turn to crime. When they did deviate from this accepted norm, they suffered a moral barrage. But the interest of male authors in female crime was limited to its moral cause and the potentially detrimental effects on wider society. What mattered was that expectations of normal feminine behaviour were being breached, not whether any rationale existed for those breaches.

Adultery Laws

These two elements of moral crime – the place of women and the use of sumptuary law to regulate behaviour – received a new articulation during the reign of Augustus. His moral laws made adultery a public, criminal offence. The law now required a husband to prosecute his wife if he discovered her having an affair, otherwise he risked being charged as a pimp. If convicted, the wife must be immediately divorced. Under the terms of the law, a father could kill his daughter and her lover provided he caught them in the act, they were having sex either in his own house or that of his son-in-law, and that he killed them both immediately. The husband was forbidden from killing his wife, and could only kill the lover if the pair were caught in his house and the lover had already suffered legal *infamia*. Adultery did not apply to all, since it depended upon the woman's status. Married men could only commit adultery with respectable married women. A wife committed adultery if she slept with any other man, even a slave. By contrast, it was impossible for a female slave or prostitute to commit adultery. As an indication of how seriously Augustus took these laws, if an accusation went to court, slaves were permitted to give evidence against their masters and mistresses.

What was Augustus trying to do with these laws? For one thing, he was making a determined effort to reinforce both the sanctity of marriage as an institution and the integrity of the family home. After two generations of civil strife during the collapse of the republic, his moral laws acted as a core part of his attempt, as the first emperor, to reinstate order to all aspects of the Roman world. In this view, political chaos had itself been a reflection of moral chaos and the family sat at the heart of his attempt to restore order. What is less clear is whether the legislation had any real impact. That slaves were able to give evidence against their owners created an easy avenue for informers (Tacitus *Annals* 3.25). As Tacitus notes, where the country once suffered from its vices, it was now in danger from its laws. One reputable married woman, called Vistilia, tried to evade the regulations by registering on the official list as a prostitute, which meant that she could not by definition commit adultery. The senate was outraged that a high-status woman would be prepared to debase herself so publicly and the law was changed as a result (*Digest* 48.5.11.2). Vistilia's husband was nearly prosecuted for allowing his wife to act in this way, while Vistilia herself was banished to the Greek island of Seriphos.

Adultery certainly seems to have generated high levels of anxiety. One of the questions contained in the *Oracles of Astrampsychus* asks, 'Will I be caught as an adulterer?' Note that the emphasis of the concern is not being an adulterer but being caught. The anxiety created by having an affair is palpable in the phrases appearing in the various possible answers: 'don't be distressed', 'don't be afraid.' As it says, being an adulterer is a 'putrid lot'. But whether this anxiety resulted not from the fear of being found out by an angry spouse but from fear of potential prosecution, is another matter. A remark by the historian Dio suggests that by the early third century AD, thousands of cases were going unprosecuted. He says that the emperor Septimius Severus tried to encourage fidelity in marriage and even passed some laws relating to adultery. This generated a huge number of indictments (so many that Dio says he found 3,000 waiting for his attention when he became consul), but very few were actually prosecuted and the emperor lost interest. The impression is given that affairs were common practice, among the Roman upper classes, at least. This is reinforced by the story of a witty remark by a visiting Caledonian woman, in which Severus's wife, Julia Augusta, teases her about the reputation of British women for promiscuity. The visitor replies that it is better to sleep openly with the best men you could find, in contrast to Roman practice, which was for women to let themselves be screwed in secret by the worst (Dio *Roman History* 77.16).

Some openly flouted the legislation, including Augustus's own daughter, Julia, who was banished to an island without, horror of horrors, access to wine (Suetonius *Augustus* 65). Ovid shows that elite authors could also delight in subverting the official position. During the reign of Augustus, Ovid wrote his poem 'The Art Of love' (*Ars amatoria*), a textbook on how to conduct a love affair, and this blatant subversion of Augustus's attempts at moral reform probably contributed to his later exile to the miserable Black Sea town of Tomis.

Overall, it seems likely that the adultery laws were aimed at the upper classes but that they gave out a strong message about the moral purpose of the new regime to Romans of all kinds. To a large degree this was a symbolic law, designed to state an aim and establish an atmosphere rather than to be meticulously prosecuted. So, no different from many Roman laws, where the ability to enforce them was severely limited by the modest resources of the state. What they also show is how the Romans maintained a general belief in the beneficial power of tradition while simultaneously recognising that things had to change. By reasserting old-fashioned values, Augustus reinvented the past to suit a very different set of political circumstances. People generally accepted this because tradition promised to deliver stability and Rome's continued success. Did Augustus's laws change what Romans got up to behind their bedroom doors? I doubt it.

Emperors Behaving Badly

How do we square these attempts at moral rebirth with the behaviour of the notorious emperors, such as Caligula and Nero, who showed little sign of any sexual restraint, or the adolescent emperor, Elagabal, who delighted in hanging out with charioteers, actors and gladiators, the kind of moral reprobates covered by the laws concerning *infamia*? Elagabal even raped a Vestal Virgin and carried out human sacrifices. Well, allegedly at least. A lot of this is genuinely sexed-up. We can never know what element of truth, if any, lies behind these stories. But the stories do highlight the peculiarity that emperors could stand above the very laws they created if they so wished.

We might think that such behaviour would undermine the law. But this kind of imperial misbehaviour was not the norm. If anything, these acts are the exceptions that reinforced society's norms. Emperors behaving badly generated a moral backlash, which we find expressed in

negative write-ups by historians such as Tacitus and Suetonius. These immoral emperors also suffered directly:
they were all assassinated and their memories were
obliterated.

Emperors as a whole reflect the kind of double standard that operated in Roman society. On the one hand,
there were repeated attempts to maintain public standards of behaviour. After sexual permissiveness and
luxury had flourished without restraint, the emperor Vespasian pressured the senate to vote that any woman who
had an affair with another person's slave should herself be
treated as a slave (Suetonius *Vespasian* 11). Domitian also
attempted a moral rebirth by introducing a slew of measures, ranging from expelling senators who had appeared
on the stage and preventing women from using sedan
chairs, to executing Vestals who had been involved in
affairs (Suetonius *Domitian* 8). The fourth-century AD
emperor, Julian, banned taverns from opening early and
from selling cooked meat, and forbade ordinary people
from heating water (in case they mixed it with wine). He
even forbade eating in public (Ammianus *Histories* 28.4.4).
I cannot believe that any of these measures were anything
but very occasionally enforced. But at the same time,
emperors also continued to indulge in all manner of
luxury and extravagance, even though the degree seems
to have varied dramatically from one emperor to the next.

It would be easy to see this as simple hypocrisy.
Another interpretation is that the Romans were concerned to enjoy the fruits of their conquests while
safeguarding their favourable relationship with the gods
– always a delicate balancing act. In addition, what

counted as luxury changed significantly over the centuries, and while most of the growing expenditure was that of the elite, the ordinary people of Rome also benefited from an increasing supply of entertainments and foodstuffs.

Perhaps the clearest example of the Roman double standard is seen with respect to prostitution. For all the Roman anxiety about female behaviour falling short of its expected standards, the Romans benefited from prostitution by taxing it. First introduced by Caligula, the tax was probably levied at the rate of the charge for a sex act per prostitute per month. When people complained about this and other new taxes the emperor imposed, saying they did not know what the laws were and so were breaking them inadvertently, Caligula had the law posted up, but in a very narrow place and in excessively small letters so that nobody could read it (Suetonius *Caligula* 40–41). Suetonius's main point is to show what an immoral emperor Caligula was. Yet the tax raised so much revenue that subsequent emperors, including Christian ones, continued to levy it until it was finally scrapped in AD 498.

By taxing prostitution, the emperors effectively legitimised it. While an element of social control was also established, through the use of soldiers to collect the tax, passive official recognition stood in stark contrast to the ongoing attempts to reassert traditional morality through the use of legislation. Some emperors felt uncomfortable about this. Severus Alexander, for example, directed that the proceeds of the tax should not be deposited in the public treasury, but should be utilised to meet the state's expenditures on the restoration of the theatre, the Circus,

the Amphitheatre and the Stadium, thereby funding
public pleasure from private pleasure in a more morally
justifiable manner. He even considered stopping the taxation of male prostitutes and banning them outright, but
supposedly feared that such a prohibition would merely
drive the practice underground (*Lives of the Later Caesars*
Severus Alexander 24). He may also have thought that the
state could do with the revenue.

Subsequent Roman emperors kept up Augustus's
interest in maintaining public morals and in doing so targeted a range of victimless crimes. It was felt to be the
duty of an emperor, as father to his people, to regulate
what they consumed. The justification for this attempted
control was the perceived need to maintain society's military strength, to limit effeminacy, to reduce economic
waste on useless pleasure, and to maintain Rome's morals
in comparison with its imagined past. Sumptuary laws,
aimed at limiting excessive luxury among the elite, also
came to target the small-scale treats of the city's taverns
and bars. In all these cases, the blame was placed squarely
on individual moral weakness, which saw people of all
classes as being led astray by the temptations of luxury
and pleasure. Taverns themselves were symbolic of the
new kind of urban culture that had arisen as Rome had
grown into a vast cosmopolitan capital. In that sense, we
can see the laws as a means of articulating concerns about
social change and possible threats to the stability of the
social hierarchy. But in reality, taverns presented no
genuine threat to social cohesion. Nor did prostitutes.
Legal stigma was an adequate way of dealing with those
involved, and, while *Infamia* may have meant public

disgrace to a few at the top of society, it was probably a far less potent penalty to lesser individuals. This lack of real threat also allowed the emperors to adopt a more practical approach to prostitution alongside their moral condemnations.

The law effectively affirmed the regime's moral aspirations without ever supposing that such high standards could be reached in practice. What we find, though, is that these moral aspirations changed over time, particularly once the empire became increasingly Christian after the emperor Constantine's conversion in AD 312. By the sixth century, the emperor Justinian was passing laws banning sodomy: those convicted would have their genitalia cut off before being paraded in public (Procopius *Secret History* 11.34). But by then the world of Roman crime had entered a very different era.

Chapter VII

WAR CRIMES

Just War

Was Rome a war criminal? Was Romulus's murder of his brother but the first in a long line of instances of immoral violence carried out in pursuance of political aims? Rome's conquests involved many acts by its armies of the utmost brutality: the mass slaughter of Gauls by Caesar's armies, the brutal destruction of great cities such as Carthage, and the crushing of the Jews in three great revolts. Rome's militaristic society glorified war. The Romans had very different attitudes to these atrocities, seeing many as being perfectly justifiable and, indeed, just. But they also possessed strong views about what was permissible in time of war. How should we judge them?

What exactly do we mean by war crime? The First Geneva Convention of 1864 set down principles for the treatment of soldiers wounded in battle. But the law of war reached a fuller articulation after the horrors of the Second World War when, in the Fourth Geneva Convention, article 147 defined war crimes as,

Wilful killing, torture or inhuman treatment, including ... wilfully causing great suffering or serious injury to body or health, unlawful deportation or transfer or unlawful confinement of a protected person, compelling a protected person to serve in the forces of a hostile power, or wilfully depriving a protected person of the rights of fair and regular trial ... taking of hostages and extensive destruction and appropriation of property, not justified by military necessity and carried out unlawfully and wantonly.

Individual soldiers were now personally liable for their actions on the battlefield. The International Criminal Tribunal in the Hague has also been heavily involved in developing thinking about war crime during its investigations into events in the former Yugoslavia. What is covered by the term 'war crime' has had to change as new forms of atrocity have been carried out. In 2001, for example, the Hague tribunal ruled that organised mass rape and sexual enslavement in a time of war constituted a crime against humanity.

The Romans didn't see things that way. If a general conquered a city, all of its inhabitants were his to treat as he pleased. The *Digest* reflects this in saying that the Latin word for slave, *servus*, derived from the verb *servare*, meaning to save, because generals had saved their captives' lives by choosing not to kill them but to sell them into slavery. Conquest for the Romans involved total subjugation of an entire population, of which the military were only a part. In a way, modern warfare has returned to this practice of targeting an enemy's entire population and not only its military personnel.

War was considered to be just if it involved repelling an invasion of Roman territory, as retaliation for raiding parties coming over the border to steal property, or in response to a breach of a treaty. Traditionally, for war to be declared, a ritual known as *rerum repetitio*, a request for reparations, had to occur. A priest-cum-ambassador pronounced a list of the Roman demands, first at the border, then when crossing the frontier, then to the first man he encountered, again on entering the enemy's city walls, and finally on reaching the forum where he would give the list to the local officials. If the demands were not met, the priest would declare war, which would then be ratified by the senate. Once the decision to go to war had been taken, a priest would return to the frontier and hurl a javelin, dipped in blood, into enemy territory and battle could commence. Clearly this was a cumbersome procedure and, once Rome faced an overseas enemy, impracticable. A column was therefore set up in Rome itself as a symbolic representation of the enemy against which a spear was thrown, and this practice was maintained until at least the end of the second century AD.

The Romans also believed in the divine right of their wars. This did not merely reflect their belief that the gods were on their side. They took active steps to involve the gods and ensure that they were fully in support of the Roman cause. Before embarking on a campaign, the senate would offer great gifts of games and money to the gods if they should grant them victory. It fell to the Pontifex Maximus, as chief priest, to make this solemn vow.

Similarly, when Roman forces marched against a town, the army's priests would pronounce another formula aimed at persuading the enemy's gods to come over to the Roman side, emphasising how well their statues would be treated and how devoutly they would continue to be worshipped afterwards. 'I pray to you and respectfully implore you, gods,' the priest would say,

> to abandon this people and city and desert their buildings, temples, and houses and fill the people with fear and terror. Come over to Rome! Our city and temples will be far more agreeable to you and we Romans will look after you so well that you will appreciate the difference ... If you do this, I vow that we will build you temples and celebrate games in your honour. (Macrobius *Saturnalia* 3.9.7–8)

So the Roman view of justness can be seen to have been related to their belief in their divine backing and their continued attractiveness to gods both old and new. They were not making a moral claim about the war producing an end that justified the loss of life and damage involved. Above all, it shows that they felt a need to have some kind of higher justification for their actions, rather than one of pure self-interest. We could easily be sceptical about these claims but it seems that the Romans were happiest fighting wars when there was a confluence of their own interests and those of the divine.

The Romans were well aware that the victims of their invasions did not share this view. In one famous speech, the leader of the Caledonians of Scotland, Calgacus, delivers a damning indictment of the suffering the Romans inflicted on others. 'They rape the whole world', he cries. 'Abduction, massacre, plunder in the name of "law and order". They bring devastation but call it peace.'

These stirring words were written by a Roman, the historian Tacitus (*Agricola* 29–31). His narrative of this defiant speech showed that the Romans themselves recognised that very different views of their power were possible, even if Tacitus's creation is constructed to press distinctly Roman concerns, such as the importance of civilised law and order over barbarian aggression. But the Romans did not see all war as always involving desolation. The surviving literature has plenty to say about how warfare should be conducted morally and what limits should be set on military behaviour.

Cicero wrote a lengthy discussion of the nature of what made a war just, and what the obligations were on combatants to ensure that the engagement was carried out according to the customs of all peoples, the *ius gentium* (*On Duties* 1.33–41). Injustice in warfare, he argues, often arises through trickery, when people fraudulently misconstrue the law. It is this kind of behaviour, Cicero says, that gave rise to the popular saying, 'More law, less justice'. He gives the example of Cleomenes, King of Sparta, who, when a truce was made with an enemy for thirty days, took to attacking their fields by night because he said the treaty had stipulated 'days' not 'nights'. Or the story told about Quintus Fabius Labeo, who was appointed by the senate to arbitrate a boundary dispute between Nola and Naples. He urged each side to make concessions, which they did, and once each had revised their suggested location for the border, a considerable strip of land remained in the middle. Fabius set the frontier as each had proposed and then awarded the remaining land to the Roman people. 'That,' says Cicero, 'is not arbitration, it is swindling.'

In war, he says, the rights of war must be strictly observed. Firstly, he advocates the principle that talk is better than conflict. Force is the characteristic of the brute and should always be the last resort. The only excuse for going to war is to live in peace unharmed. Once victorious, he goes on to argue, 'we should spare those who have not been bloodthirsty and barbarous in their warfare'. He also argues for the highest standards of integrity to be maintained with regard to acting justly to an enemy, giving the example of when a deserter from King Pyrrhus of Epirus offered to assassinate the king with poison. The senate responded by sending the deserter back to Pyrrhus, thereby showing their strong condemnation of any form of treacherous murder, even against a powerful and aggressive enemy. It is hard to square these words with the fact that they were written in 44 BC, when ambitious Roman generals such as Pompey and Julius Caesar had spent the previous two decades conquering vast tracts of Europe in order to further their domestic political aims. But that, of course, is the main point. Cicero knew that Caesar had won (Cicero was himself soon to be killed). His urgings towards good government were being made against a backdrop where constitutional rule had been replaced by dictatorship. He condemns wars fought for supremacy alone or simply for glory. We cannot, therefore, take his text as representing how Roman forces actually behaved in the field or how Romans generally felt about war.

What is clear from Cicero, though, is that the rights of the defeated were not regarded as absolute or inviolable: they were a reflection of their own behaviour during the conflict. Those who threw down their arms and surrendered to Roman generals were thought to deserve better treatment than those who fought tooth and nail. Rome became the patron of those who surrendered following a promise of safety and had a duty to protect them. Any promises made towards an enemy should be kept as a matter of honour because any other form of behaviour would be brutal and subhuman. The motivation for the war should also affect the style of its prosecution. Wars fought in search of glory should be fought with less bitterness than wars for survival. Hannibal had almost brought Rome to its knees, so when Rome finally gained the upper hand, Carthage had to be destroyed.

Types of War Crime

In reality, the Romans committed and suffered a range of atrocities against those they fought and conquered. Prisoners of war were often difficult to control and to supply with food and it is not surprising that generals sometimes decided to kill them instead. After all, Hannibal, when cornered by Roman forces on a narrow pass, immediately put to death his 5,000 prisoners in case they should try to take advantage of his predicament and help their Roman comrades (Appian *War Against Hannibal* 14). This could be excused as an act of necessity in a dire situation. More often, the mistreatment of prisoners of war was meant to send an unambiguous message to the enemy. After he put down the last stand of the Gallic forces under Vercingetorix at Uxellodunum, Julius Caesar had the right hand of every captive man amputated. Partly this served a practical aim of preventing them from raising arms ever again against Roman forces. But Caesar also dispersed them widely across the newly conquered province and, so great was the number of them, they acted as a living reminder of the fate awaiting those who dared to oppose Rome.

The historian Polybius relates an interesting story of how a group of Carthaginian rebels also deliberately mutilated their captives as part of a systematic attempt to terrorise Carthage. The mutineers passed a resolution to torture and kill every Carthaginian they captured and to send back to the capital every prisoner who was an ally of Carthage after having first cut off both their hands (*Histories* 1.81). Polybius notes how there is a particular psychology accompanying this kind of war crime. Just as there are certain kinds of tumour that afflict the body and become fierce and incurable, the same is true, he observes, of the human soul. These malignant forces can develop to such an extent in human psychology that men are capable of becoming more evil and cruel than any other animal. If treated with kindness and clemency, those afflicted simply grow ever more distrustful. If treated with brute force, the passions of the war criminal grow even stronger until there is no act so abominable or atrocious that they will not carry it out, imagining all the time that they are really displaying genuine courage. In the end, these offenders are utterly brutalised and can no longer be called human beings. Polybius blames such an outcome on a combination of factors: bad upbringing as a child, exposure to habitual violence and unscrupulousness on the part of those in authority over them.

Roman forces did not habitually mistreat their captives. In fact, a range of treatments seems to have been the norm. Clemency was often shown to the enemy, with prisoners being exchanged (for example, Livy *History of Rome* 22.23). Captives were also sometimes ransomed or were even given back for no cost. Kings were frequently pardoned and entire armies were disbanded and released, albeit after having their weapons removed. We can see this range in the handling of prisoners as representing a strategy designed to have a variety of effects on an enemy: sometimes to terrorise, sometimes to inspire loyalty, other times to offset the pain of defeat, but always the intention was to project Roman power in a way that reflected both its brute force and its mercy. Just as the law rested on its ability both to inflict exemplary punishments and to display leniency, so the Roman army knew that it could not simply destroy all its enemies; it also needed to establish the legitimate and moral basis for Roman rule.

On occasions, the Romans resorted to the use of forced population deportation and relocation as part of political, post-war settlements. In one of these cases, the Salassi, a tribe who lived in the Alps and were so bold as to act autonomously, contrary to Rome's interests, were systematically sold into long-term slavery. Rome was quite prepared to generate a humanitarian crisis by not only physically removing this obstructive people but by also destroying their collective memory and social networks. This was peacemaking as far as the Romans were concerned and those few Salassi who remained, presumably a pro-Roman faction, did benefit from the new Roman lifestyle, but only in an urban context that stamped its Romanness upon them at every street corner.

Captured spies generally faced execution but were often tortured with an aggravated cruelty in order to discourage others. Livy gives the example of a Carthaginian spy who had eluded capture for two years before being caught in Rome. His hands were cut off and he was then freed. Twenty-five slaves were crucified at the same time after another slave had informed on them for having conspired to help the enemy. The informer was rewarded with his freedom and twenty thousand sesterces (*History of Rome* 22.33).

One group thought worthy of much better treatment was envoys. Indeed, their status as representatives of the state was almost sacred. Mistreatment of Roman legates could provoke, or provide the justification for, a massive Roman response. When the Veneti detained Caesar's envoys and threw them into prison, Caesar immediately ordered large warships to be constructed and crews to be drafted. Then, as soon as the weather allowed, he himself joined the troops. The Veneti were warned of what was coming their way and they then understood the magnitude of their offences (Caesar *Gallic War* 3.9). This suggests that they had been unaware of how seriously their mistreatment of the Roman envoys would be taken. We can see that, in an international system where communications relied on such messengers, it was vital for them to be granted safe passage if the system was to function properly. But the case of the Veneti shows perhaps that some did not agree with this, or that some peoples were less experienced in dealing with other states, or indeed that they were prepared to override legates' semi-sacred status in order to make a powerful diplomatic point.

Women must often have been victims of rape during warfare. Livy (*History of Rome* 38.24) describes a high-profile example from the war between the Romans and the Tectosagi, who lived in what is now mainland Turkey. The enemy king's wife had been captured, 'a woman of surpassing beauty', and was being held under armed guard. The centurion in charge at first tried to seduce her but, when rejected, raped her. Livy himself sees no real problem with this; the woman had, by being captured, fallen to the status of a slave. In the story, the woman gets her revenge by escaping and having her own guards slit the centurion's throat and decapitate him. She then took his severed head back to her husband to show that she had avenged her assault and thereby had in some sense restored her feminine integrity. Obviously Livy thinks this story is worth recording because of the high status of the woman involved and the aggressive, masculine way in which she succeeds in reaffirming her previous identity. In reality, many women would have suffered rape at the hands of enemy soldiers and this was seen by the assailants as part of the acceptable rewards of victory. We can also assume that almost none of the victims succeeded in gaining any redress for their ordeal.

Despite these outrages, the Romans did expect certain standards of civilised behaviour. Livy's description of Carthaginian troops in the Second Punic War emphasises the sheer barbarity of these most ferocious, inhuman enemies. The Carthaginian forces were drawn from the furthest corners of the world, from beyond 'the pillars of Hercules'. They were 'not even natives of Africa'. Geographical distance from the heart of the empire was a sure sign of a lack of Roman civilised values and, sure enough, the Carthaginian mercenaries displayed this in abundance. They are described as 'destitute of all laws', even, almost, lacking language. Savage by nature, Hannibal has made them more so – and here Livy hesitates to say 'what the tongue can scarcely utter' – by teaching them to live off human flesh. What man born in Italy, he argues, would not abominate the idea of having these brutes as masters. Simply to come into contact with them would be an act of impiety because of their cannibalism. This is propaganda, of course, but it was presumably thought to be credible (*History of Rome* 23.5).

Similarly, the Romans were outraged at the war crimes carried out against those of their own troops who had been lost in the great ambush of the general Varus's troops in the Teutoburg forest in Germany in AD 9. The defeat had been so huge that Augustus was said to have banged his head against a door demanding that Varus return his lost legions (Suetonius *Augustus* 23). Tacitus records how Germanicus, when on campaign in Germany six years later, was filled with a passionate desire to pay tribute to these fallen men. This was no easy task as the ambush had occurred deep in enemy territory. Advance troops went ahead to explore the secret forest passes and throw bridges and causeways over the flooded marshes. Then they discovered Varus's camp. Bones lay bleaching in the sun, in piles according to where the men had fallen. All around lay splintered spears and limbs of horses, while human skulls had been nailed prominently on the tree trunks. In the neighbouring trees stood altars where the Germans had savagely slaughtered the tribunes and chief centurions. Survivors of the disaster had also spoken of the gibbets from which many Romans were hanged and the many torture pits. With Germanicus's arrival, a Roman army buried its comrades' bones in a spirit of rising anger against the atrocity. The general himself laid the first shovel of earth on the funeral mound made of the victims' remains (*Annals* 1.61–2).

The point of the narrative now becomes clear. Whereas Germanicus was filled with pietistic duty towards his fallen comrades, his rival, Tiberius, who was also on the campaign and was soon to succeed Augustus as emperor, is revealed as lacking in such Roman honour. Tiberius disapproved of Germanicus, arguing that by showing the soldiers such a massive Roman defeat he would be making them less keen to fight in battle themselves and would make them more respectful of the enemy. Tiberius, in other words, was doubtless a solid general, with a mind attuned to military affairs, but he had no greater spirit or higher sense of honour, something that Tacitus thought should characterise the rulers of the Roman empire. A truly great Roman, such as Germanicus, understood how such sacrilegious treatment against Roman soldiers on the battlefield needed to be dealt with.

Civilian casualties were inevitable. Actions might primarily be aimed at overcoming military opposition but this would often involve an attack on the entire population. Targeting an enemy's food supply, for instance, would inevitably cause considerable collateral damage among the civilian population. After the Gallic rebel leader, Vercingetorix, had sustained a series of losses in conventional engagements against Julius Caesar's forces, he decided to change his tactics completely. To prevent the Romans from procuring provisions he used his cavalry to destroy farms and villages that lay ahead of the Roman forces, preventing their food stores from falling into Roman hands. Any towns whose fortifications were not so strong as to make them totally secure from Roman attack were burned (Caesar *Gallic War* 7.14.1). The Romans also targeted agricultural production in military operations. When Rome declared war on an enemy it explicitly included their lands and, when necessary, such a scorched-earth policy would even be applied to Roman territory in order to impede an invader.

Cities were always major targets in any invasion and their capture often resulted in atrocities. Livy gives an account of the total devastation involved when the Romans sacked the Italian town of Alba in 672 BC. They demolished the city by pulling down all the houses, and drove the population away. Everybody left carrying whatever they could, even having to leave behind their household gods. The streets were thronged with refugees, many of whom were in tears, and who cried out in pain when they passed their temples, now in Roman hands. They felt as if their own gods had been captured (*History of Rome* 1.29).

If a city had not surrendered quickly to Roman forces,

but had had to be taken by assault, then its treatment when it finally fell was generally far worse. It was usual for the adult male population to be killed and for the women and children to be enslaved. The city itself would be plundered and razed to the ground, while its lands were confiscated and a colony of permanent Roman citizens settled. Remember that only a small percentage of the ancient population lived in towns and cities, even though many from the countryside would have sought safety within the city walls during an enemy attack. By eradicating a city, the Romans were not carrying out ethnic cleansing, but they were effectively decapitating the local population, taking away its political leadership, its wealthiest members and its principal institutions such as its temples.

The brutality involved in a hard sacking is striking. Polybius describes what happened when Roman forces took the city of New Carthage in Spain in 209 BC (*Histories* 10.15). Once they had stormed the walls, the Roman general Scipio followed Roman custom by specifically ordering his troops to target the civilian population. Once the order was given, they were to kill all they encountered, sparing nobody whatever their age. Polybius thinks the Romans followed this practice in order to inspire terror in their enemies. The result, he says, is that when towns are captured by the Romans, the streets are left littered with the corpses of civilians, and even of dogs cut in half and dismembered animals. Once New Carthage's leader had surrendered, Scipio gave the order for the killing to stop and the ransacking to begin. All the booty they snatched was collected in the marketplace for the general to divide up as he saw fit.

Although this treatment is shockingly harsh, it did still follow rules, or was meant to. Polybius makes it clear that sackings had strict limits if they were not to be seen as outrageous. 'It is one thing,' he says, 'to seize and destroy an enemy's forts, harbours, cities, men, ships, crops and other such things, because by depriving him of these resources he is weakened.' Such acts were a simple fact of life in wartime. 'But,' he continues, 'to do wanton damage to temples, statues and all such works with absolutely no prospect of any resulting advantage in the war must be characterised as the work of an insane mind at the height of its fury' (*Histories* 5.11.3). Only tyrants want to make themselves masters of other men by terror: they are hated by their subjects for doing so. If a conqueror wishes to rule over a willing people, he must earn it through acts of benevolence and humanity.

Roman atrocities are better understood as part of a range of options they had in dealing with their defeated enemies. Acts of brutality were carefully calibrated to reflect the degree of resistance shown to invading forces. This served to encourage other cities to surrender peacefully in the hope and expectation that they would receive far more favourable treatment as a result.

We have an interesting fictional example of this in a novel from the second century AD, *The Aethiopian Story*. When the town of Cyrene in North Africa was besieged by an Ethiopian army, the inhabitants realised that resistance was useless and decided to leave en masse, throwing themselves at the Ethiopians' mercy. Opening the town gates, they processed out, with those at the front holding branches as a sign of supplication and carrying pictures of

the gods for divine protection. Before they reached the
Ethiopians, they fell to their knees to entreat them for
mercy and raised a collective mournful and piteous wail
of supplication. To excite even greater compassion they
let their toddlers wander about wailing in front of them
to encourage the enemy army to show mercy. This is not
a true story, nor is it about a Roman army, but it was
written in the Roman empire and probably gives us a
good idea of the kind of thought process that went
through the collective mind of a besieged city. It was a
life-and-death decision whether to risk holding out or to
throw yourself on the mercy of your attackers.

When opponents had put up the fiercest resistance,
such as that of the Jews between AD 67 and 70, then the
level of sacking was raised to the highest to include the
obliteration of their gods. Sacred objects were taken from
the Temple at Jerusalem and brought to Rome where
they were displayed in the triumph held to celebrate
Rome's victory in Judaea. From a modern perspective,
the triumph served as a celebration of war crimes, ending
with the execution of the defeated enemy's leaders. As
Livy has one Capuan rebel declare when refusing to surrender to Rome: 'I shall not be dragged in chains through
the city of Rome as a spectacle in a triumph, so that I may
then breathe my last in the prison, or else, bound to a
stake, with my back ripped apart by rods, submit my neck
to the Roman axe.' Rather than face such a fate, he proposed to commit suicide instead (*History of Rome* 26.13).
But from a Roman perspective, the triumph acted as a
means of stating the scale of the Roman victory, of com-
municating to the citizen body the manner in which it

had been achieved, and of symbolically replacing the political leadership of the vanquished by literally decapitating them.

When Rome conquered, it could do as it pleased. Nevertheless, clear notions existed as to what level of retribution was appropriate. Terror and clemency represented two sides of the same coin and served to break the spirits of opponents and deter possible aggressors, but also to inspire loyalty in Rome's newly conquered subjects. It would be wrong to categorise the Romans as being either heartlessly cruel or surprisingly merciful. Variability was the point. But it was not random. Instead, it spoke a language of violence that carefully calibrated the consequences any opponent could expect to reap.

The Rhetoric of War

The alert reader will have spotted that most of the examples mentioned above come from the period of the republic. Partly this is simply because they happen to be the best examples and, like all historians, I have a story to tell. But this was also the period where Rome was expanding rapidly and acquiring its empire. Conflict with others was endemic. By the time of the empire, the number of wars against outsiders fell significantly (although this was to rise again in the later empire under renewed pressure from barbarians).

I suspect that not much changed in the ethical stance of the Romans as to how they prosecuted war once they had emperors. Livy's history, the source of many of these accounts, was written under Augustus and reflects a continuity in attitudes. One factor that did change significantly was that many wars were now internal, civil wars where rival claimants to the throne pitted their forces against one another. But even these were relatively rare. The reality is that, however militaristic Roman society was, by the time of the emperors the vast majority of its inhabitants went from one end of their life to the other without ever experiencing the horrors of military conflict at first-hand. This was true both as active participants, where the army numbered about four hundred thousand in a population of about 60 million (in other words, well under 1 per cent), and as civilians who suffered at the hands of invaders.

It is often said that truth is the first victim of war but in Rome the opposite seems to have been the case. It was peace that led to all kinds of rhetorical inventions being used to describe warfare. Perhaps the best example of this is Tacitus's account of the sack of the city of Cremona in north Italy, which occurred in the civil war in AD 68–69, when Vespasian besieged Vitellius's troops within the city. Forty thousand armed men burst into the town, eager to indulge in lust and cruelty. Neither social status nor age protected anyone and people were assaulted, debauched and killed without distinction. Old men and women were toyed with. Whenever a young woman or a handsome young man fell into the soldiers' hands, they were torn to pieces by the violent struggles of those who tried to grab them. Some soldiers tried to carry off the gold from temples. Others tortured the wealthy citizens to find out where they had hidden their treasure. Then they put the city to the torch (*Histories* 3.33–4). In Tacitus's account it is clear that the sacking destroyed everything that was civilised. We have a dystopic image where lust and cruelty have replaced reason, where the sacred has made way for sacrilege, and where crime has become the new law. The moral lesson Tacitus is drawing is clear: this is what happens when there are emperors. When power lies with one man, good government goes out the window and the worst kinds of atrocity are close at hand.

Despite their relative lack of exposure to such suffering, the image of the sacked city continued to resonate in the Roman imagination, with the fall of Troy serving as the original exemplar. It was like an ancient disaster movie – an image of the worst thing imaginable, where people lost everything: household, family, status and security. Its popularity and familiarity as an image also meant that writers had to work hard to make their accounts fresh and exciting. The historian Sallust describes a speech of Julius Caesar where he complains about the clichéd and boring speeches given by politicians in which they dwell on the horrors of war: 'the wretched fate of the conquered, the rape of maidens and boys, children torn from their parents' arms, matrons subjected to the will of the victors, temples and homes pillaged, bloodshed and fire'. 'In short,' he says, 'arms and corpses, gore and grief everywhere' (*On the Catiline War* 51.9). How dull. Writers therefore worked hard to sex up their accounts by adding all kinds of gory details. The first-century AD orator, Quintilian, explains the best way to do this. You cannot simply write 'the city was sacked' because this does not 'move the emotions'. Instead, the author should include dramatic images of flames racing through houses and temples, the blind panic of some, others clinging to their dear ones in a last embrace, shrieks of women and children, the frenzied activity of plunderers, the captives being driven away as slaves, and the mother who tries to keep her child with her (*Institutes of Oratory* 8.3.67–70). It did not matter whether these details were true or not and Quintilian says that it is perfectly legitimate to include invented images of the kind of thing that usually occurs when a city falls: fake news was completely acceptable.

This kind of revelling in the details of gore partly reflected the militarism lying at the heart of Roman society. This was, after all, a people who liked nothing more than watching gladiators fight to the death or condemned criminals being thrown to the wild beasts. But it does also show that it was possible to 'move the emotions', as Quintilian put it. The Romans could and did pity the dreadful fates that befell people in time of war. But it took more than just the standard sacking to arouse these feelings of sympathy. Tacitus provides us with further evidence for this by recording how nobody wanted to buy any of the captured citizens of Cremona and use them as slaves: he says, 'all Italians loathed the idea of buying slaves like these'. In response to this strong sense of public outrage, Vespasian made it illegal for anyone to enslave any captured citizen of Cremona.

If most Romans were fortunate enough not to experience what happened to Cremona, why, we might ask, were they still so interested in descriptions of sacked cities? One explanation is that these were situations where individuals were placed under the utmost pressure and so revealed their true moral character. Another is that the demilitarisation of their society raised concerns that the Romans were losing the very strength and prowess that had made them great to begin with. Tacitus notes, for example, how the army that sacked Cremona was no longer made up of Romans. There were, he complains, as many passions as there were languages and customs, because the army consisted of a mix of citizens, allies and foreigners, and no two soldiers held the same thing sacred. As a consequence, there was no crime that was held to be unlawful. Roman identity had been lost in a sea of outsiders; it was no surprise to see such a moral outrage being perpetrated on an Italian city. Coming in the civil war known as the Year of the Four Emperors, after Nero had been assassinated, the lengths individuals were prepared to go to in order to win the throne, for Tacitus at least, served to demonstrate the immorality at the heart of the imperial system.

Internal War Crimes

The fate of Cremona reminds us that not all wars were prosecuted against external enemies. The Romans faced enemies within, too. The Roman state, naturally, classified them as traitors and those caught faced the harshest possible punishments. Their actions showed that many people living in the Roman empire did not accept its writ or, at the very least, were prepared to try to live outside the law within the empire's borders.

The most extreme example of this kind of behaviour was outright rebellion. Calgacus has already suggested what motivated some of these fighters. During a revolt in

Gaul, rebel leaders gave impassioned speeches about the constant taxation, the burden of debt, and the brutality and arrogance of their Roman governors (Tacitus *Annals* 3.40). Revolts tended to break out in provinces that had been relatively recently conquered. People could still remember being free and the Roman yoke sat heavily. When revolts did erupt, the rebels generally gave the Romans no quarter. In newly conquered Britain, Boudicca and her followers massacred the Roman troops and their families who they found at Colchester, London and St Albans. But such rebellions were relatively rare during the empire, particularly in provinces where the Romans had been in authority for generations. It was Rome's own armies that were to supply a steady supply of enemies within.

The Roman army acted as a reservoir of criminal behaviour. We have seen already how many soldiers were accused of overstepping their powers and forcing individuals to hand over goods or services. But the army also supplied a steady trickle of deserters who fled into the wilderness and lived as bandits. The Roman empire had large areas that lay beyond the reach of the urban centres, such as semi-desert areas, marshlands and forests, all of which provided a largely safe haven from government forces. Some Roman army recruits clearly hated their service. One law refers to those who cut off one of their own thumbs in order to escape from military duty (they made them do paperwork to discourage the practice) (*Theodosian Code* 7.13.4–5). And they really must have hated it if the alternative was lurking in a swampy grove, eking out a living by mugging travellers. These ex-forces bandits represented a sufficient nuisance that various laws were issued against them. Deserters are referred to as going on to commit crimes such as theft, kidnapping, violent assault or cattle rustling (*Digest* 49.16.5). It was legal to kill trespassing soldiers at night, and it was particularly fine to kill deserters. Mind you, it was not always easy to know exactly who was a deserter: they might claim to have been captured by barbarians before escaping back to the empire. The same law gives guidance on how to tell whether such possible deserters are telling the truth, suggesting that their previous military record should be taken into account. If the suspect had been considered a good soldier, their claims should be believed; but if they had been lazy or negligent in carrying out their duties then they should not be believed.

Civil war produced an abundance of criminality. This included rebellion by a general, a treasonable act, and, whichever side lost, many of the defeated soldiers would melt into the countryside and live as bandits. The orator Libanius says that the fourth-century emperor Julian managed to muster an entire army from those who had been forced into banditry after fighting for the failed usurper, Magnentius, and had made a living from attacking road travellers (*Oration* 18.104). Some of the revolts were simply attempted power grabs by overly ambitious generals whose troops agreed to support them in the hope of great rewards if they succeeded. Others seem to have been little more than riots. Tacitus gives an account of a mutiny under the emperor Otho in the Year of the Four Emperors. Some of the soldiers involved had no idea of the political circumstances but were just drunk.

Others thought it would be a good opportunity to do some looting, and most of the rest were just happy to go along with any new adventure (*Histories* 1.80).

Some bandits seem to have formed into highly organised groups. As a young man, Julius Caesar was captured by pirates off Greece, which Plutarch describes as controlling the sea with large amounts of weaponry and countless small vessels. In this particular story, Caesar, once ransomed, returned to have the pirates all crucified, but in general, piracy was endemic in the Mediterranean, particularly during the late republic. Dio's account of Pompey the Great's suppression of pirates shows just how serious the threat had become (36.20). They no longer sailed in small forces, but in great fleets, and they had admirals to lead them. They robbed and pillaged those sailing the sea, even during the winter season. Pompey suppressed them successfully but Dio makes clear that this was an exceptional period. Pirates and brigands will always be known, he says, but not usually at a scale that warrants state intervention. The seas were never entirely cleared of pirates, even under the empire.

Bulla Felix was perhaps the greatest bandit the Roman world ever saw. With his band of six hundred men, he operated in Italy at the start of the third century AD, when Septimius Severus was emperor (Dio *Roman History* 77.10). His name means 'Lucky Charm' and he certainly led a charmed life. For two years, probably AD 205–207, Bulla successfully evaded Roman capture, even though he was pursued by many troops. Like some ancient superhero, Dio says he was 'never really seen when seen, never found when found, never caught when caught'. Bulla was a bandit but he had a mission. He acted fairly and justly, and rather than killing his victims, he would take only a part of their money before releasing them. He set up his band on almost socialist grounds, redistributing the money he had taken according to who had the greatest need. If his victims were artisans he would detain them for a while and get them to do jobs for him but would then release them with a generous reward.

This Robin Hood-like character was also incredibly smart. He made use of spies to find out who was travelling to and from Rome and the port of Brindisium and would then know who to rob. He surrounded himself with clever people, such as imperial freedmen who were more educated than the average ex-slave. His band also included runaway slaves who had been mistreated and so probably shared something of Bulla's passion for social justice. He was far too smart for the plodding Roman authorities. Once, when two of his men had been captured and were about to be thrown to the wild beasts, he went to their prison and pretended to be the governor of his local district; ostensibly looking for some convicts to carry out hard labour he spirited them away. Later, he went up to the centurion in charge of his capture and, pretending to be someone else, claimed he would lead him to Bulla. He then took the centurion to his camp and captured him. Here he ridiculed the Roman legal system and its injustices. He put on the dress of a magistrate, set up a fake court and summoned the centurion. He ordered part of his head to be shaved, as if he were a common criminal, before saying, 'Feed your slaves properly if you don't want them to turn to banditry!'

The emperor Septimius Severus became so embar-
rassed at his failure to defeat Bulla that he sent a tribune
to capture him under pain of the direst punishments. In
the end Bulla was only captured because a woman he was
having an affair with tipped off the authorities. Brought
before the prefect, Bulla's indomitable spirit showed itself
again: asked why he had become a bandit, his insolent
reply was, 'Why are you a prefect?' He was thrown to the
beasts in the arena, and that was the end of his merry
band.

What to make of all this? It seems relevant to note that
Dio was a senator and his history was written for an upper-
class audience. He had no reason to champion banditry or
the cause of popular justice. What else might he have
been trying to achieve? Dio contrasts Bulla's brilliance
with the emperor's lack of ability. Whereas Bulla inspired
his men by his daring example, Severus could only get his
subordinates to carry out his wishes by threatening them
with severe punishments. The bandit community was
well organised, disciplined and loyal to its leader, just like
a Roman state should be. That there were six hundred of
them was significant too – the number would have rever-
berated in Dio's readership as being the same as the
number of Roman senators. Bulla was a leader who knew
how to manage this 'senatorial' group, acting as generous
patron to all and winning their loyalty. His rule was equi-
table; he only took as much money as was fair and used
people according to their merits and skills. Implicit in all
this is a contrast with Severus's Rome, where people were
heavily taxed and cronyism was rife. Dio claims that on his
deathbed, the emperor said to his sons: 'enrich the army

and ignore everyone else.' That was what Severus's rule meant: military dictatorship with no pretence at good government. Then there is the name. A bulla was the protective amulet worn round the neck by children, a thing that kept its wearer safe. Severus, by contrast, brought only war and violence. Felix was a name adopted by all Roman emperors to emphasise the felicity – the good fortune – that they brought to the Roman state and its people. Here the happiness is being delivered by a renegade, not the official government.

Dio is writing nothing less than a damning indictment of Severus as a gangster emperor. Bulla's final flourish, demanding to know what right the prefect had to be in authority, was itself a variation on a well-known story told about Alexander the Great. The great general supposedly asked a captured pirate what drove him to cause havoc on the seas, to which the man replied, 'I am driven by the same thing that drives you to cause havoc to the world. I do it with a little boat and am called a bandit; you do it with a big fleet and are called emperor' (Cicero *On The Republic* 3.24). It was also telling that, after their charismatic leader had been executed, Bulla's band broke up: as Dio says, 'to such an extent did the strength of the whole 600 lie in him'. Severus, by contrast, only hung on to power because he had enriched the army.

Did Bulla exist? A kernel of truth may well lie at the root of his story but, for Dio, the tale becomes a vehicle for his literary embellishment, produced to damn the emperor himself. It was too subtly done to get him into trouble, but the real meaning would have been clear to his senatorial readership.

It is also unclear whether bandits were really that popular with ordinary people. It is true that the ancient bandit stories do use popular themes of injustice, poverty and corruption to express dissatisfaction with poor-quality governance. If Dio is to be believed, the local people did sympathise with Bulla. But armed bandits were typically far less noble in their aims and deeds than Bulla Felix. The biblical tale of the good Samaritan, who stopped to help a man wounded in such an attack, underlines how commonplace these attacks were and probably also how rare it was to receive any help from other travellers. Most people passed by on the other side. Bulla makes for a nice story but most people probably hated these dangerous outlaws and were delighted to see them torn apart at the games.

We probably see something closer to the reality in a more brutal bandit story from the fourth-century history of Ammianus (*Histories* 28.2.11). It tells how a large group of brigands occupied a village in Syria and used this as a base for raiding the surrounding area. They were particularly crafty because they roamed about in the guise of honest traders and soldiers. Spotting a bandit was not always easy. It would be nice to think they had green caps with feathers in the band but it was easy to pose as a legitimate traveller. Moving around unchecked by means of this ruse, they then assaulted the villas of the wealthy, their estates and even towns. They attacked randomly so that the authorities would not be able to spot any pattern in their raids. They slaughtered dozens and seemed to have enjoyed doing so, with Ammianus describing them as being 'no less greedy for blood than for booty'. Like

Bulla, they pretended to be state officials, this time a trea-surer of the state and his retinue, and used this disguise to raid the town house of one distinguished citizen. They seized his valuables and killed many of his household. Eventually a troop of the army was sent to deal with them and it was the bandits' turn to face massacre. Every last one of them was killed, as were their small children in case they should follow in their fathers' footsteps. The extravagant houses they had built with their ill-gotten proceeds were torn down. The story of their violence is probably as exaggerated in its horror as Dio's tale about Bulla was in its gentleness, but it does give a sense of how the brutal reality of banditry affected ordinary people in villages and towns. It also, as in the case of Bulla, under-lines how bandits had to pose a significant threat before emperors would direct military forces against them. These are stories of exceptional episodes and we cannot know how widespread banditry really was. But it seems that small-scale, small-group attacks carried out by a handful of runaway slaves or deserters would easily have passed under the official radar.

What we also find is that there seems to have been an increase in banditry in the third century, possibly as a response to the large-scale invasions the empire suffered at this time. Political instability resulted from the weak-ened military position of the emperor and there were frequent attempts by rebel generals to seize power. These civil wars in themselves increased the supply of defeated soldiers looking for alternative, illegal means of making a living. One mysterious group that appears for the first time is the Bagaudae. These bandits occupied the more distant regions of north-western Gaul, perhaps the closest we get to a real, live version of Asterix and his friends. One fourth-century source, Aurelius Victor, describes them as a band of country folk and bandits who destroyed estates far and wide, and took control of many cities (*On the Emperors* 39.17). This does not suggest the average small-town bandit, and the impression is reinforced by the fact that their leaders even had coins struck with imperial imagery and propaganda.

The Bagaudae disappear in the fourth century, after central imperial authority was reasserted by the emperor Diocletian and his successors, but they reappear in the fifth when the western empire was starting to collapse. One fifth-century play, *The Complainer*, written in the style of the second-century BC author Plautus (which says something about how culturally conservative the highly educated could be), makes the Bagaudae sound like a bunch of hippy drop-outs. People by the Loire, it says, live according to natural law: 'There is no deception there. Judgements are pronounced from an oak tree and are written on bone. There even yokels present cases and private citizens pronounce sentences. Everything is permitted there.' This certainly suggests that there was a perception that these groups were living outside imperial authority, trying to establish a more just society within the empire's boundaries. On the other hand, this comes from a comedy. The Christian author, Salvian, writing in the fifth-century AD, paints a very different picture of the activities of these brigands. He says that these men have been forced to run away because of the venal corruption of Roman magistrates, who have screwed whatever they could out of the locals. The Bagaudae might be called the criminals but they were forced to turn to crime. It is, he claims, the Roman state that is the real bandit (*On the Government of God* 5.5–6).

We may never get a clear picture of what these Bagaudae were up to. But what is clear is that they became sufficiently powerful to be noticed in the sources and for the empire to organise a military response. Banditry served as an index of imperial reach in the provinces: the weaker the power at the centre, the more it left a vacuum in the more distant regions where alternative leaders could fill the gap. The phenomenon of banditry also shows us that what the Roman state cared most about was military forces large enough to threaten its stability and control. And, to be fair, this may have been what mattered most to ordinary people, too. The horrors created by ancient warfare had been a regular occurrence in the world before Rome gained control of the Mediterranean. The Roman empire, to a large extent and for a long period, eradicated this threat for most of its inhabitants.

As we move into the later empire, however, we find that central control was severely challenged. Rome itself was sacked by the Goths in AD 410, an event not seen for 800 years. It is hard for us to understand how shocking this was. For the Romans, the experience of being sacked was by then as distant as the Magna Carta is for us. It is to this later world we now turn.

Chapter VIII

A REFORMED CHARACTER? CRIME AND THE CHRISTIAN EMPIRE

Towards the Later Empire

On the 28 April AD 357, the Christian emperor Constantius II entered Rome in a triumphal procession to celebrate his victory over the usurper Magnus Magnentius. It was his first visit to the eternal city. Constantius's father, Constantine the Great, had moved the capital in AD 330 to his new city of Constantinople, specifically designed to be Christian and modestly named after himself. Although Rome was no longer the seat of government, it remained the symbolic heart of the empire. In a famous description, the contemporary historian Ammianus gives a mocking account of the emperor's entrance into the city (*Histories* 16.10). Despite never having conquered a foreign enemy the emperor wished to celebrate his victory over a fellow Roman and to do so in the most grand manner. The emperor sat in a sea of attendants, soldiers and armoured cavalry, who held banners stiff with gold and dragons woven from purple thread, while the emperor himself sat alone upon a golden car studded with shimmering precious stones. The assembled force, Ammianus remarks, was so great that it would have been more suitable for a military campaign than a celebratory procession. Acclaimed by the crowd, the emperor sat motionless like a statue as if his neck were held in a vice, and, even though he was very short, stooped forward when passing through a lofty gate. He was so grand that he didn't even spit or rub his nose.

Constantius's triumphal arrival in Rome highlights some of the main developments that occurred in the later Roman empire, which were to have a significant impact on crime and its perception. Above all, the empire became Christian. I want to quickly outline how these changes occurred before asking what effect such developments had on crime in the Roman world. Did the adoption of a religion which promulgated gentleness and forgiveness mean that the empire turned over a new leaf? Just as Romulus had wept over the killing of his brother, did the later Roman empire seek to distance itself from its criminal past?

Gibbon characterised the empire of the second century as the most happy and prosperous period in all human history. This was the period when the empire faced few significant external threats, when the arts flourished and a series of good emperors reigned, all of whom carried out their job conscientiously. But the third century saw the empire face a series of invasions from a number of Germanic tribes at the same time as a reinvigorated Persian empire invaded in the east. The combined threat proved too much for the Roman military and too much for the emperor to deal with alone. Military defeat also brought political instability as multiple rivals came forward to claim the throne, resulting in frequent civil war.

Stability was restored by the emperor Diocletian, who ruled from AD 284 to 305. Recognising that the Roman state was no longer fit for purpose, he brought in a series of reforms to bring it up to scratch. He was so successful that, remarkably, he was able to retire to his palace in Split, where he reputedly tended to his cabbages until his death in 311. He increased the size of the army by something like 50 per cent and improved the empire's defences, all of which cost a lot of money. In order to raise the necessary taxes, Diocletian established a far more powerful state to extract them from the empire's inhabitants. The imperial bureaucracy ballooned, with the number of provinces almost tripling. The central civil service now kept detailed records in duplicate and charged fees for their services. The first pan-European superstate had been created.

Diocletian also realised that Rome was no longer the best strategic location for an emperor. Needing to be closer to the frontiers, he spent most of his time in Nicomedia (now in mainland Turkey). The style of his new court was completely different from that of the first emperor, Augustus. Just as the Roman government had become larger and more intimidating, so too did the image of the emperor. Instead of being styled *princeps*, 'first citizen', as Augustus had been, people now had to call Diocletian *dominus*, 'master', the same word a slave used for his owner. The emperor himself adopted a far more imposing costume, with a full purple cloak and a jewel-encrusted crown. When people approached him they were expected to prostrate themselves before him as if he were a god. The emperor now sat like a colossus at the top of a great governmental machine.

We can get a feel for this new type of government by looking at the preambles to some of their laws. Reading the start of Diocletian's *Edict on Maximum Prices*, a failed attempt of AD 301 to prevent runaway inflation, you would be forgiven for thinking that the late Roman empire was a paradise, and would not imagine that it had come close to outright failure a generation before.

> We must be grateful for the fortune of our state, second only to the immortal gods, for a tranquil world that reclines in the embrace of the most profound calm, and for the blessings of a peace that was won with great effort ... Therefore we, who by the gracious favour of the gods previously stemmed the tide of the ravages of barbarian nations by destroying them, must surround the peace which we established for eternity with the necessary defences of justice.

One of the problems that this god-like image created was that when people addressed an emperor in this period they had to be even more careful than they had been before. Fawning subservience became a requirement, which means that the evidence we have is often far removed from the underlying reality of the situation.

Diocletian was attempting to restore the health of the empire by reasserting traditional morality. He focused his attacks on a radical religious group which, plausibly to his mind, had offended the gods with their novel beliefs. In a series of edicts starting from AD 303 he banned Christian worship, ordered the scriptures to be burned, deprived Christians of various legal rights and ordered all citizens within the empire to sacrifice to the gods on pain of death. Quite how effective this legislation was is hard to say. In some parts of the empire it was enforced more rigorously than in others. It was probably relatively easy for Christians to avoid persecution by leaving their home town and going into hiding. Or they could get a fake certificate saying that they had sacrificed. The number actually executed seems to have been in the low hundreds, but many others will have suffered judicial torture.

In some ways, there was nothing new about this criminalisation of unacceptable religious practice. Major setbacks had often resulted in the state looking for scapegoats. We have seen how Nero responded to the Great Fire in AD 64 by having Christians burned. In AD 250 the emperor Decius responded to the barbarian invasions of the third-century by trying to enforce universal sacrifice to the traditional Roman gods. What was different in Diocletian's empire was the scope of the persecutions, and the attempt to assert imperial authority over the whole empire in a way that had not been seen before.

If Diocletian's reforms successfully transformed the Roman state, his religious policies were a failure. The empire needed a new form of religious expression that reflected its more centralised, all-powerful image and tapped into the growing demand for more ethically sophisticated religious belief. Against this backdrop,

Diocletian's successor Constantine had a vision. Before the Battle of the Milvian Bridge, which cemented his position as ruler of the western half of the empire, he saw a cross of light above the sun along with the words 'With this sign you will conquer'. As a result, he converted to Christianity. The Roman empire did not become Christian overnight. But the support of the world's most powerful man meant that many were attracted to switch from the traditional gods. The church grew rich from offerings and bequests, and by the late fourth century, if not before, Christianity had become the religion of the majority in the Roman empire. Jesus had gone up in the world.

Christians and Crime

To what extent did these two profound changes in the Roman state – Diocletian's superstate and its Christianisation – affect the experience and treatment of crime? Crime certainly sat at the heart of Christian teaching. The commandments of the Old Testament deal with wrongdoing such as stealing, murder, adultery, blasphemy, coveting others' possessions and being an unreliable witness. Whether Christians behaved better in practice is another matter. In one story, told by a hostile rival and so to be read accordingly, the future Pope Callistus (c. AD 217–222) started life as a slave. His owner, a friend of the emperor, instructed him to set up in business as a banker in the public fish market in Rome. Before long various Christians had deposited substantial deposits with him, since he was backed by the financial might of an emperor's associate. But Callistus secretly spent it all and found himself in a dreadful fix. When his owner demanded that he present his accounts for inspection, Callistus was so terrified that he tried to run away. He was captured and put to work on a treadmill by his master. In the end, this fraudulent slave changed his ways, became an administrator in the church and, finally, ascended to the papacy itself.

We find more prosaic evidence of Christians behaving no differently than their pagan predecessors in documents such as the guidance issued by church councils. Canon five of the Council of Elvira, held at the beginning of the fourth century, deals with women who are overcome with rage and beat their slaves to death. If the slave dies within three days of the whipping, the woman is to be banned from the church. She can be readmitted after five years if she had not intended to kill the slave, seven if she had.

We may never know whether Christian belief correlated with an improvement in actual behaviour. But did the advent of the Christian state see a move to a softer, more just government? The emperors themselves clearly thought so. Imperial decrees often refer to the support of the omnipotent Christian God and, as one Justinian law states, 'We exert every effort to preserve our subjects from all injury and slander, the subjects whose government God has entrusted to us' (*New Constitutions* 85 pref.). The church endorsed this connection between imperial state and Christian religion. The emperor was represented as God's right-hand man, an earthly parallel to Jesus, who ensured the empire was managed to promote the Christian mission and carry out God's wishes. And yet, many attitudes towards crime in the later empire show a marked continuity with previous practice.

Attitudes towards slaves, for instance, seem hardly to have changed at all. Christian sermons often assume that slaves are morally inferior to the freeborn (for example, Salvian *The Governance of God* 4.3). In the first century AD, St Paul had taken great care not to fall foul of the Roman law by harbouring a runaway slave when one turned to him for help. He sent the slave back to his master, Philemon, with a plea that he should not treat him too harshly. But as the canon of Elvira showed, Christian masters might well ignore such guidance. There was some improvement in the punishment of slaves by the courts. Crucifixion was banned, for obvious reasons, and Constantine also passed laws preventing the splitting up of slave families at sale and prohibiting slaves being used as prostitutes by their masters (*Theodosian Code* 2.25; 15.8). This last law reflects the particular Christian concern with the body as a site of morality. This meant that a master's sexual behaviour towards his slaves acquired a significance it had not held for Romans before. Runaway slaves also used to be branded on the face so that they would be easily spotted if they tried to escape again. Now this practice was banned because the face had been created in the likeness of God and so was sacrosanct. They branded the feet or legs instead.

One significant development was the recognition of ecclesiastical jurisdiction by the Roman state. Early Christians had often preferred to have their disputes settled by their bishops rather than turn to the Roman courts, but the decisions of these church courts could not be enforced.

Constantine made a bishop's judgement enforceable in Roman law. This gave the bishops an unrivalled source of authority and raised their profile even higher. They became powerful leaders in the growing Christian community. There was a downside to this, with St Ambrose complaining that his days were filled with hearing arguments about the ownership of sheep and other trifles.

One big shift came in attitudes towards the poor. The poverty of Jesus and his attitude to material wealth meant that the Christians noticed those at the bottom of the socio-economic ladder in a way that pagan Romans had not. Emperors and bishops alike styled themselves as 'Lovers of the poor'. Or, as one law put it, 'it is a feature of our humane rule to look after the interests of the destitute and to ensure that the poor do not go without food' (*Justinian Code* 1.2.12.2). The Roman state had always had an interest in granting gifts towards its citizens in the form of handouts of grain and public entertainments, but these did not take into account the recipient's wealth. Whether the later empire saw any increase in actual spending on the poor is hard to say. It may be that there was simply a shift in rhetoric, which did at least recognise the poor as a social problem. We certainly find a softer, more understanding attitude towards individuals such as immigrant beggars. If people came to the city to find work or to improve their prospects, but found themselves on the street and turned to crime as a result, they were not simply to be punished. Instead, the law said that public officials should examine them physically and, if they were unable to work, should look after them humanely. If they were fit and able to work, the officials should return them to where they came from so that they could work there. If they were beggars born in the city, they should be put to work on public projects. If they refused, in an act of indulgence, they would only be driven out of the city rather than punished (Justinian *New Constitutions* 80.4).

We find the same emphasis on the importance of public morals. All members of the clergy were forbidden from gambling with dice (Justinian *New Constitutions* 123.10). And there is even more emphasis on the need to reform the worst abuses of public office. At the end of the fourth century, the emperor Theodosius stamped out two of the worst practices in Rome on his brief visit to the city. Huge bakeries, where bread was made to distribute to the people, were run by certain unnamed corrupt officials who built taverns outside them where they also kept prostitutes. Customers of these bars, especially strangers who would not be missed, would be grabbed and bustled into the bakeries where they would be forced to work without pay and were prevented from ever going outside. Informed of this by one of his soldiers, who had managed to escape, the emperor had the bakeries pulled down. In another reform, the emperor banned the practice of penal prostitution, whereby women convicted of adultery were forced to work in filthy brothels where a little bell would ring whenever a woman had a customer in order to increase the level of her public shaming. Here was a Christian emperor cleaning up the crime-ridden old capital city of Rome (Socrates Scholasticus *Church History* 5.18).

Christian emperors certainly had different attitudes towards sex crime. The Christian emphasis on the moral importance of chastity meant that adultery laws were sometimes vigorously imposed. The pagan historian Ammianus describes with some bemusement how, under the fourth-century emperor Valentinian, many noble women were charged with adultery and executed. One of these women, Flaviana, was stripped bare of her clothes by the executioner as he led her to her death. The executioner himself was then convicted of having committed a monstrously shameful offence and was burned alive (*Histories* 28.1.28). The emperor Justinian widened the scope of adultery laws so that an aggrieved husband could kill his wife's lover in a greater number of situations than previously stipulated (*New Constitutions* 117.15). A wife, too, acquired greater powers to divorce her husband if she discovered that he had been committing adultery, or, indeed, a whole range of crimes, from murder and sedition to cattle rustling and attempted poisoning (*Justinian Code* 5.17.8.2).

Certain sex crimes seem to have acquired a symbolic significance that far outweighed the actual threat they posed. Justinian's laws of AD 528 relating to the rape of virgins, widows, and nuns spell out how heinous an offence this was, 'the worst of all crime', since it not only injured human beings but offended God. Culprits would be executed if the victims were slaves or former slaves. If the victims were freeborn women, then, in addition, all of the offender's assets would be transferred to the woman's family. Those who aided or abetted the offence would also be subject to the severest penalties, with slaves burned alive. This was actually a better fate than the first Christian emperor, Constantine, laid down for people who connived in the kidnapping of virgins or widows: they were to have molten lead poured down their throats (*Theodosian Code* 9.24.1.1).

One area where Christian emperors adopted a far more hostile attitude was homosexuality. As one law states, 'when Venus is changed into another form ... we order the laws to be armed with an avenging sword.' Just the thing to administer 'an exquisite punishment' (*Theodosian Code* 9.7.3). Justinian's laws express the harshest condemnation of what it calls 'crimes against nature' (*New Constitutions* 141). The basis for this condemnation lay in the fate of the biblical city of Sodom, which God 'caused to be consumed with an inextinguishable fire'. Not to punish such 'abominable offences, which are deservedly detested by God', risked bringing down divine wrath upon all the heads of all Romans, in the same way that punishing Christians in previous centuries had sometimes been seen as threatening to destabilise the *pax deorum*.

The Late Roman Superstate and Crime

What was the effect of the newly enlarged state on crime? One German scholar has argued that the greater power of the state meant a reduction in the overall crime rate. The development of much smaller provinces, the increase in the number of state officials, and the separation of military and civic roles all combined to make the government more effective in its task of tracking down, prosecuting and punishing offenders. Violent crime, especially, it is suggested, became less prevalent in all areas of

society, under the twin influences of Christian morality
and increased state surveillance. The state had greater
resources to target suspected murderers and, driven by a
more compassionate Christian ideology, increasingly
used prison as a way of detaining and punishing a range
of offences, from robbery and slander to adultery and
magic. This greater use of imprisonment also reflected a
reduced use of capital punishment, with this being
reserved for more heinous crimes.

There are a number of factors which might lead us to
be sceptical of this somewhat rosy view of crime in the
late Roman empire. The first is the increased economic
pressures faced by the empire's inhabitants. The pre-Dio-
cletian Roman state was small, perhaps no more than 5 to
6 per cent of the economy. Something like two-thirds of
government expenditure went on the army. The impact
of Diocletian's expansion of both the army and bureaucracy, assuming the economy stayed the same size, was to
raise the tax-take to approximately 7 to 8 per cent of economic output. This is still tiny by modern standards,
where most Western governments account for about
50 per cent of the economy. And increasing taxes by 2 to
3 per cent of the economy also seems modest, but in the
context of a small state it represented a huge increase in
percentage terms, perhaps over 30 per cent. Put up taxes
in the modern world by 30 per cent and there would be
riots in the street.

We might also reasonably expect an increase in poverty.
Most peasants in the countryside and manual labourers in
the cities probably lived at only a modest level above subsistence. They could provide their families with the basics

but little more, and they had very limited savings and resources to fall back on in times of hardship. A hefty tax hike will have hit these people hard. Many will have been driven closer to the breadline. Modern criminology suggests a strong relationship between poverty and certain kinds of crime, most notably theft and violence. Intuitively, then, we might assume that the Roman empire became a tougher place in which to make ends meet, and this would have increased criminality.

The ancient sources, regrettably, don't allow us to quantify any such rise in the overall crime rate. But one area where we do see a clear increase in violence is in the illegal usurpations of would-be emperors. The third-century crisis, for example, saw fifty-one claimants to the throne in a fifty-year period. These crises tended to be concentrated in certain periods but overall the late empire experienced a far higher level of military activity within the empire's borders than did the early empire. This was especially true after the colossal Roman defeat at the battle of Hadrianople in AD 378. Then the Goths settled within the empire's borders but retained their own military command structure, and their example was followed by various other barbarian groups after further invasions in AD 406.

We also see more periods of sustained loss of control by the central government. With its attention focused on these military threats, some more distant areas of the empire became cut off and seem to have looked to other forms of local leadership for protection. We saw this earlier in the case of the Bagaudae. Increased civil war will probably have resulted in more defeated soldiers turning to brigandage. One law refers to soldiers plundering fields by night and ambushing travellers on roads (*Theodosian Code* 9.14.2). Another seeks to prevent men from carrying arms to stop them killing each other and bans the manufacture of weapons (*New Constitutions* 85). Was this law simply a restatement of previous practice or a necessary response to more weapons being carried in the street?

The chariot-racing factions within the new Christian capital of Constantinople provide us with a clear indication of a lack of state authority. The sixth-century historian, Procopius, gives a gruesomely vivid account of their increasing power. The whole empire was thrown into confusion by the hooliganism of the fans and 'both the laws and orderly government were completely overturned' (*Secret History* 7).

The population had for a long time been divided into two factions, supporting either the Blues or the Greens. The gladiatorial combats had been banned at the end of the fourth century and, in the late empire, it was the chariot races in the circus that became the focus of popular entertainment. Their political importance was reflected in the location of the circus in Constantinople: next to the imperial palace, from which a passage afforded the emperor direct access. In such a divided society it might have been wise for the emperor to remain neutral. But Procopius claims that the sixth-century Justinian supported the Blues. This stirred up the animosity between the two sides to unprecedented levels: it emboldened the Blues to attack the Greens, while it made the Greens feel resentful and keen to avenge the injuries done to them. As

Procopius says, 'Men who are wronged are likely to become desperate.'

The effect of imperial backing was to shake the city 'as if an earthquake had hit it'. First, some of the rebels on the Green side changed their hairstyle. They wore it long, except at the front where they cut it short across the forehead, and grew Persian-style beards and moustaches, in a look they called the 'Hun' style. Then the fans started dressing in outrageous fashions. They put the purple stripe on their togas, a colour restricted to the emperor, and swaggered about as if they were high-ranking officials. The young men had special sleeves on their tunics that billowed out when they waved their arms. There is a sense here of an alternative gang culture, revelling in the coolness of a powerful external enemy and rejecting the authority of their own government.

But the factions were far more dangerous than this dandyism might suggest. For one thing, Procopius says that they nearly all carried swords openly at night. In daytime, they concealed small two-edged daggers along the thigh under their cloaks. They gathered at dusk and went about robbing the better-off of their clothes and jewellery, accosting their victims in narrow alleyways and snatching their cloaks, gold brooches and whatever else they were carrying. They killed some to stop them informing the authorities. Everyone was outraged by these attacks, but the city government paid no attention, with the result that people stopped carrying anything valuable and stayed at home once it was dark. The criminals grew increasingly daring: as Procopius explains, 'when crime is permitted, there are no limits to its abuses'.

People fled the city, and everyone was drawn into the civil war even if they had shown no interest in the racing factions previously. At first the factions targeted only the other side. But as matters deteriorated, they started to murder randomly. Many people took advantage of the mayhem by bribing the factions to target their enemies. This also started to happen openly during the day all over the city, even during church services. With the criminals having no fear of punishment, nobody was safe. Family members would be murdered by their own relatives. All arguments were now settled by violence. The gangs even started to knife people simply to prove their manhood.

The reign of terror was so great that judges stopped trying to deliver justice. They simply convicted or acquitted according to whether the defendant was a Blue. Otherwise the judge himself would be targeted by the faction. Many Blues refused to pay their bills if they owed money to a Green. The social dystopia was such that some were forced to free their slaves, while some women even had slaves start telling them what to do. Children started to force their fathers to transfer property to them while some fathers were even compelled to prostitute their own wives and sons to the Blues. One attractive woman was on a boat with her husband when they encountered some of the Blues. The fans jumped aboard and grabbed her. As she was forced to board their vessel she whispered to her husband that he should not worry that she would allow herself to be dishonoured, then threw herself into the water and vanished beneath the waves. Such was reign of the criminal gangs of Constantinople.

How reliable a witness do we consider Procopius to be? We should bear in mind that his *Secret History* claimed to lift the lid on the real Justinian, a man whom he likens at one point to a demon. Nevertheless, the atmosphere of chaos is persuasively evoked. The government seemingly couldn't even control the popular gangs of the factions on the imperial palace's doorstep. But it was what Justinian was doing to the state that Procopius claims people were really worried about.

The late Roman state was certainly not more gentle than before. If anything there seems to have been an increase in judicial savagery. It can be argued that this was in part a rhetorical shift, with fewer criminals suffering more aggravated punishments in order to act as examples to others. And perhaps the increase in the rhetorical severity of the punishments served to compensate for the state's declining ability to control marginal groups like the Bagaudae and the factions. But it is also impossible to quantify such things. Is a government gentler if it executes fewer people in a more gruesome way?

What is certainly clear is that the law changed. The more variegated legal culture of the early empire, where imperial edicts sat alongside local customs, slowly transformed into an ideal of a universal law. This was given an added boost by the creation of a stronger, more centralised state. Codifying the law into a single coherent body fitted in with the centralising tendencies of the late Roman government.

The new law produced a more hierarchical society, where the haves received more and the have-nots had legal privileges taken away. This was a slow process but it resulted in legal status reflecting an individual's social status, and both the privileges and penalties varied accordingly. Citizenship itself had been almost worthless since AD 212 when Caracalla granted it to all free men in the empire. By the third century, people were also now formally divided in law between the elite who were 'more honourable' (*honestiores*) and those who were 'more humble' (*humiliores* – literally 'closer to the ground'). This legal divide became stronger, and by the fifth century had developed into one between the 'weaker people' (*tenuiores*) and the 'more powerful' (*potentiores*).

One consequence was that the vast majority of people became liable to harsher punishments. Even local landowners could face floggings if they failed in their duties, such as raising tax. This represented a dramatic shift from the days of the republic and early empire when a Roman citizen could not be punished physically. Even if it is true that the more severe punishments, such as pouring molten lead down the throat, were very rarely carried out and represented an attempt to make a strong moral statement, the late empire saw most people living under fear of far more vigorous reprisals than before. Other laws also tied freeborn peasants to the land where they were registered. They and their families became like serfs, bound to their land in perpetuity to ensure a steady flow of taxes into the treasury's coffers. The law may have looked and sounded stronger but liberty was on the retreat.

Corruption

One area where there seems to have been a clear increase in crime was in government corruption. The late Roman empire was notoriously venal. One civil servant, John Lydus, earned a salary of only nine gold coins for his first year as a junior official but pocketed a thousand in extra fees for providing people with access to the government's services. This seems like straightforward corruption, but the situation was more complicated. It has been argued that the government turned a blind eye to the practice so long as it was done within certain limits for the simple reason that it kept the cost to the government low by transferring it onto the users. It also served to restrict access to government to those who could afford it. Even the enlarged late Roman state was relatively small and its capacity to deal with petitions and other business was very limited. Charging fees effectively made sure that the powerful, those whom the government had to listen to, could get access when they needed it. The vast majority of subjects could do little more than send in a petition and hope to get a response. The government made sure that there was regular staff turnover so as to limit a bureaucrat's power and maximise the number of officials who could benefit from earning governmental fees. In the republic, the crime of *ambitus* had referred to attempts at electoral bribery. Under the late empire, it came to refer to the practice of hanging on to office for as long as possible to maximise one's take.

How did ordinary people feel about this? Did they see it as corruption? Did the practice reduce the legitimacy of the state because accessing the courts was now based more on money and less on the justness of the case? One interesting example comes from the fifth-century writer Priscus, who went on a diplomatic mission to the court of Attila the Hun. While there, he met a Greek merchant who had been captured in war but who subsequently chose to live with the barbarians. When questioned as to why, the merchant lists various reasons, several of which relate to the lack of justice the common man could expect in the empire. Taxes are high, he complains, and the law does not apply to all equally. Criminals escape if they are rich and powerful whereas they are punished if they are poor – if they do not die first because the proceedings take so long. Worst of all, he says, is to have to pay officials in order to gain access to a court to seek justice (11.2.407–510). Priscus replies that proper legal process takes time and that it is better to deliver justice slowly than injustice fast. In the text, the merchant naturally ends up agreeing with Priscus, but the story still says something about the reservations people might have had.

Another text talks of runaways who were happy to abandon the Roman empire altogether, preferring 'to endure a poor freedom among the barbarians rather than the harried condition of a taxpayer among the Romans' (Orosius *History* 7.41). Many of those who fled became brigands within the empire's borders. The writer of the fourth- or fifth-century *On Military Matters* wrote to the emperor to suggest various ways in which he might improve the empire's situation (he wisely did not put his name to the document). He complains that corrupt provincial governors are 'all the more burdensome in that injustice proceeds from the very persons from whom a remedy should have been expected', and warns that tax and injustice are driving the poor to crime:

> the poor have been driven by their afflictions into various criminal enterprises, and losing sight of all respect for the law, all feelings of loyalty, they have entrusted their revenge to crime. For they have often inflicted the most severe injuries on the empire, laying waste the fields, breaking the peace with outbursts of brigandage, and stirring up animosities. (2.3; 4.1)

Others complain about officials taking more than they should in tax. One petition from an Egyptian peasant to the District Magistrate in AD 298/9 complains, 'The laws have repeatedly said that no one should be made to suffer oppression or illegal exaction ... Now I have had exacted from me unjustly and audaciously three grams of gold and eight of silver by Acotas ... not to benefit the collection of taxes, but to steal my property contrary to the imperial laws.' As it goes on to say, 'if arrogant men are successful in this way, all men of modest means would have been destroyed long ago' (*P. Cair. Isid.* 65–7). Emperors made various attempts to stamp out this malpractice. In AD 331 Constantine commanded that,

> The grasping hands of officials shall immediately be stopped, they shall stop I say; for if after due warning they have not stopped, they are to be cut off by the sword. Access to the governor's court should not be for sale; entrance should not be purchased ... the ears

of the governor shall be open equally to the poorest
and to the wealthiest. (*Theodosian Code* 1.16.7)

But in reality, emperors needed their officials to earn
money by charging fees in order to keep down the costs
to the state, so probably the aim was simply to try to
prevent them from charging too much.

Repeated imperial laws refer to officials taking advantage of their power to extort money from those beneath
them. One from Justinian refers to the prefects of the
Nightwatch employing various criminals and then turning
a blind eye to their activities, presumably in return for a
cut of the ill-gotten proceeds. If only they would 'hate
and avoid such people' and use men of good character
then 'there will be no thieves, stolen property will be
easily recovered, the guilty will be caught', and there will
be magistrates 'whom no one can purchase with money'
(*New Constitutions* 13.4). There is a good deal of wishful
thinking in these decrees.

Clearly people did feel some degree of hostility
towards the state for the use of fees, primarily because the
system was easily abused. But people may also have had
low expectations of government in general. They did not
expect efficiency and so may not have lost faith in the
system if it failed to deliver. The degree of muddle is
sometimes pretty marked. On Christmas day AD 409, a
rescript from the emperor Honorius to the praetorian
prefect dealt with the minor officials known as eirenarchs.
These officials policed local areas, especially in the eastern
provinces, and had been established independently of the
central government by various cities. Honorius set out

the conditions for their appointment, referring to the eirenarchs as men who 'cause harmony to arise throughout
individual territories for the protection of the peace and
quiet of the provinces'. On the same day another rescript
to the same praetorian prefect abolished the post: 'the
title of eirenarch, who under the pretence of maintaining
the protection of peace and quiet of the provinces did not
allow harmony to arise through individual territories,
should be utterly removed' (*Justinian Code* 10.77; *Theodosian Code* 12.14.1). It is possible that there is something
wrong with the text. The two laws were probably just
lumped together later by chancery officials and given the
same date because they dealt with the same subject. Even
so, the imperial responses show that at the same time as
the Roman state was facing greater threats to its control,
from bandits to barbarians, it thought it a good idea to
abolish local policemen, who were regarded as somehow
contrary to the maintenance of law and order. It shows
the strain between central government and the local landowners who were still expected to carry out many of the
tasks of local government. On the one hand, the state
expected them to raise tax and maintain order, on the
other it did not trust them to do so and looked down on
them as 'humbler'.

The new reliance on money to access the courts was
in some sense fairer than the traditional practice of
patronage, which we might also see as corrupt. In the
early empire, getting things done had always relied on
having contacts in the right places. At least money allowed
anyone who had the cash to access the governmental services they required. In reality, patronage remained a major

force in the later empire, except that now what was vital was having contacts with those in the imperial court and the central bureaucracy. Often there was a clash between these two forms of power. The fourth-century orator Libanius complains about villagers paying officials who enjoy a relationship with the governor to protect them from the tax demands of the local councillors, the curials (*Oration* 47.7–8).

What the increased use of money really showed was that the nature of patronage itself had changed in line with the new governmental structure. Patronage had always involved networking with local elites but what mattered in the later empire was having links with the centralised state. Money represented the best way to deal with this more distant, faceless, revolving bureaucracy. So the new system did not simply replace patronage. After all, money is not a neutral medium of exchange but an expression of society's economic and political ordering. Money was a way for patronage to work when greater distance, both geographical and social, existed between the local landowners and the central elite. It allowed the wealthy in Roman society to build networks of interdependence that could benefit them all, even when there was no direct personal relationship between those involved. Rather than try to eliminate corruption, the state started to regulate it.

Criminal Christians

The combination of an enlarged state and its adoption of Christianity probably changed the rhetoric concerning crime more than crime itself. What it also meant is that the Christian religion lost much of its previous radical edge. Being in bed with the emperor made the church much richer. This brought great benefits, such as a huge church-building programme and some increase in poor relief. And now that the church was respectable, men of talent and ambition wanted to join it. The church was transformed from an underground religion of the oppressed to a comfortable home for the wealthy. For many ordinary Christians, it had sold out to the very state that used to persecute it.

Some Christians strongly resisted the new Constantinian catholic church. In North Africa, many in the local community refused to accept back into the church those who had betrayed it during Diocletian's persecutions. Constantine insisted that they should. They broke away from the orthodox church and set up their own places of worship. Soon most towns and cities had two bishops – orthodox and rebel, known as Donatist. Within a few years of his conversion to Christianity, Constantine found himself in the perverse situation of threatening and persecuting minority Christian groups because they refused to follow the official line. The most radical Donatists, known as Circumcellions, attacked catholic property owners and freed their slaves. Revering the Christian martyrs of the days of the pagan persecutions, some of them even burst into law courts and tried to provoke the judges into executing them.

Another effect of Constantine's conversion was that the emperor himself became involved in all kinds of religious disputes. When an Egyptian clergyman named

Arius argued that the Trinity was not composed of three equals – the Father, the Son and the Holy Ghost – but that the Father must be superior to the Son, many thought his idea made sense: the father/son relationship was one of the core building blocks of Roman social relations, and God had also created Jesus and sent him down from heaven, meaning that he must have pre-existed him in some way. The problem was that all this smacked of a return to pagan polytheism. For Constantine, who by now was sole ruler of the whole empire, this division was unacceptable. He wanted his Christian empire to have one God whose sole representative on earth was the one emperor, himself. Constantine summoned all Christian bishops to solve the issue. Two hundred or so poured into the city of Nicaea in northern Greece to thrash the matter out. In the end it was the emperor himself, not, of course, a bishop, who supposedly came up with the solution. It was agreed that all three parts of the Trinity were 'consubstantial', all of the same matter. The bishops who refused to go along with this were excommunicated and then exiled.

This imperial involvement in matters of theology meant that debates about orthodoxy and heresy acquired a political aspect. Heretics could find themselves facing legal penalties. Religious error became a crime. The intensity of these doctrinal arguments grew as Christianity became more widely followed and as the political consequences of being on the losing side became apparent. In one of the most famous controversies, St Augustine made a systematic effort to have the radical teachings of Pelagius condemned as heretical by the emperor.

Pelagius was probably born in Brittany in the early 350s and is unflatteringly described by St Jerome as 'a fat man weighed down by Irish porridge'. In Rome he promoted a very hair-shirted form of Christianity, leaving the city only after it was sacked by the Goths in AD 410, an event that gave these theological debates an added urgency. Were the Romans being punished for their sin and for allowing heresy? (The pagans, meanwhile, argued that it was because the empire had abandoned the old gods.) Once in Africa, Pelagius came into direct contact with Augustine but his teachings could not have been more different. Augustine favoured a broad church under imperial patronage, one that helped the weak individual sinner to achieve salvation. Pelagius placed the burden of effort squarely on the individual, who was urged to live a pure life, devoid of riches. 'Riches can hardly be acquired without injustice', he argued, 'Riches are evil' (*On Riches* 7.3; 5.1). Even when the rich gave alms to the poor, Pelagius argued, they were merely returning a little of the great wealth they had extorted from the poor in the first place. 'Is this really their own wealth?' he asked, when it has been acquired by 'the violence of servants of the emperor and governors, who despoil through the use of their official power' (Jerome *Commentary on Ezechial* 6.8).

Augustine recognised the potency of this radical message. In a series of church councils in the 410s, Pelagius was condemned as a heretic. But such condemnation counted for nothing without the backing of the emperor to enforce it. Augustine and other orthodox African bishops sought to get the pope in Rome to support their case and allegedly sent eighty thoroughbred horses as bribes to the imperial court. It helped that some of Pelagius's supporters had been associated with riots in the streets of Rome; threats to orthodoxy were one thing but public order was another. In AD 418, therefore, Honorius condemned Pelagius for his heresy and for promoting sedition in the streets. Pelagius went off to Egypt and was never heard of again. 'The case is finished' (*causa finita est*), Augustine remarked (*Sermon* 131).

The Pelagian controversy was largely non-violent. Other church rivalries spilled over into large-scale street riots. In the late fourth century, the supporters of two rival claimants to become pope, Damasus and Ursinus, clashed in a series of bloody protests. The pagan historian Ammianus delights in the ambition of these Christians, their bitter strife and their use of violence. Damasus's faction won in the end, but only after his supporters fought their rivals in the basilica of Sicinius, causing 137 deaths (*Histories* 27.3.12–13). Shortly before, in Constantinople, the bishop Macedonius forcefully pushed an Arian agenda against his more orthodox rivals. The emperor, Constantius II, whose entry into Rome we saw earlier, had Arian leanings and this encouraged Macedonius's supporters all the more. He seized the bishopric and sought to suppress any opposition. He used torture to force men, women and children to accept the sacraments from him. If any resisted they were flogged. Women who refused had their breasts sawn off, a torture that the historian Socrates Scholasticus says was 'unknown even among barbarians but invented by those who professed to be Christians'. The Macedonian faction demolished rival churches and the bishop even managed to persuade the emperor to send in troops against orthodox believers in one region. (This backfired when the locals, armed only with pitchforks and religious zeal, fought back and killed most of the soldiers.) In the end, Macedonius lost Constantius's support by trying to move the remains of his father, Constantine, to another church. This caused such a massive riot that great loss of life occurred and 'the churchyard was covered with gore, and the well which stood in it overflowed with blood'. Once again, public disorder spurred an imperial response. Macedonius lost his job (*History of the Church* 2.38).

Christians did not fight only among themselves. As Christianity asserted itself more vigorously, paganism was repressed. Temples were closed and sacrifice outlawed. When the famous Serapaeum and other temples were demolished in the Egyptian city of Alexandria at the end of the fourth century AD, it provoked a violent response from the many pagan worshippers who still lived in the city. They rushed the Christians and murdered many. The number of wounded on both sides was countless (Socrates Scholasticus *History of the Church* 5.16). These outbursts of violence were not the norm, of course; they were extreme events, which is why historians thought them worth recording.

Pagans and Christians of various kinds coexisted peaceably for the most part. But the stories do still underline how religion in the late empire became a periodic source of violence, and of accusations of criminality and legal dispute. Above all, what constituted unacceptable religious belief and behaviour was now up for debate and had acquired an unavoidable political dimension.

Perhaps the biggest change relating to crime in the later empire was how it was put to a new, more sophisticated metaphorical purpose. In his *Confessions*, Augustine recounts a famous story of how he used to go stealing pears with his friends (*Confessions* 2.4–10). He describes how, in his youth, he used to hang out with a gang of other boys and would play games in the street until late at night (1.18.30; 2.8.16). He recalls how they were so competitive that they would cheat in order to win. When he caught others cheating, Augustine was outraged and quarrelled with them fiercely, even though he was himself guilty of the same. But Augustine had a more profound theological purpose in using such imagery. As people grow up, he argues, these sins are transferred from harmless games to the behaviour of magistrates and kings. Augustine's quarrels over cheating also show that the boys shared a strong sense of communal justice, however far short of this ideal they fell individually. Each boy expected the others to act honestly towards one another and observe a common code of good conduct even if in practice the desire for status meant that they were perfectly prepared to cheat. Christians needed to maintain this sense of justice.

Augustine emphasises the importance of peer pressure on his misspent youth. He tells us that he engaged in acts of minor theft from his parents' cellar and table partly so that he would have something to swap for trinkets among his group of friends. He loved stealing because of the camaraderie it engendered and says that he would not have done it on his own. What Augustine's text shows is how the image of the thieving child could now serve as a metaphor for the weak Christian individual soul as it struggled to attain salvation in the face of multiple earthly temptations. The whole point of the theft of the pears was simply destructive, since the boys had no desire to eat the fruit but would simply throw them to pigs. As Augustine says, the fact that it was forbidden 'pleased us all the more'. All Christians, in Augustine's view, were therefore in need of God's guidance and correction to keep them on the straight and narrow. Humans had an in-built weakness to be led astray by temptation. They actually desired to do what was sinful. We would all end up as spiritual criminals if it were not for the help of the Christian church, through which God's grace was channelled.

Irreverent Rome

When looking at the grand, terrifying image of late Roman emperors, it is easy for us to be cynical about the heaven on earth that they claimed to have established. But an emperor's own subjects were also capable of criticising him, especially when he failed to live up to these claims. In that regard the late empire marked no change. When taxes were too high or food in short supply, the ordinary people of the empire could vent their ire against the very imperial images that in other circumstance they were happy to revere. During one tax riot in Antioch in the late fourth century, the crowd threw stones at the many painted pictures of the emperors that were hanging at various places in the city and jeered as they were smashed. The statues of the emperor and empress were then thrown down and dragged through the city and, 'as is usual on such occasions, the enraged multitude uttered every insult which passion could suggest' (Sozomen *History of the Church* 7.23).

The later emperors were if anything even more keen than their predecessors to know what people thought about them. One law states that all who spoke against the emperor were foolish, insane, malicious or plain drunk, but they were not to be punished. The emperors wanted to hear everything 'with all details unchanged' (*Theodosian Code* 9.4.1). The fourth-century emperor Gallus used to wander the streets of Antioch in disguise, asking people what they thought of him (Ammianus *Histories* 14.1.9).

There was, as Ammianus himself noted, something ridiculous about the grand image of Constantius arriving at Rome: a small man pretending to be a statue to make people think he was divine. Static, rigid and self-important, perhaps Constantius is meant to symbolise the late Roman state itself. Ammianus claims that the people had no desire to see such a spectacle. When Constantius later went to the games in Rome, he had to put up with jokes at his expense. In fact, when he first saw the forum, he stood amazed as his eyes rested on the dazzling array of marvellous sights. That was Constantius: a bumpkin, awed by Rome when he himself should have been awe-inspiring.

The late Roman empire has been dominated by Gibbon's narrative of decline and fall. In his view, it was Rome's immoderate greatness that led to its eventual demise. Can we shake off these preconceptions that it was somehow inevitable that the Roman empire would collapse? It became a lesson for later empires, such as

Britain's, to learn from. The fall of Rome supposedly showed what happens when an empire loses its moral purpose and its government becomes locked in internecine squabbles. The reality was far more complex. For one thing, the eastern half of the empire (always the more populous and prosperous area) survived for another thousand years. Later called the Byzantine empire, its rulers saw themselves as the eastern Romans, the direct descendants of the Romans of the republic. For another, the late empire had become Christian. If this represented a moral improvement, as our Christian sources assure us it did, then why did God allow the Christian empire to fall? There was much more to the late Roman world than simple decline: many new forms of art flourished, the Christian church expanded its mission, and for the first time the law was codified into the great collections that formed the basis for many later European legal systems. The creation of a central body of law itself reflected an increased distance between the emperor and his people. A new kind of rhetoric was used to establish the emperor's superhuman qualities, his proximity to God and the justness of his rule. The reality of how crime was dealt with disappears into that widening gulf of power and the grandiose rhetoric it encouraged. If we are to judge the late Roman empire, we will have to take into account all these factors. But one thing is clear: for all these changes, crime and images of crime continued to sit at the heart of how the people understood their relationship with their emperor.

THE

VERDICT

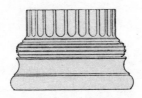

ROME: GUILTY OR
NOT GUILTY?

The accusation, then: Rome was a habitual offender. It was riddled with crime but did little to help victims gain redress. Injustice, as Rome saw it, was an occupational hazard of controlling an empire. We have seen how crime affected people of all social levels, right across the empire and all through its long history. We have seen how even the emperor, who was head of the legal system, the highest judge and ultimate source of Roman law, was able to behave like a common thug. Being rich was no protection. When the emperor Tiberius was short of money, he made a rich man named Gnaeus Lentulus Augur leave him everything in his will and then forced the poor man to commit suicide (Suetonius *Tiberius* 49). Nobody was safe.

Life for the poor could be just as dangerous. An Egyptian papyrus dating from AD 188 is a petition sent to the local Roman governor by a man called Andromachus, who had been the victim of violent robbery at the hands of his neighbours. It details how two brothers had burgled his home and stolen items including a white tunic, a cloak, a pair of scissors, some beer and, probably, some salt (the text is unclear) (*P. Tebt.* 2.331). Another Egyptian petition from five years later was sent by a man who had a piglet stolen. He claimed that the animal was worth 100 drachma. In reality, this was about five times what piglets usually cost. Clearly even victims were trying to cheat.

Can they be blamed? We know what to do if we fall victim to a crime: call the police, get a lawyer, go to court, and so on. The experience of Romans depended significantly upon their social status, whether citizen or slave, man or woman, rich or poor. Most people could do little. Their responses were not just to turn to the courts but to the local community or to religion, or to resort to direct acts of vengeance.

How do we judge Roman law? It was surely an extraordinary achievement, built up incrementally over centuries, but it relied largely on the victim to seek justice and redress. The cost and difficulty of this served to deter most. Direct means of appeal, such as petitions to local governors, had little chance of success. What was the governor who received 1,804 petitions on his annual two-day visit to a single town in Egypt meant to do with them all? The difficulty of gaining legal redress coupled with widespread corruption meant that the law could do little to deliver justice to most victims of crime. But even if Roman law did not succeed in stamping out crime, it did still make a powerful symbolic statement about its unacceptability.

We have also seen that Roman law was mainly about private concerns: private property, business contracts and family inheritance. This is called the civil law, the law relating to civilians. Criminal law, by contrast, concerns those offences that are seen as a wrong against all of society. Anyone who commits one will face a public legal action. If convicted, they will face a punishment that again is decided by the state, whether a fine or imprisonment. To be convicted is regarded as a social stigma. So the standard of proof is set high. Most Anglo-Saxon countries follow the formulation of a prosecution case having to be proved beyond reasonable doubt.

Civil law is different. It relates to dealings between individuals and corporations. If someone agrees to do a service for someone else for a certain price then a contract exists between them that can be enforced by the courts. Sometimes the two types of law overlap. So if you run someone over while drunk you can face a criminal prosecution for being drunk and a civil one for damages for injuries resulting from the incident. The aim of civil law is to redress the negative effect of any wrongdoing. So, in the case of a contract, if someone fails to pay the agreed price then the civil law will simply ensure that the correct fee is paid, possibly with some element of compensation for any other negative effects of the non-payment. By contrast, the aim of criminal law is to punish the wrongdoer. The purpose of this punishment is to prevent others from carrying out similar offences, and to reform the criminal so that he or she does not commit such acts again. (It may also be to satisfy public demand for revenge: those who harm the common good should suffer some kind of public retribution.)

We have found that Roman law was almost entirely

civil. Of the fifty large books of the *Digest* – the huge compendium of previous legal cases collected on the order of
the emperor Justinian in the sixth century – only one is
concerned with criminal law. In other words, it is
98 per cent about private matters. This, like the practice
of law itself, reflected the fact that the law was fundamentally concerned with the propertied class. It was much
less concerned with illegal acts that involved the state or
were judged to have a public dimension. Roman law did
not have as its main aim the establishment and maintenance of generally agreed standards of socially acceptable
behaviour. It existed to enforce the profoundly unequal
and steeply stratified social hierarchy.

How important is this emphasis on civil law? Did it
reflect indifference towards the majority of crimes that
affected most people in the empire?

Roman criminal law also had a very different view of
what constituted criminal behaviour. The criminal law
dealt primarily with the most heinous offences, acts so
offensive or subversive that the state felt compelled to
respond. Treason ranked high on the list, and the penalty
was death and the subsequent erasure of all record of the
offender. Murder demanded a public prosecution,
whether it had been carried out using weapons, poison or
magic, and a range of violent acts, from riot to rape, were
treated as offences. Rapists were to suffer capital punishment, and kidnapping could result in the death penalty,
depending on the severity of the case. But the criminal
law also dealt with non-violent acts such as forgery, with
a particular interest in forged wills. Again, we see the
importance of family and the transmission of wealth

from generation to generation. Also noteworthy is the fact that the law made special mention that slaves who forged wills were to be killed. It was common for owners to free their slaves on their death and so the law recognised that slaves would have a special temptation to insert a false clause into their master's will granting themselves freedom.

Theft of money or property that belonged to the state counted as a criminal offence, and this included officials who embezzled public funds. Likewise, stealing from temples was an offence, since it risked turning the gods against the community as a whole. The law criminalised those who tried to corrupt elections by resort to bribery and those who fraudulently drove up the price of grain by hoarding supplies. Grain was the staple food, and in a huge city such as Rome where a million inhabitants relied on the grain ships making the perilous journey across the Mediterranean Sea, supply of this basic commodity was always a hot political issue, something that the law reflected in its treatment of those who might be tempted to fiddle with its price.

If an individual in Rome was successfully prosecuted for a criminal offence, then they suffered infamy (*infamia*), lowering their legal status to reflect the harm they had done to the community. If they managed to win a civil case against someone else, they could get compensation, but that was an end to the matter. To qualify as a crime in ancient Rome, the act had to have broad social consequences. This meant that many acts of wrongdoing that we would classify as crimes were treated differently in Rome. Most thefts and assaults were seen as a private matter (known as delicts, they roughly equalled the legal idea of a tort). The state had no interest in individual suffering. Then again, Roman law was constantly evolving. Under the empire, the state got more and more involved in different areas of public and private legal life and punishments often became more severe.

The Roman state did nothing more than provide the judicial machinery for the settlement of civil disputes. The state had no further interest in the action. Even in criminal cases, the justice system was less a system than a collection of individuals. Today, a public authority prepares the criminal charge, runs the trial, and, if the prosecution is successful, receives judgement in its favour. In Rome, the prosecution was brought to court by magistrates or by the wronged persons themselves. It seems strange to us that a victim should have to pursue redress for a serious crime. In Rome, it was normal.

To what extent should we allow modern ideas about crime to affect our judgement? Our outlook is heavily dependent on developments in the nineteenth century. Robert Peel first established a dedicated professional police force in London in 1829, and their job was to prevent and investigate crime. The prison system expanded, placing an emphasis on the rehabilitation of criminals rather than on punishment, and the new science of criminology was established to study the phenomenon of crime and learn what caused it. Mass journalism turned crime into a newsworthy commodity and a genre of popular literature emerged that invented mysterious and shocking crimes to entertain the reading public. By the end of the nineteenth century, the foundations for what we understand as crime were in place. But the Romans had almost none of this.

There are subtler differences, less easily traced to particular historical innovations. Today, the criminal legal process is based on narrow definitions of particular offences. They are investigated by agents of the state and the facts of the case are presented to a court to determine whether a crime has indeed been committed. Roman law, by contrast, set out broad categories of wrongdoing. We have seen that it was largely up to the individual to prosecute anyone who fitted those categories and the state merely provided the means for this dispute settlement. The nature of what counted as evidence also differed. We would expect the facts of the case to be established, whereas one of the prime concerns of Roman judges and jurors was the moral character of the accused – was he or she the kind of person likely to have carried out the crime?

Is it possible to come to a conclusion about what exactly constituted crime? We will have to move beyond the narrow definition of Roman criminal law. Women, for example, had no part in public law but it would be wrong to think that they were unaffected by or had no views on crime. We have seen that crime could consist of a wide variety of rule-breaking behaviour: acts which broke laws or breached generally accepted norms, local customs, informal agreements or traditions. The Romans themselves had no single term for crime. The Latin term *crimen*, from which we derive our word, meant reproach or accusation and came from the word *cernere*, meaning to decide or judge. In other words it was about communal disapproval. But Latin also contains a variety of other words for wrongdoing: *scelus*, *maleficium*, *facinus*, *nefas*, *peccatum*, *delictum*. These different kinds of wrongdoing could generate a range of responses, such as formal trials, lynchings, gossip or thunderbolts from the gods.

Then there is the problem of the reliability of our witnesses. We have seen that the Romans were fascinated by crime. Theft, robbery, sexual offences, desertion, murder, treason – they all pepper the works of Roman historians. As we know well today, though, reported crime does not yield any easy insights into patterns of actual criminal behaviour. Statistics tell us that in the real world, crimes occur in inverse proportion to their seriousness. Thefts happen by the million, muggings by the thousand and murders by the hundred. For the news, however, the more heinous the offence the better. So too for the ancient authors. When they write about crime, their accounts are biased by their own political and social prejudices, by religious beliefs and by a lack of hard evidence. Often their accounts were written to serve ulterior purposes. Roman historians were generally not interested in the problems of ordinary people; history was too important to be concerned with everyday victims. Then we have impressionistic sources such as legal disputes mentioned in letters and fiction, which can give us a sense of how the law was perceived but not necessarily of how it actually operated. Finally there are hundreds of administrative documents, most notably papyri rescued from the sands of Roman Egypt, which show how the system functioned in one particular province. But we usually do not have all the documents relating to a case, or they are literally full of holes. And how representative was Egypt of the rest of the empire?

The Romans thought that crime was explained by personal morality. Roman accounts are often sprinkled with tales carefully selected to deliver an appropriate moral message for their readership, not the facts of the case. The emphasis on what a crime revealed about the perpetrator is also reflected in the government's behaviour. What mattered was not the truth of the allegations but whether the acts were thought to pose a moral hazard to society at large. In a society such as Rome, which venerated tradition, any social change was likely to be interpreted as a seed of moral breakdown. Crime was just the thin end of the wedge.

What should we make of these witnesses? Did they exaggerate their evidence to give the impression that danger lurked around every street corner? Does their testimony reflect genuine fears? We know that anxiety about crime affects far more people than crime itself. But what is it, exactly? Is it a loss of confidence in your neighbours? A fear of strangers, or a sense that the nation's standards of behaviour are in decline? And is it qualitatively different from other daily concerns, such as the fear of being run over? Fear of crime was probably as common in Rome as it is today. A list of crimes that most concern modern westerners would probably include sexual assault, burglary and violence; all of these worried Romans too. But their concerns often centred on issues of status and of public loss of face, and the need for a public retribution. How important a factor was such fear?

Speaking truth unto power is always a dangerous activity and the Roman empire was no different. We must be careful not to accept everything people said about the emperors and their regimes. To do so is simply to regurgitate the ideology of the state. When we read that taverns closed in mourning on the death of emperors and that, 'all over the city, expressions of grief are displayed', it is easy to believe that the people held the emperors in genuine affection (Tertullian *On Idolatry* 15; Herodian *History of the Empire since the Death of Marcus Aurelius* 4.2). That these expressions of grief were 'combined with festivals' suggests that the people did still feel able to enjoy themselves. But the fact that the emperors used secret police and disguises in an attempt to learn what people were really thinking suggests too that people could talk critically about their emperors. And popular enthusiasm seems at odds with the hard-nosed scepticism they sometimes displayed towards their superiors in sayings and proverbs: 'A change in ruler is just a change in master for the poor' (Phaedrus *Fables* 1.15).

We have had to confront the two paradoxes found operating throughout Roman society. If Roman law was largely ineffective both as a deterrent to criminals and as a protection for most of its citizens, why did the Romans devote such time and thought to perfecting it that, two thousand years later, it provides the basis for European law? And secondly, why was the Roman empire so long-lasting and stable when even its rulers and officials were often involved in rank criminality and corruption? We could conclude that Rome and its leaders presided over what appears at times to be a lawless anarchy. If so, we must ask ourselves what it was that kept the empire together, that allowed it to grow, and which maintained the *pax Romana* that brought peace and prosperity to most of Europe.

How are we to judge a Roman state that was very limited in comparison with the modern Western world? It had no interest in providing healthcare, education, or widespread social security benefits, but nobody expected it to. It existed primarily to defeat enemies without and maintain civil order within. Rome was remarkably successful on the first count. But on the second, the evidence clearly reveals the limitations of state power. Officials could disregard laws from above and corruption, by modern standards, was rife. A considerable gap therefore existed between the emperors' rhetorical claims and the reality of what they could deliver. In this pre-industrial, relatively unsophisticated society, the purpose of the law was not simply to function and be effective. Rather it served as a powerful symbol of the justness of emperors, designed to impress the empire's inhabitants of the legitimacy of their rulers. The development of an idea of a universal legal umbrella was also part of the glue that held the Roman empire together, even in the face of widespread crime and little hope of justice for most. Do we think that most people would have thought this perfectly normal, and were broadly happy with the level of security the empire maintained?

Rather than seeing the empire's inhabitants as either fully supportive of the emperors or fully hostile, we could view them as having been capable of adopting different stances according to the situation. Many, particularly the

elite, generally accepted the regime and its laws. They
had no fundamental reason to resist the state's aims and
may have largely accepted the emperor's claims to deliver
just government. But the Roman people were also capable
of adopting a more utilitarian attitude to the emperor. As
with bread and circuses, they could treat this as a game to
be played for their own benefit. Similarly, provincials
might turn to Roman courts for a legal means to settle
their disputes not because they had any fundamental
belief in the justice of the system but because that was
the way to get what they wanted. Finally, there might
have been times when individuals would resist the imperial state and reject its laws, either by actively opposing
them or trying to evade their reach.

The emperors seem to have accepted the limitations
on what they could in practice deliver by relying on a mix
of cruelty and clemency: the latter to the most deserving
of those criminals they caught, the former to the very
worst offenders. Emperors themselves could be both virtuous rulers and wicked crooks, which reflected the
imperial system's lack of controls on executive power. It
also reflected the two sides to imperial rule. The emperors wanted to be leaders of a well-ordered, disciplined
society that obeyed the law. Augustus had shown this by
making the crowd sit according to social status at the
games, where the vicious punishments meted out to condemned criminals publicly reaffirmed these social ideals.
But the emperors' power was such that they also had
carte blanche to express their dominance over Roman
society by acting as they wished.

How much influence did ordinary people have on

these powerful autocrats? In one incident, a woman stopped the emperor Hadrian as he passed by her and asked him to hear her petition. When he said that he was too busy, she replied, 'Then stop being emperor.' She called out the emperor's claim to deliver just government and used his own imagery against him. Needless to say, he felt obliged to hear her complaint (Dio *Roman History* 69.6.3). Was this remarkable tale an anecdote invented by elite writers to legitimate the imperial system? Or did the story reflect, if not an actual event, the kind of tactic ordinary people could employ to try to work the system in their favour?

And what about us? How fit are we to sit in judgement? Rome's own split personality is perhaps one of the main reasons we are so fascinated by it: it reflects our own world's contradictory tendencies. The decent position would be to admire Rome's great achievements and of course – of course! – shudder at its bloodthirsty games and brutal treatment of slaves. But is that us? People have long used the ancient world as a vehicle for all kinds of fantasies. It is a distant place where very different moral and sexual mores operated: it offers us an imaginary escape route from our own world. The favourite book of the decadent and reclusive anti-hero of *A Rebour* ('Against Nature'), was the *Satyricon*, because its author Petronius revealed 'the petty existences of the people, their encounters, their bestialities, their passions'. The dazzling luxury of elite Roman life probably attracts some of us, too; as Nero remarked when his Golden Palace was completed, 'Now I can start to live like a human being.' Rome provides both an early inspiration for the consumer individualism of the modern world and a revolting example of what happens when it gets out of control.

What we love about Rome is what we also hate about it. Its classical architecture provides a warm glow of familiarity by reminding us of many of our own public buildings. It tells us we are looking at a world of order, authority and stable government. Other constructions tell us we are entering a world of technological progress (something with which we are comfortably familiar), one which saw aqueducts supply fresh water to cities, and communications improve thanks to the straight roads that criss-crossed the countryside. But we know that these developments came at a price. The Roman world could not have functioned like it did without slave power. Many millions were conquered by Rome's brutally efficient armies and forced to acquiesce to Roman rule. Far from feeling any qualms about these realities, Rome openly celebrated them in magnificent public games and festivals. How better to vicariously experience the joy of conquest than by seeing a gladiator's throat slit in the Colosseum?

The Christian tradition likes to think that it improved on the morals of the Roman world. But that very Christian tradition was shaped by the world it inherited. Early Christians had no issue with owning slaves, for instance. We might like to think that the modern world has improved because slavery is now illegal in every country but, according to one estimate, there are almost thirty million slaves in the world today, a far higher figure than Rome ever possessed. Do we simply turn a blind eye to these crimes in the same way that the Romans did about petty acts of violence against the person?

A Roman would probably argue that the modern Western lifestyle requires similarly drastic inequalities in order to be maintained. Over 70 per cent of the world's population live on less than $10 a day, and half of global wealth is held in the hands of the top 1 per cent. The eight richest men own as much as the poorest 3.6 billion. It is a level of inequality that is, if anything, far worse than existed in the Roman world. We in the West simply keep our low-cost producers out of sight, housed in factories located in faraway countries. At least the Romans faced up to the social hierarchy that helped generate the wealth and leisure that allowed them to enjoy themselves at the baths and games. I suspect the Romans would feel that their values and ours were in many ways the same: a belief in the pursuit of personal fulfilment and wealth, regardless of the cost to others. All Roman citizens felt that they had the right to the benefits that Roman power brought them. And all of them had the potential to climb the social ladder. Not many plebs became multi-millionaires, of course, but neither do many of the poorest become billionaires today. Are they really that different?

Rome: brutal offender or lawful policeman of the world? Despotic ruler over a chaotic, crime-ridden society or a legitimate government that did a good job given the standards of the day? Can we decide?

FURTHER READING

The subject of crime has received only limited attention from ancient historians. Below are listed the main works that can help those interested in digging deeper. By contrast, the field of Roman law is vast and only a selection of what I have found most useful is included. I have concentrated on works that are easily accessible in English but also include some of the most important foreign-language texts. Throughout the text, I have used the standard abbreviations for the various collections of papyri and inscriptions (such as *P. Oxy.* for the Oxyrhynchus papyri and *CIL* for the *Corpus Inscriptionum Latinarum*).

General

A useful place to start for those looking to understand better the theories of criminology is I. Marsh (ed.) *Theories of Crime* (London, 2006). Those interested in the broader role of justice in society should read B. Moore, *Injustice: The Social Bases of Obedience and Revolt* (London, 1978). An important landmark in the study of society's treatment of criminality is the French philosopher Michel Foucault's analysis of the theories that lay behind the development of penal systems in the modern world: M. Foucault, *Discipline and Punish: The Birth of the Prison*, trans. A. Sheridan (London, 1979). A fascinating study of the ways in which law interacts with ordinary life to leave people living 'in the shadow of the law' can be found in P. Ewick and S. S. Silbey, *The Common Place of Law: Stories from Everyday Life* (Chicago, 1998).

Numerous studies exist about crime in other periods of history. Their findings cannot simply be applied to antiquity but they raise many of the same questions we can ask of the ancient evidence. The following are only a selection but are all excellent: T. Dean, *Crime in Medieval Europe 1200–1550* (Harlow, 2001); T. Astarita, *Village Justice: Community, Family, and Popular Culture in Early Modern Italy* (Baltimore, MD, 1999); D. Hay et al., *Albion's Fatal Tree: Crime and Society in Eighteenth-Century England* (London, 1975); C. Emsley, *Crime and Society in England 1750–1900* (London, 1987); and V. A. C. Gatrell, *The Hanging Tree: Execution and the English People 1770–1868* (Oxford, 1994). And for a modern look at urban theft: G. Manaugh, *A Burglar's Guide to the City* (London, 2016).

The view that Rome's games were 'holocausts' can be found in M. Grant, *Gladiators* (London, 1967: 8 & 124). The comparative data for the murder rate in medieval London comes from S. Pinker, *The Better Angels of Our Nature: a History of Violence and Humanity* (London, 2012). The data for infanticide in Victorian Britain are discussed in L. Rose, *Massacre of the Innocents: Infanticide in Britain, 1800–1939* (London, 1986).

Crime in Antiquity

The best general work on Roman crime is by the German scholar Jens-Uwe Krause: *Kriminalgeschichte der Antike* (Munich, 2004). There is an important review of this book by Joerg Fuendling in the online *Bryn Mawr Classical Review*, which makes a range of astute criticisms. Krause has also published other impressive works in the field of crime, such as the use of imprisonment in Rome, *Gefängnisse im Römischen Reich* (Stuttgart, 1996). R. A. Bauman, *Crime and Punishment in Ancient Rome* (London, 1996) examines the crime of treason (*crimen maiestas*); while J. Boriaud, *Crimes à l'Antique* (Paris, 2012) focuses on murder in the world of high politics. The collection of essays brought together in K. Hopwood, *Organised Crime in Antiquity* (London, 1999) looks at various local forms of criminal activity. The best study of criminal behaviour in the Greek world is D. Cohen, *Law, Violence and Community in Classical Athens* (Cambridge, 1995).

Roman Law

The primary sources for Roman law divide into various types. First there are the early laws introduced by the kings, the Leges regiae, and The Twelve Tables (Lex duodecim tabularum), which are the republican laws dating from the mid-fifth century BC. From the later republican period we have various public laws (Leges publicae) as well as the praetor's edicts and decrees of the senate (Senatus consulta). The early empire is generally considered as the 'Golden Age' of Roman law and is found in the writings of three principal jurists: Gaius, whose *Institutes* date from the second century AD; Ulpian, who lived from AD 170 to 223/4 and wrote the *Regulae*; and Paulus, whose *Sententiae* date from around AD 200. The various imperial legal pronouncements were later collected in various codes, such as the *Codex Hermogenianus* covering the year AD 293–294, and the *Theodosian Code* which contains imperial enactments from AD 312 to 438. Above all, the *Corpus Juris Civilis* (body of civil law) was collected on the orders of the emperor Justinian and issued between AD 529 and 534 and consists of four parts: the *Digest*, *Institutes*, *Code*, and *New Constitutions*. The first three served as revisions of existing law, while the final part dealt with Justinian's own enactments. Examples of declamations, the training speeches used to educate would-be lawyers, can be found in the collection of Seneca the Elder's *Controversiae*, in the declamations of Calpurnius Flaccus, and in the Major and Minor Declamations traditionally, although erroneously, attributed to Quintilian.

Useful introductions to Roman law can be found in D. Johnston, *Roman Law in Context* (Cambridge, 1999) or in greater detail in D. Johnston (ed.), *The Cambridge Companion to Roman Law* (Cambridge, 2015) and P. J. du Plessis, C. Ando and K. Tuori (eds), *The Oxford Handbook of Roman Law and Society* (Oxford, 2016). Other good introductions are A. Watson, *The Spirit of Roman Law* (Athens, GA, 1995), and A. M. Riggsby, *Roman Law and the Legal World of the Romans* (Cambridge, 2010). A detailed textbook on Roman law itself from its 'Golden Age', can be found in F. Schulz, *Classical Roman Law* (Oxford, 1951). The various criminal laws are detailed in O. F. Robinson, *The Criminal Law of Ancient Rome* (London, 1995). Two books that do an excellent job of contextualising the laws are J. Crook, *Law and Life in Ancient Rome* (Ithaca, NY, 1967) and J. Harries, *Law and Crime in the Roman World* (Cambridge, 2007), while S. Connolly, *Lives Behind the Laws* (Bloomington, IN, 2010) tries to see what the *Codex Hermogenianus* can tell us of the realities of life in the third-century empire. The relationships between emperors, politics and the law is analysed by R. A. Bauman, *Lawyers and Politics in the Early Roman Empire* (Munich, 1989) and T. Honoré, *Emperors and Lawyers* (Oxford, 1994).

The details of the petition system can be found in T. Hauken, *Petition* and *Response: An Epigraphic Study of Petitions to Roman Emperors, 181–249* (Athens, 1998). The differing ways in which the law treated those of unequal status are analysed in P. Garnsey, *Social Status and Legal Privilege in the Roman Empire* (Oxford, 1970). Examples of family law can be found in B. W. Frier and T. A. J. McGinn, *A Casebook on Roman Family Law* (Oxford, 2004). An introduction to ancient theories of property can be found in P. Garnsey, *Thinking about Property: from Antiquity to the Age of Revolution* (Cambridge, 2007). A detailed overview of Roman penal practice can be found in O. F. Robinson, *Penal Practice and Penal Policy in Ancient Rome* (London, 2007), while S. Schwartz, *From Bedroom to Courtroom: Law and Justice in the Greek Novel* (Groningen, 2016) looks at how the fictional legal scenes of ancient novels may reflect the actual legal ideas concerning family and sexuality.

The use of myth in executions is discussed in K. M. Coleman, 'Fatal charades: Roman executions staged as mythological enactments' (*Journal of Roman Studies* 80, 1990: 44–73).

Roman Egypt

An excellent introduction to the unique world of Roman Egypt is given by P. Parsons, *City of the Sharp-nosed Fish: Greek Lives in Roman Egypt* (London, 2007). The crimes of Roman Egypt were first looked at in B. Baldwin, 'Crime and criminals in Graeco-Roman Egypt' (*Aegyptus* 43, 1963: 256–63); R. W. Davies, 'The investigation of some crimes in Roman Egypt' (*Ancient History* 4, 1973: 199–212); R. S. Bagnall, 'Official and private violence in Roman Egypt' (*The Bulletin of the American Society of Papyrologists* 26, 1989: 201–16); and D. W. Hobson, 'The impact of law on village life in Roman Egypt', in B. Halpern and D. W. Hobson (eds.), *Law, Politics and Society in the Ancient Mediterranean World* (Sheffield, 1993: 193–219). The crime data drawn from the papyri is taken from this source. Since then there have been two important studies of the social context of litigation, to which I have been much indebted: B. Kelly, *Petitions, Litigation, and Social Control in Roman Egypt* (Oxford, 2011) and A. Bryen, *Violence in Roman Egypt: a Study in Legal Interpretation* (Philadelphia, PA, 2013). The case of the stolen fish is to be found in Kelly, pp. 54–5. The case of Daimon the cook is from Bryen, p. 96. See Hobson for the discussion of the use of the terms 'bia' and 'hubris'. For example papyri taken from these sources, I have used their translations with some minor alterations of my own.

Popular Interaction with the Law

The text and a translation of the spoof will, the Piglet's Will (*testamentum porcelli*) can be found in D. Daube, *Roman Law: Linguistic, Social and Philosophical Aspects* (Edinburgh, 1969: 77–81). J.-J. Aubert 'Du lard ou du cochon?: the "Testamentum Porcelli" as a Jewish Anti-Christian Pamphlet', in *A Tall Order: Writing the Social History of the Ancient World* (Munich, 2005: 107–41) contains a useful introduction but then proposes what to me looks like a far-fetched theory. Other useful commentaries are E. Champlin, 'The Testament of the Piglet' (*Phoenix* 41, 1987: 174–83), and B. Baldwin, 'The Testamentum Porcelli', in Baldwin, *Studies on Late Roman and Byzantine History* (Leiden, 1985: 137–48).

On laws relating to taverns, see J. Toner, *Leisure and Ancient Rome* (Cambridge, 1995). On popular notions of justice, see T. Morgan, *Popular Morality in the Early Roman Empire* (Cambridge, 2007). On ideas about popular justice contained in the ancient novel, see F. Millar, 'The World of the Golden Ass' (*Journal of Roman Studies* 71, 1981: 63–75).

Popular Resistance

An overview of this topic can be found in J. Toner, *Popular Culture in Ancient Rome* (Cambridge, 2009) chapter 5 'Popular Resistance'; and R. MacMullen, *Enemies of the Roman Order: Treason, Unrest, and Alienation in the Empire* (Cambridge, MA, 1966) chapter 6 'The Outsiders'. For a list of primary resistance texts, see G. E. M. de Ste. Croix, *The Class Struggle in the Ancient Greek World: From the Archaic Age to the Arab Conquests* (London, 1981: 441–52). The most useful discussions of these are J. Barns, 'Shenute as a historical source', in J. Wolski (ed.), *Actes du Xe Congrès International de Papyrologues, Varsovie, Cracovie, 3–9 Septembre, 1961* (Wrocław, 1964: 151–59); and L. Koenen, 'The prophecies of a potter: a prophecy of world renewal becomes an apocalypse' (*American Studies in Papyrology 7*, 1970: 249–54). Jewish views about Roman rule can be found in N. R. M. de Lange, 'Jewish attitudes to the Roman Empire', in P. Garnsey and C. R. Whittaker (eds), *Imperialism in the Ancient World* (Cambridge, 1978: 255–81). The anonymous letter of complaint known as 'On Military Matters' is discussed in E. A. Thompson, *A Roman Reformer and Inventor: Being a New Text of the Treatise De rebus bellicis* (Oxford, 1952). Of comparative interest for the way in which peasants go about resisting their subordinate position in life, see the excellent J. Scott, *Domination and the*

Arts of Resistance (New Haven, CT, 1992) and *Weapons of the Weak: Every-day Forms of Peasant Resistance*, (New Haven, CT, 1985).

Crowd violence is best discussed in P. J. J. Vanderbroeck, *Popular Leadership and Collective Behavior in the Late Roman Republic ca. 80–50 B.C.* (Amsterdam, 1987). See also T. W. Africa, 'Urban violence in Imperial Rome' (*Journal of Interdisciplinary History* 2, 1971: 3–21). On the importance of food crises in popular politics, see P. Garsney, *Famine and Food Supply in the Graeco-Roman World: Responses to Risk and Crisis* (Cambridge, 1988), and for a comparative perspective, see the classic article by E. P. Thompson, 'The moral economy of the English crowd in the eighteenth century' (*Past & Present* 50, 1971: 76–136).

War and Banditry

Banditry is examined in T. Grünewald, *Bandits in the Roman Empire: Myth and Reality*, trans. J. Drinkwater (London, 2004) and the two works by B. Shaw: 'Bandits in the Roman Empire' (*Past & Present* 105, 1984: 3–52) and 'Rebels and outsiders' (*Cambridge Ancient History* 11, 2000: 361–403). See also R. C. Knapp, *Prostitutes, Outlaws, Slaves, Gladiators, Ordinary Men and Women ... the Romans that History Forgot* (London, 2011) chapter 9 'Beyond the Law' on bandits and pirates. On the Gallic context for the later Bagaudae, see J. Drinkwater and H. Elton (eds), *Fifth-Century Gaul: A Crisis of Identity?* (Cambridge, 1992). On broader peasant revolts, see E. A. Thompson, 'Peasant Revolts in Late Roman Gaul and Spain' in M. I. Finley (ed.), *Studies in Ancient Society* (London, 1974) chapter 14; and the two articles by S. L. Dyson, 'Native revolts in the Roman Empire' (*Historia* 20, 1971: 239–74); and 'Native revolt patterns in the Roman Empire' (*Aufstieg und Niedergang der römischen Welt* 2.3, 1975: 138–75). The only work dealing with ancient wartime atrocities is an unpublished PhD by Mars McClelland Westington, 'Atrocities in Roman warfare to 133 BC' (University of Chicago, 1938). L. Matthews discusses the case of the Salassi, who were systematically sold into extended slavery, in 'A Manmade Humanitarian Crisis: Augustus and the Salassi' in R. Riera, D. Gómez-Castro and T. Ñaco del Hoyo (eds), *Ancient Disasters and Crisis Management in Classical Antiquity* (Gdansk, 2015: 99–119)

Women and Religion

The relationship between law and women is detailed in T. A. J. McGinn, *Prostitution, Sexuality, and the Law in Ancient Rome* (Oxford, 2003). Rape is studied in K. F. Pierce and S. Deacy, *Rape in Antiquity* (London, 1997). For the later empire, see A. Arjava, *Women and Law in Late Antiquity* (Oxford, 1996). A comparative view is best found in L. Zedner, *Women, Crime, and Custody in Victorian England* (Oxford, 1991).

Religious crimes are analysed by R. A. Bauman, *Impietas in Principem: A Study of Treason against the Roman Emperor with Special Reference to the First Century AD* (Munich, 1974) and C. Ando and J. Rüpke (eds), *Religion and Law in Classical and Christian Rome* (Stuttgart, 2006). For the later empire, there is also the work by M. Gaddis, *There is no Crime for Those who have Christ: Religious Violence in the Christian Roman Empire* (Berkeley, CA, 2005). On the widespread use of curses to try to gain redress, see E. Eidinow, *Oracles, Curses, and Risk among the Ancient Greeks* (Oxford, 2007) and for the best collection, J. G. Gager, (ed.), *Curse Tablets and Binding Spells from the Ancient World* (Oxford, 1992). I have indicated in the text examples taken from this source. On the ways in which Romans interacted with each other and their tendency to turn to violence, see M. Peachin (ed.), *The Oxford Handbook of Social Relations in the Roman World* (Oxford, 2011). The curse of the victim Maslik is to be found in H. S. Versnel in 'Punish Those Who Rejoice in Our Misery: on Curse Tablets and Schadenfreude', in D. R. Jordan, H. Montgomery, and E. Thomassen (eds), *The World of Ancient Magic* (Bergen, 1999: 125–62, p. 128). See P. Ripat, 'Expelling misconceptions: astrologers at Rome' (*Classical Philology* 106, 2011: 115–54) for a full list of interpreters being exiled.

Moral Crime

On perceptions of luxury, see A. Dalby, *Empire of Pleasures: Luxury and Indulgence in the Roman World* (London, 2000); A. Wallace-Hadrill, *Rome's Cultural Revolution* (Cambridge, 2008); A. Wallace-Hadrill, 'The Senses in the Market-place: The Luxury Market and Eastern Trade in Imperial Rome' in J. Toner (ed.) *A Cultural History of the Senses in Antiquity*, (London, 2014: 69–89); E. Zanda, *Fighting Hydra-like Luxury: Sumptuary Regulation in the Roman Republic* (London, 2013); M. Zarmakoupi, *Designing for Luxury on the Bay of Naples: Villas and landscapes (c.100 BCE–79 CE)*

(Oxford, 2014); and for a comparative perspective, D. Weir, *Decadence and the Making of Modernism* (Amherst, MA, 1995).

Roman Government

Perhaps the best way for the non-expert to get a feel for the nature of Roman rule is the slightly mad work of K. Hopkins, *A World Full of Gods: Pagans, Jews and Christians in the Roman Empire* (London, 1999), which includes time travellers going back to Pompeii and finding themselves in court. His more straightforwardly academic discussion can be found in K. Hopkins, *Conquerors and Slaves* (Cambridge, 1978). A good general introduction is B. Levick, *The Government of the Roman Empire* (London, 2000). The ways in which the Roman authorities maintained control are analysed in W. Nippel, *Public Order in Ancient Rome* (Cambridge, 1995); J. E. Lendon, 'Social control at Rome' (*Classical Journal* 93, 1997: 83–8); and C. J. Fuhrmann, *Policing the Roman Empire: Soldiers, Administration and Public Order* (Oxford, 2011), who argues for a higher level of local policing by means of stationing small numbers of soldiers in towns and villages. S. H. Rutledge, *Imperial Inquisitions: Prosecutors and Informants from Tiberius to Domitian* (London, 2001) examines the evidence for state informers (*delatores*), while R. S. Rogers, *Criminal Trials and Criminal Legislation under Tiberius* (Middletown, CT, 1935) looks at the use of treason trials to control the aristocracy.

The ideology of Roman rule and the role of the law in creating it, are analysed by L. C. Colognesi, *Law and Power in the Making of the Roman Commonwealth*, trans. L. Kopp (Cambridge, 2014) and by C. Ando, *Law, language, and Empire in the Roman Tradition* (Philadelphia, PA, 2011). See, above all, C. Ando, *Imperial Ideology and Provincial Loyalty in the Roman Empire* (Berkeley, CA, 2000) for what I would regard as an overly optimistic view of the reception of Roman rule on the ground. For the view that people loved their emperor see P. Veyne, *Bread and Circuses: Historical Sociology and Political Pluralism*, trans. B. Pearce (London, 1992: 295–6).

The Late Roman Empire

The best introduction to the law of the later empire is J. Harries, *Law and Empire in Late Antiquity* (Cambridge, 1999). J. N. Dillon, *The Justice of Constantine: Law, Communication, and Control* (Ann Arbor, MI, 2012) gives an upbeat assessment of the legal innovations of the first Christian emperor. The article by R. MacMullen, 'Judicial savagery in the Roman empire' (*Chiron* 16, 1986: 43–62) and his book, *Corruption and the Decline of Rome* (New Haven, CT, 1988) provides something of an antidote to this, arguing the case for a destructively high level of venality. C. Kelly, *Ruling the Later Roman Empire* (Cambridge, MA, 2004) argues for a more neutral reading of corruption, seeing it as the grease that helped a relatively inefficient pre-industrial system to function. He contains a detailed discussion of the text of the ancient bureaucrat, John Lydus. See Kelly also (note 1 to p. 114) for various references to the story about Hadrian and the woman demanding that her petition be heard. Jens-Uwe Krause has also written on violent crime in the late Roman empire, *Gewalt und Kriminalität in der Spätantike* (Munich, 2014), which, I argue, gives a far too positive assessment on the level of violence. The muddle concerning the post of eirenarch is discussed in Hopwood, *Organised Crime*, pp. 192–3. Violence is analysed at a popular level by T. E. Gregory, *Vox Populi: Popular Opinion and Violence in the Religious Controversies of the Fifth Century A.D.* (Columbus, OH, 1979); and more broadly in H. Drake (ed.), *Violence in Late Antiquity: Perceptions and Practices* (Aldershot, 2006: 179–96), which includes a chapter on religious violence: B. Shaw, 'Bad Boys: Circumcellions and Fictive Violence'. The use of agents to help the state maintain order is discussed in the article by W. G. Sinnigen, 'Two branches of the Later Roman Secret Service' (*American Journal of Philology* 80, 1959: 238–54).

ACKNOWLEDGEMENTS

My interest in Roman law and whether it delivered justice was first stimulated over twenty-five years ago by Keith Hopkins, whose brilliant course on Roman Egypt introduced me to a whole other ancient world. The aim of this book is to provide an accessible analysis of the broader subject of crime in the Roman empire that also tries to see Rome from another angle. It tries to show Roman society in all its guises: practical, flexible, innovative, brutal. Writing a book always generates debts of gratitude and I would like to thank the following people for their support and encouragement: Gavin Ayliffe, Pierre Caquet, Jason Goddard and Emma Widdis. Peter Garnsey, as ever, helped me enormously in focusing my ideas. My wife, Anne, and children, Arthur and Florence, have all put up with me while I researched and wrote the text. I am grateful to everyone at Churchill College for all their interesting discussions and I also want to thank the staff of Cambridge University Library and the Classics Faculty who are always so helpful. My editor at Profile, Ed Lake, really helped me tighten up the text and shape it for a wider audience. The project began, though, with John Davey as editor. John was a man of great intellect and charm and his death robbed me of a good friend. This book is dedicated to his memory.

INDEX